NVivo 11 Essentials

Your Guide to the World's Most Powerful Data Analysis Software
2nd Revised Edition

By Bengt M. Edhlund & Allan G. McDougall

FORM & KUNSKAP AB
INFORMATIONTECHNOLOGY

§45 06 STALLARHOLMEN • SWEDEN • +46 152 201 80
OM • WWW.FORMKUNSKAP.COM

FOREWARD

The 2nd Edition of NVivo 11 Essentials is here. As we write, NVivo 11 is currently on its fourth major update (version 11.4.1 to be precise). These updates have involved numerous improvements and upgrades to software functionality and the user interface. To ensure our readers are up to date, we undertook a major revision of this book. We hope you enjoy.

The book has two authors, and we each share a distinct lens to NVivo 11. Bengt Edhlund is a software trainer with decades of experience teaching and writing about research software. Dr. Allan McDougall is a qualitative researcher who has worked with NVivo 8 through 11 on projects ranging from text-based discourse analysis to ethnography. We have co-authored this book to provide instruction to NVivo 11 users of all skill levels and experience with both qualitative data analysis and qualitative research methods. We break down the functional components of this intricate software while striving to provide practical, anecdotal advice for using NVivo 11 for every stage of your research project. Further, we strive to provide advice on using NVivo 11 in a collaborative environment, a topic on which we are aware many of our colleagues are interested.

Form & Kunskap AB, founded by Bengt in 1993, is a training company focused on software solutions for academic researchers. We believe any single product cannot be the sole solution for researchers and research teams. Research is like woodworking: a quality product will always be the result of combining several tools and techniques. We believe it is important to always select market leading software products that follow recognized industry standards. We believe in teaching vertically, cutting across the planes of single software solutions. Our clients receive well written literature followed by professional support, and many years of teaching and support has helped us understand how to teach our clients to productively tackle complex research topics.

Please enjoy our book and feel free to contact us at any time at: info@formkunskap.com

TABLE OF CONTENTS

1. INTRODUCING NVIVO 11

Welcome to NVivo 11 Essentials

Welcome to NVivo 11 Essentials, your guide to the world's most powerful qualitative data analysis software. The purpose of this book is to provide a comprehensive guide to every feature of NVivo 11. For beginners, you will find explanations of key concepts and recommendations for starting your first NVivo project, importing your data, analyzing your data, and sharing your findings with collaborators. Some people find it hard to wrap their heads around NVivo, and you might be one of those people. Perhaps you have been playing around with the software already and you don't really 'get it'. This book offers that one simple description of what to do with NVivo and how you can make it work for you. There is no one right way to use NVivo, but we have enough collective experience to offer some best practices that will help you along your journey.

For advanced users, you will find a comprehensive introduction to NVivo 11's latest features, including the ability to work with social network analysis. You may wish to skip to page 19 for our summary, What's New in NVivo 11?

Whatever your skill level using NVivo is, this book has been written by two authors who combine theory and practice to offer readers a guide towards both technical capability and practical application.

Bengt M. Edhlund

Bengt Edhlund is the author of several books, including *NVivo 10 Essentials*. He is Scandinavia's leading research software trainer. As a former telecommunications engineer, Bengt has published 22 books on academic informatics tools such as NVivo, EndNote, PubMed, and Excel. All of Bengt's books are available in English and Swedish. He has trained researchers from every corner of the globe, including Canada, Sweden, Norway, China, Egypt, Uganda, and Vietnam. A trainer who takes pride in his students' success, Bengt provides all of his clients with customized NVivo support solutions via Skype or email.

Allan G. McDougall, PhD

A former student of Bengt's, Allan is a qualitative researcher with extensive NVivo experience. He has used NVivo in a collaborative academic environment on diverse projects related to his area of qualitative health research and health professional education. While Bengt knows every facet of NVivo's various functions, Allan is a NVivo user who provides practical tips based on personal experiences applying NVivo to create dozens of qualitative research solutions.

What is NVivo 11?

NVivo 11 allows researchers to organize and analyze a wide variety of data, including but not limited to documents, images, audio, video, questionnaires and web / social media content.

Whether you work with grounded theory, phenomenology, ethnography, discourse analysis, attitude surveys, organizational studies or mixed-methods approaches, you will at some point need to bring order and structure to your data. We have worked with researchers tasked with analyzing hundreds of interviews and focus group discussions, and researchers tasked with analyzing thousands of surveys blending quantitative and written data. Although at one time researchers were able to analyze data using paper-based systems, NVivo allows for the fast and easy analysis of large datasets for both individuals and multi-user teams..

Key Components of an NVivo 11 Project

The purpose of this section is familiarizing you with some of the terminology you will need to understand to work with NVivo 10. **Sources**, **Nodes**, **Coding**, and **Queries** are the building blocks of an NVivo project. This book provides in-depth explanations of these concepts whether you decide to read linearly through the chapters, or use the glossary at the end of the book to pick and choose topics of interest.

Below is a simplified diagram of an NVivo project's key components:

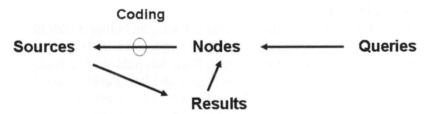

Simply put, **Sources** are your data. Sources can be documents, audio, video and image files, memos, websites, research articles, or entire surveys. Sources can be imported into NVivo, or they can be linked from other locations like the web. Some Sources, like documents, can also be created directly inside NVivo using it's built in word processor.

A key feature of NVivo is that discrete units of data can be organized into highly flexible containers, or **Nodes**. Nodes can be actual parts of your data, like a snippet of audio or a passage of text. Nodes can also be concepts or organizational structures based on your own ideas to designate properties, phenomena, or keywords that characterize aspects of your data. Importantly, Nodes allow for the addition of meta-data that can apply tangible information about your dataset, such as demographic or geographic information, to support organization and analysis. Later in the book, we will explain the important distinction between two types of Nodes: **Theme Nodes** and **Case Nodes**—suffice it to say for now that Case Nodes use meta-data to organize the practical components of your research, while Theme Nodes use conceptual information to relay analytic findings.

Coding is the activity of building nodes. Coding means that words, sentences, paragraphs, audio snippets, video segments, or survey comments organized with Nodes. We'll discuss how you can code data yourself or use the power of auto-coding to automatically organize large portions of your dataset.

Queries are the backbone of qualitative data analysis with NVivo. Queries are basically special searches and filters that can be saved and reused as your project develops. Results of queries can also be saved, used to generate Nodes, data matrices, and data visualizations like charts and word clouds.

A Crucial Note on NVivo Projects

When working with NVivo, it is important to understand that the word project has two meanings. The first, more conventional meaning is simply your research project. But in this book we will use another meaning for the term: when we say **Project**, we mean an NVivo **Project file**. As we discuss below, NVivo creates a single file that will serve as an amalgamation of your Project Items, which include Sources, Coding, Queries, and a host of other analytic units like Diagrams and Sets. NVivo allows you to organize your data into both **Project Items** and then to arrange them into folders.

Importantly, items and folders in NVivo are 'virtual' in relation to a Windows-based or Mac-based environment. In an NVivo Project, folders are similar to Windows or Mac OSX folders, but NVivo has special rules for how folders are handled—for example only certain types of folders are allowed to be organized hierarchically, and certain types of folders can only accommodate certain types of items. Like a computer operating system, Project Items and folders can be edited, copied, cut, pasted, deleted, moved, etc. But whatever changes you make, they are all localized to the Project file.

Visualizing your Project

An overall picture of how a project can be developed is:

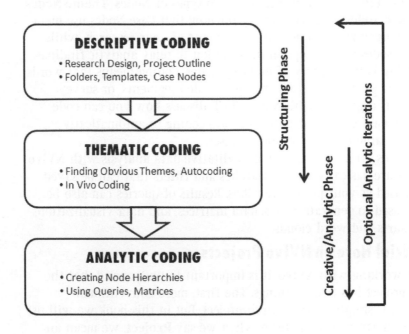

NVivo helps to organize data so that analysis and conclusions will be safer and easier. The ultimate goal may be described as follows:

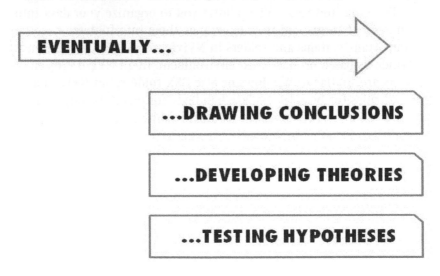

- ◆ -

Exploring this Book

This book begins by describing the system requirements for NVivo 11. Chapter 2 describes how NVivo's user interface is designed and basic settings for optimizing your software. Chapter 3 explains how to create, save and backup your NVivo Project file.

Chapters 4 - 8 cover how to import, create and edit text, audio, video, and picture data. Chapter 9 outlines how to create Memos and Links. Chapters 10 - 12 explain Nodes, Classifications and Coding—the lifeblood of qualitative data analysis with NVivo. Chapters 13 and 14 discuss creating Queries, saving them and creating Nodes from Query results.

Chapter 15 deals with NVivo's powerful functionality to support literature reviews and bibliographic data, with Chapter 16 describing the Framework Method of conveniently viewing and summarizing your data in Framework Matrices. Chapter 17 moves into managing surveys and questionnaires, called Datasets in NVivo.

Chapter 18 describes capturing data from the web and social media and Chapter 19 describes how to handle Social Network Analysis and Sociograms. Chapter 20 and 21 highlight NVivo's functionality for working with Evernote and OneNote 2010. Chapter 22 talks about finding and sorting various items within an NVivo project. While Chapter 23 deals with important aspects of collaboration using NVivo when you are a part of a research team. Chapters 24 - 26 describe how to graphically illustrate a project using Maps, Charts and Diagrams. And Chapter 27 describes building reports and extracts from your NVivo Projects.

Finally, Chapter 28 reviews the help functions available in NVivo 11, and Chapter 29 contains our glossary.

Furthermore, as one of the news in NVivo 11 is the introduction of three software editions, Starter, Pro and Plus, each with a given facility level, we have decided to add a suffix to the applicable chapter and section titles as follows:

- Only for Pro & Plus
- Only for Plus

All other chapters and sections are valid for all three editions.

Graphic Conventions

In this book we have applied some simple graphic conventions with the intention of improving readability:

Convention	Example	Comment
Commands	Go to **CONCEPT MAP	Item	Add Project Items**	Ribbon menu **CONCEPT MAP** and Menu group **Item** and Menu option **Add Project Items**
Menus	Go to **FILE → Options**	Main menu and options with **Bold**
Mouse functions	Right-click and select **New Query → Compound...**	Right-click with the mouse and select menu and sub-menu with **Bold**
Tabs	Select the **Layout** tab	Optional tabs with **Bold**
Functions	Select *Advanced Find* from **Options** drop-down list	Variable with **Bold**, the value with *Italic*; Heading with **Bold**, options with *Italic*
Buttons	Confirm with **[OK]**	Graphical buttons within brackets
Keyboard commands	Use the **[Del]** key to delete	Key is written within brackets
Typing	Type `Bibliography` in the textbox	`Courier` for text to be typed
Text	`..[1-3]` is shown in the textbox	`Courier` for shown text
Keyboard shortcuts	.. key command **[Ctrl]** + **[Shift]** + **[N]**	Hold the first (and second) key while touching the last

Before you Install NVivo 11

Your present Windows version decides if you should install 32-bit or 64-bit version of NVivo 11. The 32-bit version can be installed on all the below-mentioned Windows versions. The 64-bit version can only be installed when you have a 64-bit version of Windows.

Installation is made in two steps: The 'installation' which requires a license key and then the 'activation' which requires a communication with QSR preferably over the internet. The activation registers the user data in a customer database at QSR and is a license control function.

Should you need to change computer at a later stage then you need to deactivate your license **before** you uninstall NVivo in the old machine. Then you can reinstall NVivo in the new computer with your license key followed by a new activation procedure.

System Requirements

- 2 GHz dual-core processor or faster
- 4 GB RAM or more
- 1680 x 1050 screen resolution or higher
- Microsoft Windows 7 or later
- Approximately 8 GB of available hard-disk space or more depending on data storage need
- Internet Explorer 11 or later (for NCapture)
- Google Chrome 44 or later (for NCapture)
- Internet Connection

We recommend that your machine complies with those recommendations even if you are working with smaller projects.

Some Notes on NVivo and Macintosh Computers

There are crucial differences between installing NVivo 11 on your Mac and using the software called NVivo for Mac. These tools are not the same. The commercial release of NVivo for Mac took place in 2014. The software was released as a stripped-down version of NVivo 10 that was missing many of the software's core features such as the ability to handle surveys and questionnaires—called Datasets in NVivo parlance. Since then, a number of important updates have allowed NVivo for Mac to come closer to the functionality offered by NVivo 10. However, the drawbacks of NVivo for Mac's feature list were made plainly clear on the release of NVivo 11.

The purpose of this book is to describe NVivo 11 and its functions. While many of the functions are available in NVivo for Mac, many more are not. At the present time, it goes beyond the purposes of this book to compare and contrast the features of NVivo for Mac and NVivo 11—these comparisons are available on the developer's website. Suffice it to say, we believe that this book can still be a resource for

Mac users insofar as it can give some sense of what is available and what is missing.

Below, we discuss some methods Mac users use to install the fully functional version of NVivo 11 on their Mac computers. While the solutions may not be perfect, they at least allow Mac users the ability to use NVivo 11. We wish to reiterate though that this software is designed for PC, and the Mac version falls well short of meeting the full functionality of its PC predecessor.

Requirements for installing NVivo 11 on a Mac

NVivo 11 will operate on a Macintosh (Mac) computer. First, the user must set up some method of accessing Windows on their Mac. This can be done using dual-boot software (where a Mac computer has both Windows and a Mac operating system installed) or using virtualization software (where the Mac 'tricks' NVivo into believing it is operating on a Windows computer). Historically, Mac users have found three tools most useful: Boot Camp, Parallels and VMware Fusion.

Boot Camp

Boot Camp is a dual-boot software utility that has been included in Mac operating systems since 2007. Mac users utilizing Boot Camp must ensure their system requirements specified for NVivo 11 on Windows should be met. Again, Boot Camp allows Mac users to 'boot up' their Mac computer to run either a Mac operating system or a Windows operating system. Boot Camp is not popular with all Mac users running NVivo because it requires users switch between operating systems to use NVivo. Conversely, Boot Camp is an included Mac feature and there is free to run.

Parallels & VMware

Parallels and VMware are virtualization software that ostensibly 'trick' NVivo 11 into believing it is operating on a Windows-based computer. The advantage for Mac users here is that, unlike Boot Camp, they are not required to switch between a Mac and Windows operating system on their computer. However, Mac users should be aware that when using Parallels or VMware Fusion (or similar products), they may be required to have a Mac computer with higher system specifications than those detailed above. These emulation programs require increased memory and processor functions because they are simultaneously running a Mac operating system and a 'virtual' Windows system as well. Feel free to contact the authors if you have any questions about whether or not your computer's resources pose and challenges for NVivo 11 functionality.

Handling Other File Formats

NVivo can convert certain other file formats to its native format. This takes place when such file is selected for opening with NVivo or when NVivo intends to import such file into its project.

In some cases NVivo will ask for certain software for the conversion and may suggest direct download with a link.

File formats presently possible to convert are:

- Earlier versions of NVivo
- NVivo for Mac
- Atlas.ti
- MAXQDA

Atlas.ti and MAXQDA are subject to restrictions depending on software versions and releases. When you are considering such conversions, you are welcome to contact support@formkunskap.com

What's New in NVivo 11?

You'll learn all about what's new in NVivo 11 throughout this book, but we thought it would be important for our more advanced readers to have a guide to find out the ins and outs of NVivo's new features:

- Three software editions: Starter, Pro and Plus
- An updated user interface and start screen
- Expanded language support for English, Chinese, French, German, Japanese, Portuguese, and Spanish
- Clearer visual distinction between Case Nodes and Theme Nodes (see pages 1377 and 1499)
- More options for visualizing your data, including comparison diagrams, explore diagrams, hierarchy charts, mind maps, concept maps, and project maps
- Powerful new autocoding functions, including coding for themes, sentiments and patterns
- New features supporting social network analysis, including the ability to produce sociograms
- New functionality for exporting a codebook

2.   THE NVIVO 11 INTERFACE

This chapter is about the architecture of the NVivo screen, which resembles the interface of Microsoft Outlook. Appendix A, The NVivo Screen (see page 383), shows an overview of the main NVivo window. We will use Area 1, Area 2, etc. to represent the various sectors of the NVivo window. A work session usually starts in Area 1 with the selection of a Navigation Button corresponding to a group of folders. In Area 2, you select the folder relevant to your analysis, which leads to Area 3 where you can select a certain Project Item. Area 4 appears when you open a Project Item. In Area 4 where you can study that item's content.

> **Tip:** We suggest simply opening your NVivo 11 software and experimenting with the interface. Challenging yourself to play around in NVivo is a great way to learn!

Project work is done through the Ribbon menus, keyboard commands or via the menu options brought up by right-clicking your mouse. For more information about these commands, Appendix B (see page 385) is a summary of NVivo's keyboard commands.

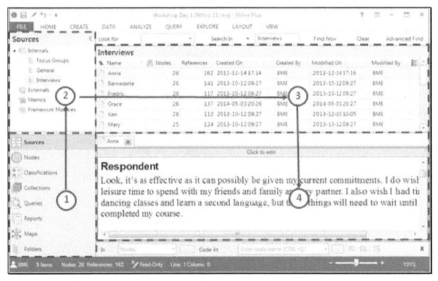

You will also find a Status Bar below the four areas comprising the main NVivo screen. The Status Bar displays contextual information that depends on the cursor position of your mouse. It can display the number of items in a folder, number of Nodes and references associated with a Project Item, or the row number and column number in a Dataset.

Area 1 – The Navigation Window

Area 1, the Navigation Window, contains 8 navigation buttons. Each button will display a specific folder in Area 2. The [**Folders**] button allows you to display all available NVivo 11 folders.

Another option for controlling the Navigation Window is selecting **HOME | Workspace | Go** as seen in the image to the right.

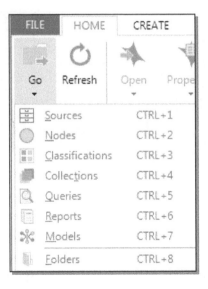

Area 2 – The Virtual Explorer

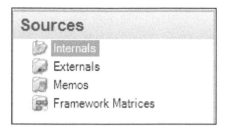

Each Navigation button contains a number of folders where relevant Project Items are stored. The folders associated with each Navigation Button are displayed in the Virtual Explorer, Area 2.

Virtual file paths are called Hierarchical Names. Only folders and Nodes have hierarchical names in NVivo. In the NVivo environment, hierarchical names are written with a double backslash between folders and a single backslash between a Node and its child Node.

For example:

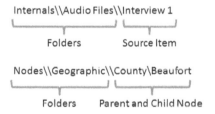

> **Did you know?** NVivo folders are called *virtual folders* as opposed to folders in a Windows environment. NVivo folders are *virtual* because they exist only in the NVivo project file. In most cases, *Virtual folders* perform like any Windows folder - you can create sub-folders, drag and drop project items into allowable folders, copy and paste folders. Certain folders are predefined in the NVivo project template and cannot be changed or deleted whereas other folders can be created by the user.

Creating a New Folder

NVivo contains a core set of template folders that cannot be deleted or moved. Users can create new subfolders under some of these template folders: Internals, Externals, Memos, Framework Matrices, Nodes, Relationships, Node Matrices, Source Classifications, Node Classifications, Relationship Types, Sets, Search Folders, Memo Links, See Also Links, Annotations, Queries, Results, Reports, Extracts, and Maps:

1. Select one of the navigation buttons in Area 1 and then select the folder in Area 2 under which a new subfolder will be created.
2. Go to **CREATE | Collections | Folder**
   or right-click and select **New Folder...**
   or **[Ctrl] + [Shift] + [N]**.

For each new folder, the **New Folder** dialog box appears:

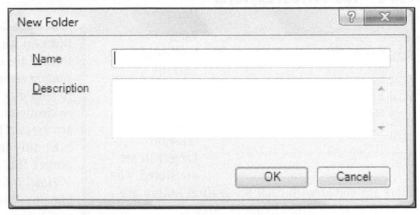

3   Type a name (compulsory) and a description (optional), then [**OK**].

Deleting a Folder

Deleting a folder also deletes its subfolders and all contents (all items in Area 3) therein.

1   Select the folder or folders in Area 2 that you want to delete.

2   Go to **HOME | Editing | Delete**
or right-click and select **Delete**
or [**Del**].

3   Confirm with [**Yes**].

Area 3 – The List View

Area 3 appears similar to a list of files in Windows, but NVivo calls these Project Items within an Item List. All folders are Project Items. All Project Items in the Internals, Externals and Memos folders - and their subfolders - are *Source Items*.

During the course of a project, you may need to revise the item lists when items are created, deleted or moved. At times it may be necessary to refresh the item list:

1   Go to **HOME | Workspace | Refresh**
or [**F5**].

Item Properties

All items have certain characteristics that can be changed or updated through the item's properties menu:

1 Select the item in Area 3 that you want to change or update.
2 Go to **HOME | Item | Properties**
or **[Ctrl] + [Shift] + [P]**
or right-click and select <**Item type**> **Properties**.

An item properties dialog box (in this case, **Document Properties**) may look like this:

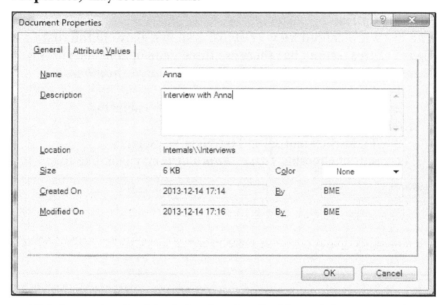

All information in this dialog box is editable and the text in the text boxes **Name** and **Description** is also searchable with the **Find** function, see Chapter 22, Finding and Sorting Project Items. Most experienced NVivo users know the project properties shortcut off by heart because this is fastest way to reach an item's Descriptions, a profoundly useful function in NVivo we'll spend more time on in Chapter 23, Collaborating with NVivo.

Setting Colors

Source items, Nodes, relationships, attribute values or users can be color marked individually. NVivo has seven pre-defined colors. Colors serve as visual cues for project researchers and as a result they can be used for a number of reasons. Most importantly, a color assigned to a Node will be visually represented in coding stripes (see page 193). The color marking is shown in the List View of Area 3.

1 Select the item or items (without openeing) that you want to color mark.
2 Go to **HOME | Item | Properties → Color → <select>**
or right-click and select **Color → <select>**.

Classifying an Item

All Source Items (except Framework Matrices) and Case Nodes can be classified and thus associated with meta-data. We'll discuss this further in Chapter 11, Classifications, but for now this is a reminder that working with items takes place in the List View, Area 3.

1   Select the item or items that you want to classify.

2   Go to **HOME | Item | Properties → Classification → <select>**
     or right-click and select **Classification → <select>**.

Viewing Options

The List View default view (*Details*) is shown above in the first figure of this section. But there are three more options for viewing items in the List View: *Small, Medium and Large Thumbnails*.

1   Click on any empty space in Area 3.

2   Go to **VIEW | List View | List View → <select>**.

alternatively

2   Right-click and select **List View → <select>**.

The result of choosing *Large Thumbnails* may look like this:

Sorting Options for a List

There are several ways to sort a list in Area 3.

1   Click on any empty space in Area 3.
2   Go to **LAYOUT | Sort & Filter | Sort by →** <select>.

You can also perform a custom sort for sources or nodes by moving items in the list.

1   Go to **LAYOUT | Sort & Filter | Sort by → Custom**
2   Select one or more items in Area 3.
3   Go to **LAYOUT | Rows & Columns | Move Up** ([Ctrl] + [Shift] + [U]).

alternatively

3   Go to **LAYOUT | Rows & Columns | Move Down** ([Ctrl] + [Shift] + [D]).

Your custom sorting is saved so it can at any later stage be resumed by going to **LAYOUT | Sort & Filter | Sort by → Custom**.

Customizing the Item List

You can customize the columns associated with Project Items. The **Customize Current View** dialog box allows you to remove unnecessary columns or add additional ones.

1   Click on any empty space in Area 3.
2   Go to **VIEW | List View | List View → Customize...**

alternatively

2   Right-click and select **List View → Customize...**

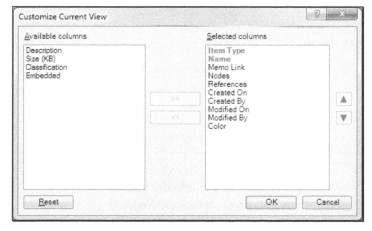

The detailed layout of this dialog box varies depending on which type of items is shown.

Tip: Some videos begin with a black frame, making the List View thumbnail a black square. But thumbnails of video items can display the specific frame that you want.

1   Move the playhead the frame you want to display.
2   Klick in the video fram.
3   Go to **Media | Selection | Assign Frame as Thumbnail**.

The selected frame is displayed as a thumbnail in Area 3 and when using the Video tab for a Node that the Video Item is coded at.

To reset all customizations for all types of items go to **VIEW** | **List View** | **List View** → **Reset All Customizations** or alternatively right-click and select **List View** → **Reset All Customizations**.

Printing the Item List

Printing the Item List can be a valuable contribution to discussions in project team meetings:

1   Go to **FILE** → **Print** → **Print List...**
     or right-click and select **Print** → **Print List...**
2   Select printer and printer settings, then [**OK**].

Exporting the Item List

Exporting your item list as an Excel spreadsheet or a text document is also possible:

1   Go to **DATA** | **Export** | **Export** → **Export List...**
     or right-click and select **Export** → **Export List...**
2   Select file format, folder and name, then [**OK**].

Deleting an Item

You can delete items from Area 3. When you delete a parent Node you also delete its child Nodes. Likewise, deleting a Classification also deletes its Attributes.

1   Click the appropriate navigation button in Area 1.
2   Select the appropriate folder in Area 2 or its subfolder.
3   Select the item or items in Area 3 that you want to delete.
4   Go to **HOME** | **Editing** | **Delete**
     or right-click and select **Delete**
     or [**Del**].
5   Confirm with [**Yes**].

Area 4 – The Detail View

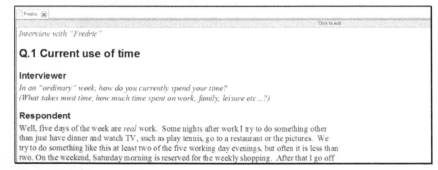

The above image is an example of an open Project Item, which can include documents, audio clips, videos, pictures, memos, or Nodes.

Each time a Source Item is opened it is Read Only. The document is made instantly editable by clicking on the Click to edit link at the top of an open item. Alternatively, you can go to **HOME** | **Item** | **Edit** or **[Ctrl]** + **[E]** which is a toggling function.

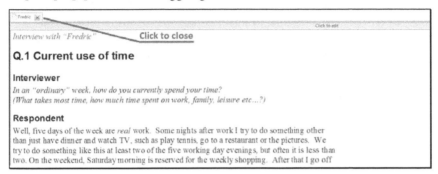

Each item has its own tab when several items are opened at the same time. By default, Project Items are 'docked' inside Area 4. You can undock an open item as a standalone window:

 1   Go to **VIEW** | **Window** | **Docked**.

Any undocked item can be docked again:

 1   Select the undocked item.
 2   Go to **VIEW** | **Window** | **Docked**.

Any undocked window can preferably be maximized with the conventional Maximize button.

Undocking items can only take place during an open work session; when you reopen a project all undocked windows are closed. However, you can go to **FILE → Options** and in the **Application Options** dialog box, select the Display tab, under the Detail View Defaults section, beside Window, you can select *Floating* (see page 42) so that an item window is always opened in undocked mode.

Tip: When you have several open project items, you can undock these items as seperate windows:

 1   Go to **VIEW** | **Workspace** | **Undock All**.

Conversely, if you want to dock all of your open items, click outside any of the undocked items:

 1   Go to **VIEW** | **Workspace** | **Dock All**.

While any docked window can be closed by clicking x on the right side of its tab, all windows can be closed simultaneously:

 1   Go to **VIEW** | **Workspace** | **Close All**.

Copying, Cutting, and Pasting

Standard conventions for copying, cutting, and pasting text and images prevail in NVivo. In addition, NVivo can also copy, cut, and paste complete Project Items like documents, memos, Nodes, etc. However, it is not possible to paste Nodes into folders meant for documents and vice versa (this would breach the software's folder template conventions). It is only possible to paste an item into the folder appropriate for that type of folder (e.g., paste a Node within the Nodes folder, a Query within the Queries folder, etc.). To cut and paste within NVivo:

1　Select an item (document, Node etc.)
2　Go to **HOME | Clipboard | Cut**
　　or right-click and select **Cut**
　　or [**Ctrl**] + [**X**].

alternatively

2　Go to **HOME | Clipboard | Copy**
　　or right-click and select **Copy**
　　or [**Ctrl**] + [**C**].
3　Select the appropriate folder or parent Node under which you want to place the item.
4　Go to **HOME | Clipboard | Paste → Paste**
　　or right-click and select **Paste**
　　or [**Ctrl**] + [**V**].

Paste Special

The normal **Paste** command includes all those elements. But after copying or cutting of some items (excluding Nodes) you can decide which elements from the item that should be pasted:

1　Copy or cut the item or items that you want to paste into the new position.
2　Select the target folder.
3　Go to **HOME | Clipboard | Paste → Paste Special...**

The **Paste Special Options** dialog box appears:

4   Select the item elements that you want to include.
    Additional context-based options may also appear: *Media
    content* and *Transcript* are valid for video and audio items
    and *Log entries* is valid for picture items.

5   Confirm with [**OK**].

Creating New Sets

You'll find Sets in the parent folder **Sets**. These are customizable
groups of shortcuts to various Project Items or groups of Project
Items. A Set is considered a subset or collection of Project Items that
allow you to access organized groups of items without moving or
copying those items.

1   Go to [**Folders**] or [**Collections**] in Area 1.

2   Select the **Sets** folder in Area 2.

3   Go to **CREATE | Collections | Sets**
    or right-click and select **New Set...**
    or [**Ctrl**] + [**Shift**] + [**N**].

The **New Set** dialog box appears:

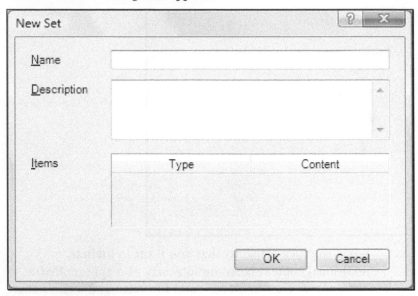

4 Type a name (compulsory) and a description (optional), then [**OK**].

Next, you need to define the members of your set:

1 Select the item or items that will form a set.
2 Go to **CREATE** | **Collections** | **Add To Set**
   or right-click any Project Item and select **Add To Set...**

The **Select Set** dialog box appears:

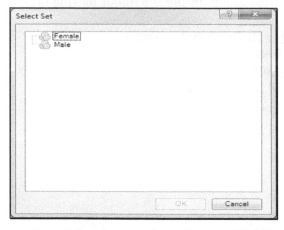

3 Select a set and confirm with [**OK**].

You can also select items or shortcuts from any folder and paste them into a Set. When using **Find**, **Advanced Find**, or **Grouped Find** the result can easily be added to a Set. Sets can be used as an alternative to storing results in a subfolder to **Search Folders**:

1 Select an item (shortcut) or items (shortcuts) that will form a new set.
2 Go to **CREATE** | **Collections** | **Create As Set**.
The **New Set** dialog box is shown.
3 Type a name of the new set.
4 Confirm with [**OK**].
Editing Sets involves Copying, Cutting, Pasting, Sorting, Moving, Deleting Set members as with other project items.

Sets are a powerful organizational tool in NVivo, but beginning and intermediate users are sometimes confused by their functionality. The main function of Sets is to allow users the flexibility of organizing project items into temporary or permanent groups.

For example, we are involved in a project involving interview data, focus group data, writing samples, and social media data for a group of 20 undergraduate social science students. As a team, we could organize these data sources according to type of data source (e.g., an interview folder, a focus group folder, etc.) or we could organize these data sources according to student (e.g., a folder for Student 1, a folder for Student 2, etc.). While each method of organization has its merits, Sets allows us to organize project items according to type of data source AND create a Set organizing data sources according to student. As alternative methods of organizing text items present themselves, more and more sets can be generated.

Undo

The undo-function can be made in several steps backwards. Undo only works for commands made after the last save:
1 Go to **Undo** on the **Quick Access Toolbar**
or [**Ctrl**] + [**Z**].
The arrow next to the undo-icon makes it possible to select which of the last five commands that shall be undone. When you select the first option only the last command is undone and when you select the last option all commands will be undone.

The option **Redo** (Undo – Undo) is available in Word but not in NVivo.

The Ribbons

Commands are organized into logical groups, collected together under tabs. Each tab relates to a type of activity, such as creating new Project Items or analyzing your source materials.

The **HOME, CREATE, DATA, ANALYZE, QUERY, EXPLORE, LAYOUT**, and **VIEW** tabs are always visible. The other tabs are 'contextual' which means that they are shown when needed. For example, the **PICTURE** tab is shown when a picture is opened.

Within each tab, related commands are grouped together. For example, the **Format** group on the **HOME** tab contains commands for setting font size, type, bold, italics and underline.

The ribbon is optimized for a screen resolution of 1280 by 1024 pixels, when the NVivo window is maximized on your screen. When the NVivo window is not maximized and the ribbon is smaller, you may not see all the icons or text.

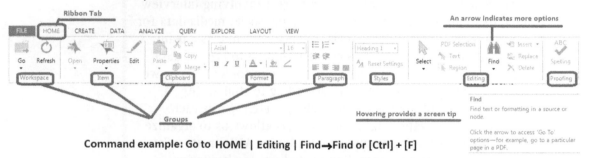

Command example: Go to HOME | Editing | Find→Find or [Ctrl] + [F]

The **Quick Access Toolbar** is always visible and provides quick access to frequently-used commands. By default, the Save, Edit and Undo commands are available in Quick Access Toolbar. You can customize the Quick Access Toolbar by adding or removing commands. You can also move the Quick Access Toolbar above or below the ribbon by clicking the small arrow:

Select the options *Show Above the Ribbon* and *Minimize the Ribbon*. The menu tabs are shown again as soon as you point at any menu alternative.

The **HOME** tab provides commands related to formatting (e.g., paragraph styles) and workflow (e.g., cut and paste):

The **CREATE** tab provides commands related to making new Project Items (e.g., creating a new Node):

The **DATA** tab provides commands related to importing and exporting Project Items:

The **ANALYZE** tab provides commands related to coding, linking, and annotating:

The **QUERY** tab provides commands related to searching and querying your data.

The **EXPLORE** tab provides commands related to analytic representations.

The **LAYOUT** tab provides commands related to list views and tables:

The **VIEW** tab provides commands related to visual aspects of the Project Item interface (e.g., docking and coding stripes):

- ◆ -

The following tabs are context dependent, meaning they only become available depending on the Project Item type that is open.

The **NODE/CASE/RELATIONSHIP/SENTIMENT** tab provides commands related to Nodes/Cases/Relationships/Sentiment:

The **FRAMEWORK MATRIX** tab provides commands related to Framework matrices:

The **MEDIA** tab provides commands related to audio and video:

The **PICTURE** tab provides commands related to images:

The **REPORT** tab provides commands related to the Report Designer:

The **MIND MAP** tab provides commands related to creating and modifying Mind Maps:

The **PROJECT MAP** tab provides commands related to creating and modifying Project Maps:

The **CONCEPT MAP** tab provides commands related to creating and modifying Concept Maps:

The **CHART** tab provides commands related to creating and modifying charts:

The **HIERARCHY CHART** tab provides commands related to creating and modifying Hierarchy Charts:

The **WORD TREE** tab has commands handling and modifying Word Trees:

The **CLUSTER ANALYSIS** tab provides commands related to conducting and formatting cluster analyses:

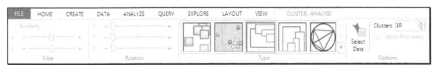

The **COMPARISON DIAGRAM** tab provides commands related to modifying Comparison Diagrams:

The **EXPLORE DIAGRAM** tab provides commands related to modifying Explore Diagrams:

The **SOCIOGRAM** tab provides commands related to modifying sociograms:

The **TWITTER SOCIOGRAM** tab provides commands related to modifying sociograms from Twitter.

Application Options

NVivo project settings can be adjusted for an individual project or for the NVivo software overall. **Application Options** adjust settings for the software overall, and some changes you make only apply to new projects and will therefore have an effect on the **Project Properties** (see page 55) settings for future projects:

1   From the NVivo Welcome Screen or in an open project go to **FILE → Options**.

The **[Reset]** button will change the options back to the default settings and cannot be undone. Your username, initials, user interface language and server connections will be preserved.

> **Tip:** Display plain text for Nodes with <value> or more sources ensures better performance for large projects. Restore source formatting by going to **VIEW | Detail View | Node → Rich Text**.

The General Tab

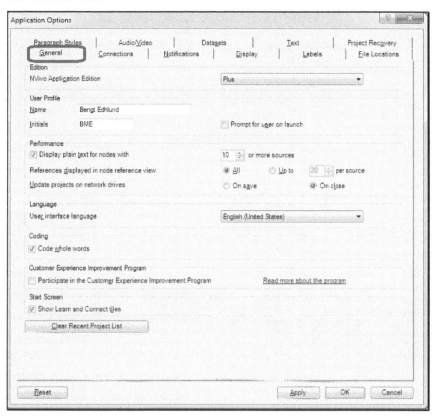

The **General** tab contains default options for working with the NVivo interface such as Application Edition, user interface language and coding properties.

The setting of NVivo Application Edition is made here: Starter, Pro or Plus depending on your current license.

Settings made here take immediate effect in an ongoing project and will also become default for new projects. Here you can change the user interface language.

The Connections Tab

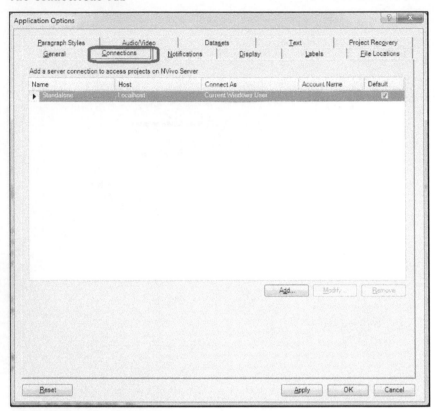

The **Connections** tab contains settings pertaining to NVivo for Teams – additional QSR proprietary teamwork software (see page 323).

The Notifications Tab

The **Notifications** tab contains default options for save reminders and software update checks.

All settings under this tab take immediate effect on an ongoing project.

Tip: Why take a chance on losing valuable work? We recommend that a save reminder displays every 10 minutes, instead of the default 15.

The Display Tab

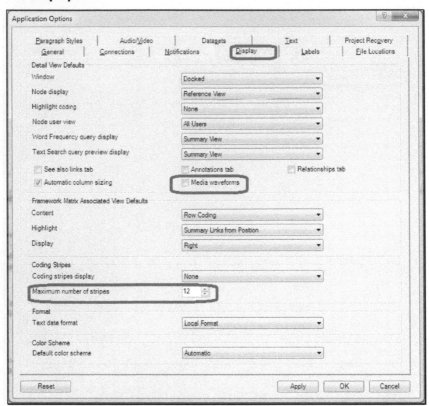

The **Display** tab contains default options for visual cues in NVivo such as coding stripes, highlighting, and tabs.

We suggest unchecking the display of Media waveforms as the waveform often disturbs other graphic information like coding stripes, links and selections.

We also suggest increasing the maximum number of coding stripes beyond the default number which is 7. The number of stripes cannot be extended beyond 200.

In case you prefer always to open your windows undocked, then set Detail View as Window *Floating*.

For settings related to Framework Matrix, see page 259.

All settings under this tab take immediate effect on an ongoing project.

The Labels Tab

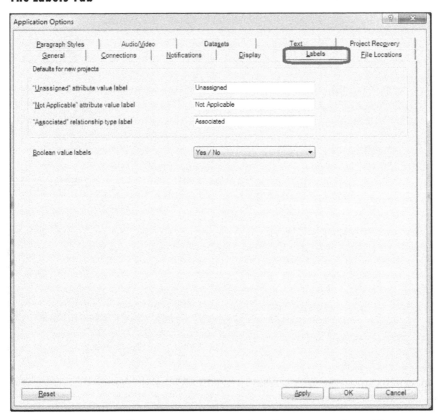

The **Labels** tab allows you to customize the names of attributes, values and the Associated relationship type.

Settings made here will take effect next time a project is created. If you want to make changes in the current project, use **Labels** tab in **Project Properties** dialog box (see page 57).

The File Locations Tab

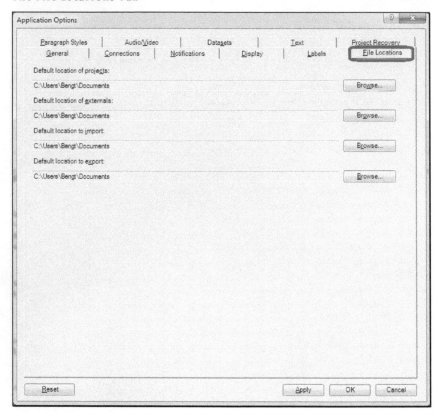

The **File Locations** tab contains default file locations of projects, externals and the default locations of imported and exported Project Items and data.

The preferred location for ongoing project files is the native harddisk, the C-disk. After each work session you are recommended to create a security backup copy in a safe location in your network or in a cloud service, see page 67. When you need to access such backup copy of your project file either copy the file to your local drive or create a new project and import the backup project. Never open a project file from a USB memory or any cloud service.

All settings under this tab take immediate effect on an ongoing project.

The Paragraph Styles Tab

   The **Paragraph Styles** tab contains default options for NVivo styles (see page 80). Changes made under Application Options will be available next time a new project is created. Existing project settings can be modified under the **Paragraph Styles** tab in **Project Properties** (see page 60).

The Audio/Video Tab

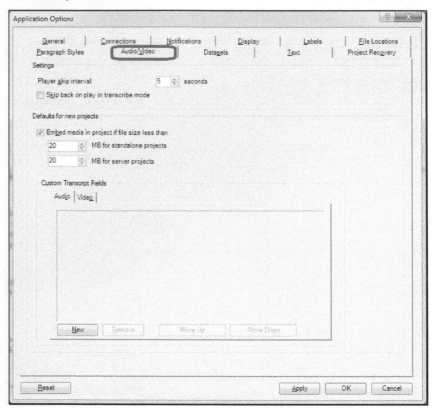

Tip: Settings for the threshold value of embedded audio and video files are set under: *Embed media in project if file size less than <value> MB.* Max is 40 MB for single users. Embedded or not, you can always code, link and create transcript rows in a media item.

The **Audio/Video** tab contains settings for the skip interval for skipping forward and skipping backward. The threshold value for embedding is set here. These settings have an immediate effect on an open project. You can also create custom transcript fields (or columns) for audio and video items. However, these fields will come into effect for new projects. To create custom transcript fields in an existing project go to **FILE → Project Properties**, and select the **Audio/Video** tab, see page 61).

The Datasets Tab

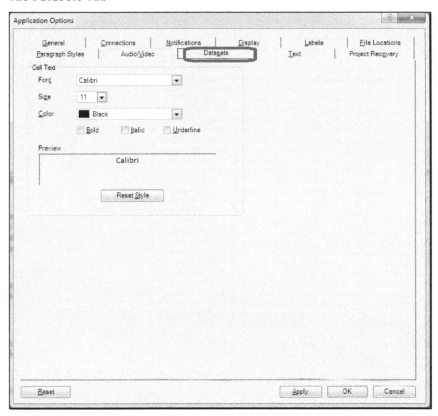

The **Datasets** tab allows you to adjust the font, size and color of cell text. Modifications made here will take effect next time a Dataset is opened.

The Text Tab

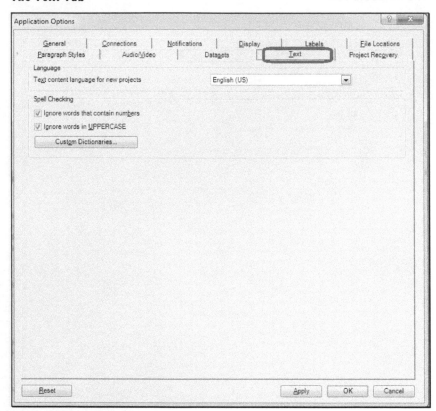

The **Text** tab allows you to make settings for the content language and the spell checking dictionaries that you want to use. The setting of language does not have an effect on the ongoing project. For the next new project the chosen language will be default. If you want to change content language for the current project go to the **General** tab of **Project Properties** dialog box (see page 55).

The supported languages are: Chinese (PRC), English (UK), English (US), French, German, Japanese, Portuguese and Spanish. If you use any other language then you can set the language as *Other*.

The button [**Custom Dictionaries...**] can be used to appoint one specific folder for each language which can include the custom dictionary, **<filename>.DIC**. This is a normal text-file and can be opened and edited with Notepad. If you already have a custom dictionary from before you can name it **<filename>.DIC** and store it in the defined folder. Even the setting *Other* can have its own custom dictionary.

Project Recovery Tab

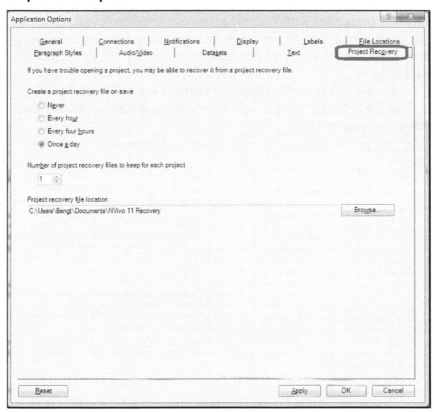

The **Project Recovery** tab allows you to set the frequency of recovery files and the number of such files.

As you update and save your project, these settings will let NVivo create a 'project recovery file' to protect against loss of data. This is useful in situations where your project is compromised and you cannot open it—you will have the option to restore it from the project recovery file.

Alternate Screen Layouts

Sharing the screen with four windows can sometimes make reading Area 4 difficult. But NVivo offers an alternate screen layout to split the screen space vertically instead of horizontally between Area 3 and Area 4.

    1   Go to **VIEW | Workspace | Detail View → Right**.

The Right Detail View is very handy when coding with drag-and-drop (see page 167).

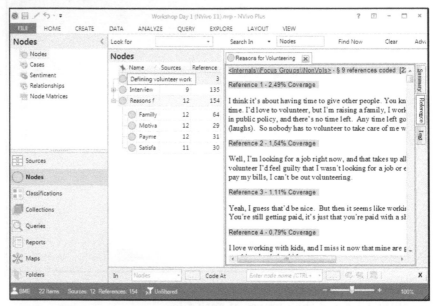

To revert to original setting of the screen:

    1   Go to **VIEW | Workspace | Detail View → Bottom**.

New to NVivo 11, your **Detail View** setting preference can now be saved in between sessions.

For more screen space it is also possible to temporarily close Areas 1 and 2.

1   Go to **VIEW | Workspace → Navigation View** or **[Alt] + [F1]**, which is a toggling function.

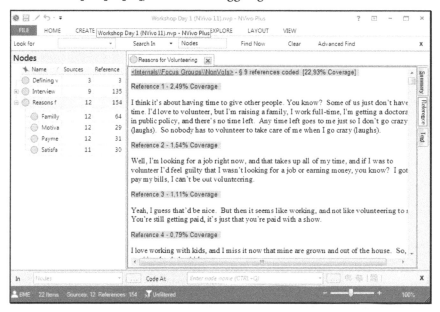

One option is hiding with the small arrow in the upper right corner of Area 2:

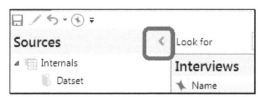

This setting is saved during current session even if you open another project. You can navigate to other folders by going to **HOME | Workspace | Go key → <select>** or **[Ctrl] + [1 - 8]**.

3. BEGINNING YOUR PROJECT

An NVivo project is a term used for all source documents and other items that altogether form a qualitative study. Importantly, a project is also a computer file that houses all those Project Items.

NVivo can only open and process one project at a time. It is however possible to start the program twice and open one project in each program window. Cut, copy, and paste between two such program windows is limited to text, graphics and images and not Project Items like documents or Nodes.

A project is built up of several items with different properties. There are internal sources (i.e., documents, memos), external sources (i.e., web sites), Nodes and queries.

Creating a New Project

The Welcome screen will greet you each time you launch NVivo, and it is from here that you have the option to create a new project file (Blank Project):

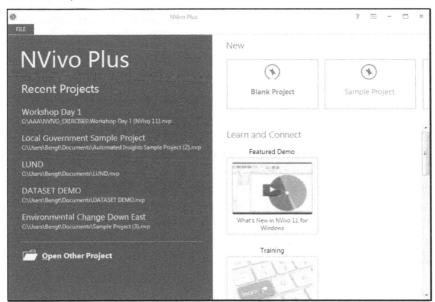

Your most recent projects are listed on the Welcome screen. You can also create a new project while navigating inside an existing project:

1   Go to **FILE → New**
      or [**Ctrl**] + [**N**]

      or the icon  on the Quick Access
      Toolbar.

The **New Project** dialog box appears:

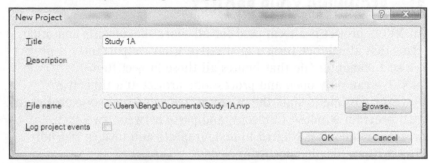

You must type a name for your project file, but the description is optional. The file path for your project is seen in the **File name** box. Click **[Browse]** to select a new location for your project file. The default location of the project file is determined in the **Application Options** dialog box, under the **File Locations** tab (see page 44). The preferred location for ongoing project files is the native harddisk, the C-disk. About security backup, see page 67.

The name of a project can later be changed without changing the file name. Any open NVivo projects will be closed as NVivo opens a new or an existing project.

Sources & Project Size

NVivo is capable of importing and creating a variety of file types as data (e.g., text sources, tables, images, video, PDFs, etc.) Collectively, these items care called *Sources*. We'll discuss sources at length over the next few chapters, but for now it's important you understand that NVivo can either *import* Sources to a project file or *link* Sources externally to a Project file.

Files that are imported into NVivo are amalgamated by the software, which means that they become a part of the NVivo project. These are called *Internal Sources*. For example, any changes you make to imported sources (e.g., a text Source) are not reflected in the original document (e.g., a Microsoft Word text file).

Files that are linked into NVivo are only referenced by the software, which means that they exist independently of the NVivo project. These are called *External Sources* and cannot be coded, only the external item (the text inside NVivo) can be coded.

Audio- and video files are special as they can either be embedded or remain stored outside NVivo. If such files remain outside NVivo they can still be handled as if they were embedded, that is you can link and code, etc. Therefore, even not embedded media files are *Internal Sources*. It is the size of such files that decides if it should be embedded or not. A threshold value set by the user decides. The threshold value however, cannot exceed 40 MB (read more on page 102).

An NVivo 11 Project file size is maximum 10 GB provided the storage is of type NTFS. Bear in mind that large Project Items (e.g., audio and video files) can be stored outside the project file. Linking to external files allows you to keep the project file size down. Using NVivo for Teams (see Chapter 23, Collaborating with NVivo) allows for a maximum project file size of 100 GB or larger if storage space is available.

Project Properties

When a new project is created some settings from the **Application Options** dialog box are inherited. This dialog box opens by going to **FILE → Options**, and the settings that are inherited are found under these tabs: **Labels**, **Paragraph Styles**, **Audio/Video** and **Text**. Modifications and templates which are made in the **Project Properties** dialog box are only valid for your current project:

    1   Go to **FILE → Info → Project Properties**.

The General Tab

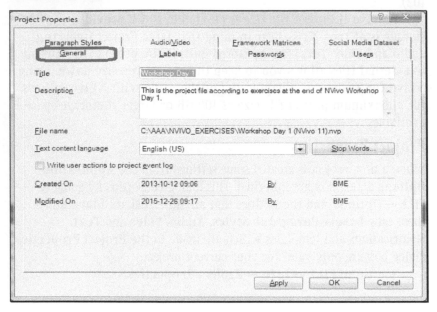

In this dialog box it is possible to modify your project name, but not the NVivo project file name. From the **Text content language** drop-down list you will, if available, select the language of the data used in the project, otherwise select *English* or *Other*. Your content language will be the default language for spell check, as well as an important setting for Text Search Queries and Word Frequency Queries. For all languages except *Other* a default stop words list is built in. The stop words list can be edited using the **[Stop Words]** button or while using Word Frequency Queries (see Chapter 13, Queries). Such customized stop word lists are only valid for the current project. Even when the content language setting is *Other* you can build a customized stop words list.

Tip: Your stop words list can be edited with the button **[Stop Words]**. Remember, customized stop words are only valid for the current project. Google on "stopwords swedish" or an applicable language to copy and paste other stop words lists.

Other language dependent functions are: Similar words (stemmed, synonyms, specializations, generalizations), autocoding of Themes and Sentiments (NVivo 11 Plus), Spell check (see pages 48 and 82).

The Description (max 512 characters) can be modified. *Write user actions to project event log* is optional. When activated you can open this log with **FILE → Info → Open Project Event Log** or delete with **FILE → Info → Clear Project Event Log**.

The Labels Tab

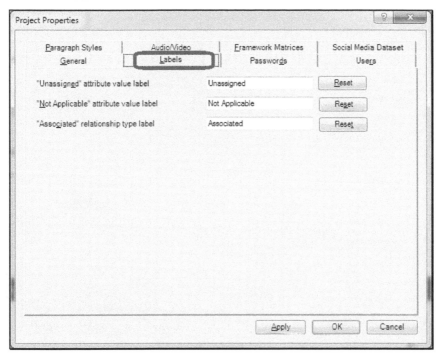

Under the **Labels** tab you can change some of your project's 'labels'. The [**Reset**] buttons reset to the values defined in the **Application Options** dialog box, under the **Labels** tab (see page 43).

The Passwords Tab

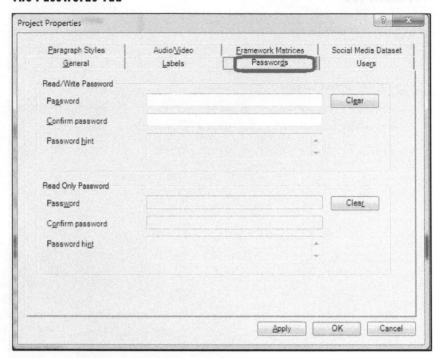

Under the **Passwords** tab you can define separate passwords for opening and editing your current project.

The Users Tab

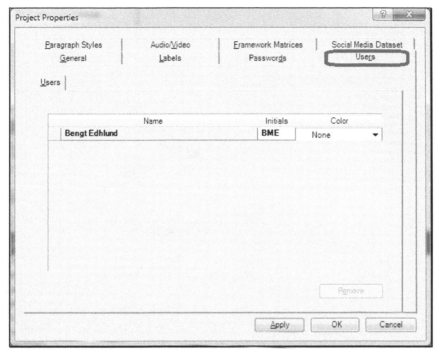

All users who have actively worked in the current project are listed here. The current user is identified by bold letters. You can replace a user with someone else on the list by selecting the user who shall be replaced (triangle) and using the **[Remove]** button. Select who will replace the deleted user by selecting from the list of users.

Users can also be given an individual color marking. Use the drop-down list in the Color column and select color. This color marking can be used when viewing coding stripes per user.

The Paragraph Styles Tab

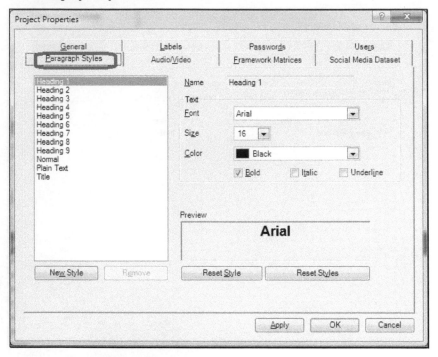

Under the **Paragraph Styles** tab, you can redefine your paragraph styles. The [**Reset Styles**] buttons reset to values defined in the **Application Options** dialog box, (see page 45).

The Audio/Video Tab

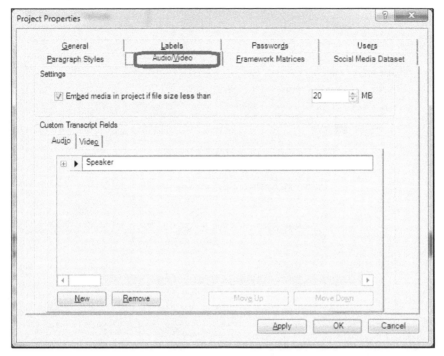

The settings for new projects are inherited from the **Application Options** dialog box, the **Audio/Video** tab (see page 46). Modifications made here are only valid for the current project.

When you need to create Custom Transcript Fields in your current project then you may use this dialog box. The [**New**] button defines more fields like Speaker, Affiliation with separate fields for Audio and Video.

The Framework Matrices Tab

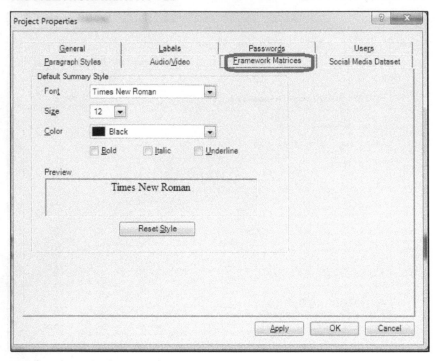

The settings here for new projects are inherited from the style Normal in the **Application Options** dialog box, the **Paragraph Style** tab (see page 45). Modifications made here are only valid for the Framework Matrices summaries in the current project.

The Social Media Dataset Tab

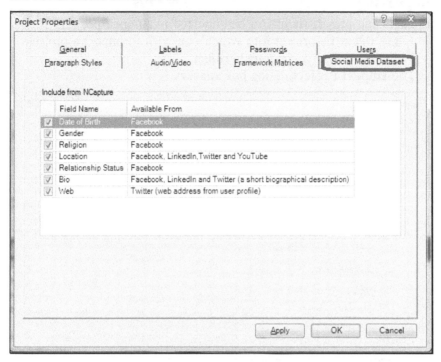

The Social Media tab: Social Media Datasets can be imported via NCapture files containing Facebook, Twitter, LinkedIn or YouTube data. This tab allows you to toggle the types of data you wish to capture from each social networking site.

Importing Projects – Only for Pro & Plus

Projects and project items can be imported to an open project:
1   Open the project into which you wish to import a project.
2   Go to **DATA | Import | Project**.

The **Import Project** dialog box appears:

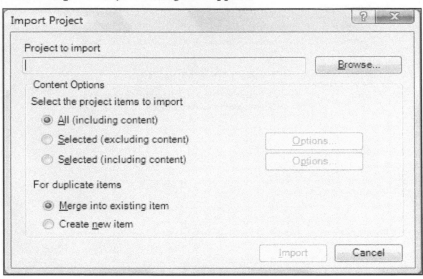

3   The [**Browse...**] button opens a file browser. Search for the project file to be imported.
4   Select the item options that you need for the import.
5   Confirm with [**Import**].

The options of this dialog box are very important to understand. When you need to merge two projects you simply first create a new project and then import one project after another applying the default settings of the **Import Project** dialog box.

When you for example need to import only folders, Nodes, and Cases but not content (data) then you select *Selected (excluded content)* and the [**Options...**] button opens the **Import Options**

dialog box:

Tip: For users who don't have access to NVivo for Teams, merging projects is a useful function for teams collaborating on the same project. Users can independently make changes to their project and, later, import their changes into a project 'master' file.

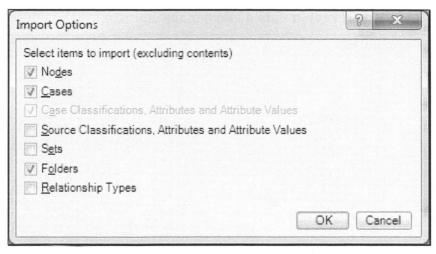

After choosing the applicable options, click [**OK**] and then [**Import**]. The result of such import can be used as a project template and is an easy way to inherit node and folder structures from one project to another.

An **Import Project Report** is now shown each time an import has taken place listing all imported items.

Exporting Project Data – Only for Pro & Plus

All Project Items (except folders) can be exported in various file formats. For example, project Memos can be created in NVivo and then exported as .DOC or .DOCX files so they can be shared with collaborated over email:

1   Open a project.
2   Go to **DATA | Export | Project**

The **Export Project Data** dialog box appears:

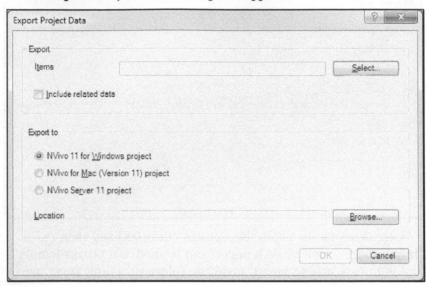

At **Export items** and the [**Select**] button you decide what items that shall be exported and at **Export to** and the [**Specify**] button you decide the name and location of the exported project data.

The option *NVivo for Mac* requires a Project Converter to be installed.

Saving Projects

You can save the project file at any time during a work session. The complete project is saved; it is not possible to save single Project Items.

1   Go to **FILE → Save**
     or [**Ctrl**] + [**S**]

     or the icon 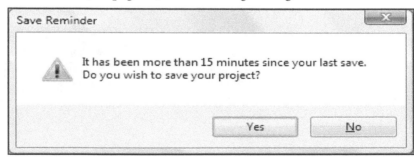 on the Quick Access Toolbar.

If the option *Enable project save reminders every 15 minutes* has been chosen (see page 41) the following message will show:

Save Reminder

⚠ It has been more than 15 minutes since your last save. Do you wish to save your project?

Yes   No

2   Confirming with [**Yes**] saves the whole project file.

Security Backup

Security backup of your NVivo project is important yet easy since the whole project is one file and not a structure of files and folders. Use Windows native tools for backup copies and follow the backup routines that your organization applies. The command **FILE → Copy Project** creates a copy of the project at the location that you decide while the current project remains.

It is advisable to include the current date in the file name of the backup copy so you can easily identify and open earlier versions of your project.

When you need to access such backup copy of your project file either copy the file to your local drive or create a new project and import the backup project. Never open a project file from a USB memory or any cloud service.

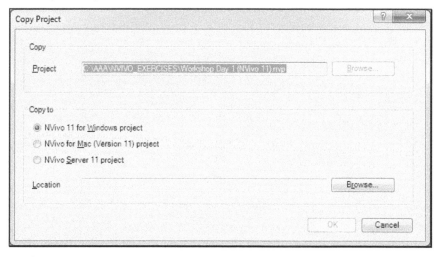

The option *NVivo for Mac* requires a Project Converter to be installed.

Closing NVivo

After each work session save your project file and close NVivo. Close with:

FILE → Close

or the icon 🌐 → **Close**
or [**Alt**] + [**F4**].

Security Backup

Security backup of your Myro project is important yet easy since the whole project is one file and not a structure of files and folders. Use Windows native tools for backup copies and follow the backup routines that your organization applies. The command File → Copy Project creates a copy of the project at the location that you decide while the current project remains.

It is advisable to include the current date in the file name of the backup copy so you can easily identify and open earlier versions of your project.

4. HANDLING TEXT SOURCES

Documents

From interview transcripts to government white papers, text data makes up the majority of qualitative research data. Text items can be easily imported from files created outside NVivo, like Word documents or text notes from Evernote. Text items can also be created by NVivo as most word processing tools and functions are incorporated in NVivo software, which we'll discuss in the next chapter.

Importing Documents

This section is about text-based sources that can be imported and these file types are: .DOC, .DOCX, .RTF, .TXT, and text-only Evernote export files (.ENEX). When text files are imported into NVivo, they become Project Items within the Source folder:

1   Go to **DATA | Import | Documents**
     Default folder is **Internals**.
     Go to 5.

alternatively

1   Click on [**Sources**] in Area 1.
2   Select the **Internals** folder in Area 2 or its subfolder.
3   Go to **DATA | Import | Documents**.
     Go to 5.

alternatively

3   Click on any empty space in Area 3.
4   Right-click and select **Import → Import Documents...**
     or [**Ctrl**] + [**Shift**] + [**I**].

alternatively

3   Drag and drop your file's icon from an outside folder into Area 3.
     Go to 5.

In each case, the **Import Internals** dialog box appears:

5   The [**Browse...**] button gives access to a file browser and you can select one or several documents for a batch import. To select multiple documents use [**Shift**] + left click.

6   When the documents have been selected, confirm with
     [Open].
The **[More >>]** button offers several options:

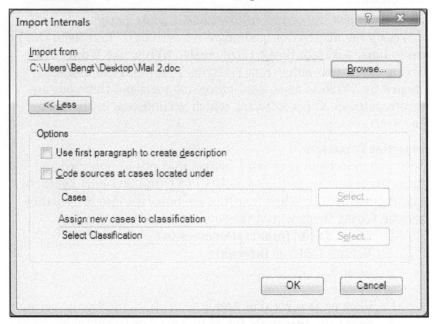

Use first paragraph to create descriptions. NVivo copies the first
paragraph of the document and pastes it into the Description field.
   Code sources at cases located under. Each Source Item will be
coded at a Case with the same name as the imported file and located
in a folder or under a parent Node that has been selected. Also you
must assign the Nodes to a Classification when importing (see
Chapter 11, Classifications).
7   Confirm the import with **[OK]**.

When only *one* document has been imported, the **Document Properties** dialog box appears:

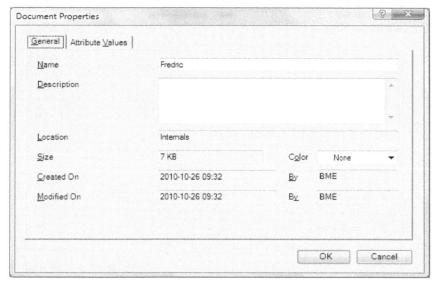

Within this dialog box you can modify the name of the Source Item and optionally add a description.

    8   Confirm with [**OK**].

Creating a New Document

You can also create your own text items within NVivo, much the same as creating a Word document or text note in Evernote.

    1   Go to **CREATE | Sources | Document**
        Default folder is **Internals**.
        Go to 5.

alternatively

    1   Click on [**Sources**] in Area 1.
    2   Select the **Internals** folder in Area 2 or its subfolder.
    3   Go to **CREATE | Sources | Document**
        Go to 5.

alternatively

    3   Click on any empty space in Area 3.
    4   Right-click and select **New Internal → New Document...**
        or [**Ctrl**] + [**Shift**] + [**N**].

The **New Document** dialog box appears:

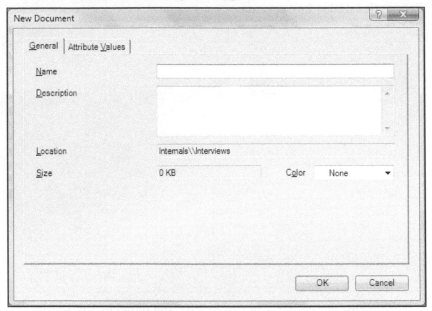

5 Type a name (compulsory) and a description (optionally), then **[OK]**.

Here is a typical list view in Area 3 of some Source Items:

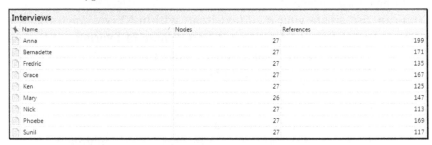

Opening a Document

Now that you have imported or created a list of Source Items, you can easily open one or more items anytime you see fit:

1 Click on **[Sources]** in Area 1.
2 Select the **Internals** folder in Area 2 or its subfolder.
3 Select the document in Area 3 that you want to open.
4 Go to **HOME | Item | Open**
  or right-click and select **Open Document...**
  or double-click on the document in Area 3
  or **[Ctrl] + [Shift] + [O]**.

Please note, NVivo only allows you to open one document at a time, but several documents can stay open simultaneously.

Exporting a Document

As mentioned, you may wish at some point to export a text Source Item, such as a Memo you wrote inside NVivo but now need to email to a collaborator.

1   Click [**Sources**] in Area 1.
2   Select the **Internals** folder in Area 2 or its subfolder.
3   Select the document(s) Area 3 that you want to export.
4   Go to **DATA | Export | Items**
    or right-click and select **Export → Export <Item>**
    or [**Ctrl**] + [**Shift**] + [**E**].

The **Export Options** dialog box appears:

5   Select the options that you want. Confirm with [**OK**].
6   Decide file name, file location, and file type. (.DOCX, .DOC, .RTF, .TXT, .PDF, or .HTML. Confirm with [**Save**].

Remember, coding made on text items cannot be transferred when a Source Item is exported.

External Items – Only for Pro & Plus

For any number of reasons, you may wish to refer to external items outside of your NVivo project (i.e., a web site, a file too large or a file type that is incompatible). NVivo allows you to create external items that can act as placeholders or links.

Creating an External Item

1 Go to **CREATE | Sources | External**
 Default folder is **Externals**.
 Go to 5.

alternatively

1 Click on [**Sources**] in Area 1.
2 Select the **Externals** folder in Area 2 or its subfolder.
3 Go to **CREATE | Sources | External**.
 Go to 5.

alternatively

3 Click on any empty space in Area 3.
4 Right-click and select **New External...**
 or [**Ctrl**] + [**Shift**] + [**N**].

The **New External** dialog box appears:

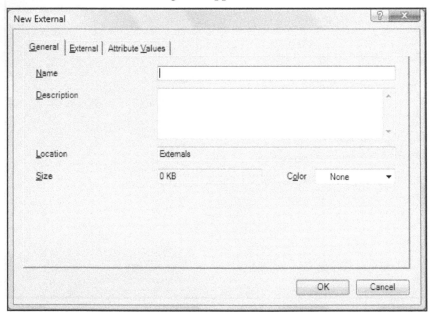

5 Type name (compulsory) and description (optional), then go to the **External** tab.

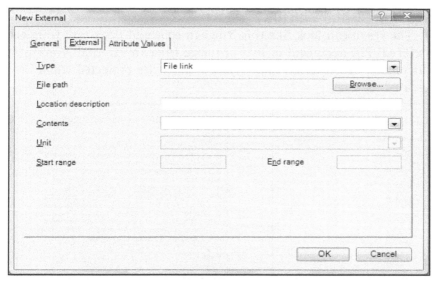

6   At **Type** select *File link* and then use the [**Browse...**] button to find the target file. Alternatively, at Type select *Web link* and type or paste the URL in the text box below. For non-digital items select *Other*.

7   At **Location description** type the location of the external file, like 'my computer' or physical place.

8   At **Contents** the options are *Audio, Image, Printed Document* or *Video*.

When you select Printed Document the **Unit** options are hapter, Page, Paragraph, Section, Sentence and Verse.

9   At **Start range** and **End range** you can put the first and the last page of an external document, like this:

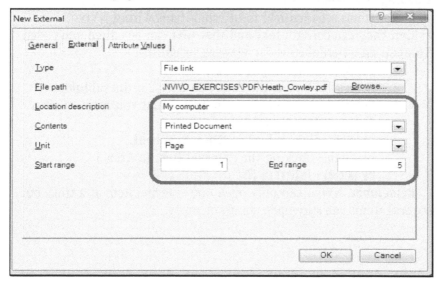

10   Confirm with [**OK**].

The result can look like this. You can copy and paste text from an external PDF-document or text or image from an external Word-document. The external source item is not write-protected when created:

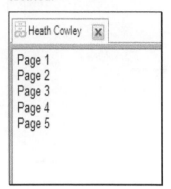 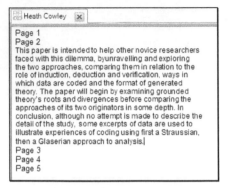

The text you enter or paste can be coded but not the content of the external file.

This is a typical list view in Area 3 of some external items:

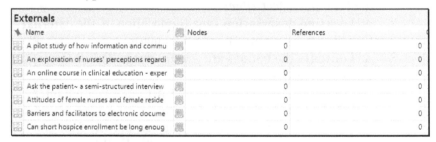

Opening an External Item

External items act identical to internal items within NVivo's Sources folder: they can contain text and that text can be edited and coded. To open an external item for viewing or editing:

1   Click on [**Sources**] in Area 1.
2   Select the **Externals** folder in Area 2 or its subfolder.
3   Select the external item in Area 3 that you want to open.
4   Go to **HOME | Item | Open**
    or right-click and select **Open External...**
    or double-click on the external item in Area 3
    or [**Ctrl**] + [**Shift**] + [**O**].

Remember, NVivo can only open one external item at a time, but several items can stay open simultaneously.

Opening an External Source

Unlike internal items, external items are necessarily linked to external sources, which can be opened through NVivo:

1   Click on [**Sources**] in Area 1.
2   Select the **Externals** folder in Area 2 or its subfolder.
3   Select the external item in Area 3 that has a link to the external file or URL that you want to open.
4   Go to **HOME | Item | Open → Open External File**
    or right-click and select **Open External File**.

Editing an External Source or Link

1   Click on [**Sources**] in Area 1.
2   Select the **Externals** folder in Area 2 or its subfolder.
3   Select the external item in Area 3 that you want to edit.
4   Go to **HOME | Item | Properties**
    or right-click and select **External Properties...**
    or [**Ctrl**] + [**Shift**] + [**P**].

The **External Properties** dialog box appears.

5   Select the **External** tab and if you want to link to a new target file use [**Browse...**]. If you want to modify a web link change the URL.

Exporting an External Item – Only for Pro & Plus

Similar to internal items, external items can be exported. However, the linked external file or the web link is not included in the exported item, only the external item text contents are exported.

1   Click on [**Sources**] in Area 1.
2   Select the **Externals** folder in Area 2 or its subfolder.
3   Select the external item or items in Area 3 that you want to export.
4   Go to **DATA | Export | Item**
    or right-click and select **Export → Export <Item>**
    or [**Ctrl**] + [**Shift**] + [**E**].

The **Export Options** dialog box appears.

5   Select the options that you want. Confirm with [**OK**].
6   Decide file name, file location, and file type. Possible file types are: .DOCX, .DOC, .RTF, .TXT, .PDF, or .HTML. Confirm with [**Save**].

5. EDITING TEXT IN NVIVO

Whether you import a text document or create a new one, NVivo 11 contains most of the functions of modern word processing software. Notwithstanding the fact that text document files are often imported, understanding how to edit text in NVivo is useful. Aside from its ability to edit existing source documents, you can use NVivo's word processing functionality to compose Memos, Externals, and Framework Matrix summaries.

Formatting Text

Remember, each time a Source Item is opened it is Read-Only. Therefore, click *Click to edit* (or **HOME | Item | Edit** or [Ctrl] + [E]) at the top of a Source Item before editing.

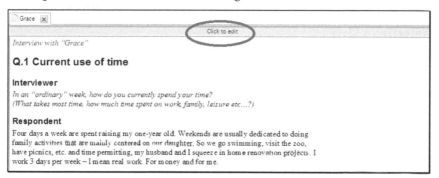

Selecting the whole document:
1. Position the cursor anywhere in the document.
2. Go to **HOME | Editing | Select → Select All** or [Ctrl] + [A].

You can also select any paragraph like his:
1. Position the cursor in the current paragraph.
2. Go to **HOME | Editing | Select → Select Paragraph** or triple-click with the mouse.

Tip: Selecting Text
Select a passage of text by holding left-click and mousing over it. Double left-clicking on a single word highlights just that word. And did you know that triple left-clicking on a single word selects the whole paragraph? Both of these shortcuts can be when coding.

Changing Fonts, Font Style, Size, and Color

1   Select the text you want to format.
2   Go to **HOME | Format → Font...**

The **Font** dialog box appears:

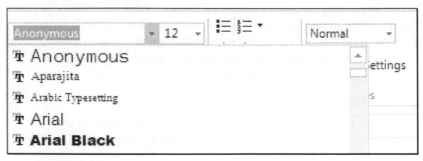

3   Select the options you need with immediate effect.

Selecting a Style

1   Position the cursor in the paragraph you want to format.
2   Go to **HOME | Styles**.
3   Select from the list of styles.
4   Confirm with **[OK]**.

Resetting to previous style is possible as long as the project has not been saved after the last change:

1   Position the cursor in the paragraph you want to reset.
2   Go to **HOME | Styles | Reset Settings**.

Aligning Paragraphs

Selecting Alignments

1   Position the cursor in the paragraph you want to format.
2   Go to **HOME | Paragraph**.
3   Select from the list of alignment options.

Selecting Indentation

1   Position the cursor in the paragraph for which you want to change the indentation.
2   Go to **HOME | Paragraph**.
3   Select increased or decreased indentation.

Creating Lists

1 Select the paragraphs that you want to make as a list.
2 Go to **HOME** | **Paragraph**.
3 Select a bulleted or numbered list.

Finding, Replacing and Navigating Text

Finding Text

1 Open a document.
2 Go to **HOME** | **Editing** | **Find → Find...**
  or **[Ctrl]** + **[F]**.

The **Find Content** dialog box appears:

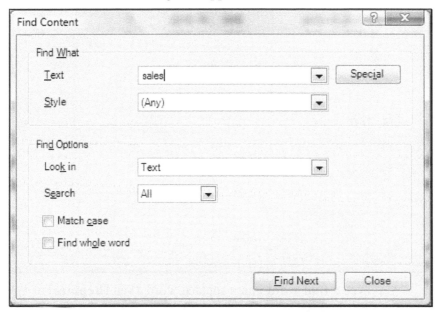

3 Type a search word, then click **[Find Next]**.

The **Style** option makes it possible to limit the search from *Any* to a certain style.

Please note the option *Match case* which makes it possible to exactly match *UPPERCASE* or *lowercase* and the option *Find whole word* which switches off the free text search.

Searching and Replacing

1 Open a document.
2 Go to **HOME | Editing | Replace**
   or **[Ctrl] + [H]**.
The **Replace Content** dialog box appears:

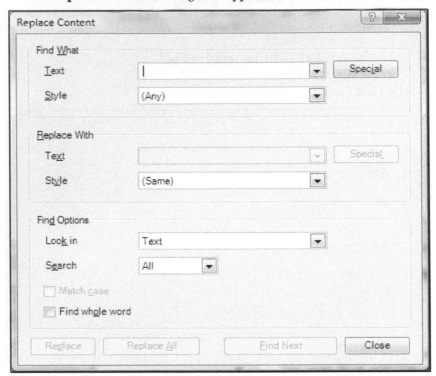

3 Type a find word and a replace word, then **[Replace]** or
   [Replace All].

The option Style near **Find What** makes it possible limit the search from All to any given style and the option Style near **Replace With** makes it possible to replace the found word as well as change the style from Same to any given style.

Please notice the option *Match case* which makes it possible to exactly match *UPPERCASE* and *lowercase* and the option *Find whole word* which switches off the double-sided auto truncation.

Spell Checking

NVivo comes with built-in dictionaries for English (UK), English (US), French, German, Portuguese and Spanish. If your source materials use specialized terms or abbreviations that are not in the built-in dictionary, you can add these words to a custom dictionary. Each of these languages can have its own custom dictionary.

When you spell check a source, NVivo flags words that are not in the built-in or custom dictionary. You can decide whether you want to ignore flagged words, correct them or add them to the custom dictionary.

You can spell check source content when the source is open in edit mode. You can spell check:

- Documents
- Memos
- Audio and video transcripts (the Content column only)
- Picture logs (the Content column only)
- Framework Matrices
- Externals

You can also spell check Annotations in any type of source, including non-editable source types such as Datasets and PDFs. You can also spell check annotations displayed in Node Detail View.

You can set your spell check preferences in NVivo's application options—for example, you can choose whether or not to flag all uppercase words (e.g. USA) as spelling mistakes.

1   Open a Source Item in Edit mode.
2   Go to **HOME | Proofing | Spelling**
      or [**F7**].

The **Spelling: <Language>** dialog box appears:

The meanings of these buttons are:

[Ignore Once]	Ignore and move to next
[Ignore All]	Ignore all instances in the whole source and move to next
[Add To Dictionary]	The word is added to the custom dictionary and will not be flagged from now on
[Change]	Changes the spelling to the highlighted suggested word
[Change All]	Changes the spelling to the highlighted suggested word at all instances in the whole source and move to next
[Cancel]	Stops the spell checking

When you want to spell check any Annotation, open the annotations window and keep the cursor within the annotation. If you have more than one annotation in the same source the spell checker will run through all of them. The source itself need not be in edited mode when you spell check an annotation.

For more on settings for content languages and dictionaries (see page 48).

Selecting Text

Selecting text: Click and drag
Selecting one word: Double-click
Selecting a paragraph:
1   Position the cursor in the paragraph you want to select.
2   Go to **HOME | Editing | Select → Select Paragraph**
    or triple-click.

Selecting the whole document:
1   Position the cursor anywhere in the document.
2   Go to **HOME | Editing | Select→ Select All** or **[Ctrl] + [A]**.

'Go To' options vary depending on the source type (e.g., Documents, PDFs, Datasets, Pictures, and Audio or Video). Possible Go To options include Paragraph, Character Position, See Also Link and Annotation (above), as well as Dataset Record ID, Log Row, Page, Source, Time, and Transcript Row.

Go to a Certain Location

1   Go to **HOME | Editing | Find → Go to...** or **[Ctrl] + [G]**.

The **Go to** dialog box appears:

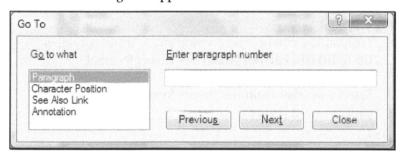

2   Select option at **Go to what** and when required, a value.
3   Click on **[Previous]** or **[Next]**.

Creating a Table

1   Position the cursor where you want to create a table.
2   Go to **HOME | Editing | Insert → Insert Text Table...**

The **Insert Text Table** dialog box appears:

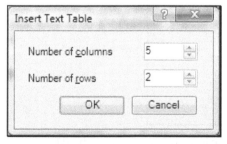

3   Select number of columns and number of rows in the table.
4   Confirm with **[OK]**.

Inserting Page Breaks, Images, Dates, and Symbols

Inserting a Page Break

1   Position the cursor where you want to insert a page break.
2   Go to **HOME | Editing | Insert → Insert Page Break**.

A page break is indicated with a dotted line on the screen.

Inserting an Image

1   Position the cursor where you want to insert an image.
2   Go to **HOME | Editing | Insert → Insert Image...**
3   Select an image with the file browser. Only .BMP, .JPG and .GIF file formats can be inserted.
4   Confirm with [**Open**].

Inserting Date and Time

1   Position the cursor where you want to insert date and time.
2   Go to **HOME | Editing | Insert → Insert Date/Time**
    or [**Ctrl**] + [**Shift**] + [**T**].

Inserting a Symbol

1   Position the cursor where you want to insert a symbol.
2   Go to **HOME | Editing | Insert → Insert Symbol**
    or [**Ctrl**] + [**Shift**] + [**Y**]
3   Select a symbol from the **Insert Symbol** dialog box, confirm with [**Insert**].

Zooming

1   Open a document.
2   Go to **VIEW | Window | Zoom | Zoom...**

The **Zoom** dialog box appears:

> **Tip:** Our preferred method of zooming in NVivo is [**Ctrl**] + mouse wheel. [**Ctrl**] + moving the mouse wheel forward allows zooming in; [**Ctrl**] + moving the mouse wheel backward allows zooming out.

3   Select a certain magnification and confirm with [**OK**].

Alternatively, you may also use the Zoom-slider in the status bar below on the screen.

Alternatively, [**Ctrl**] + your mouse wheel allows zooming in or out.

You can also zoom in or out in predetermined steps:

1   Open a document.
2   Go to **VIEW | Window | Zoom | Zoom In**
        or **VIEW | Window | Zoom | Zoom Out**.

Print Previewing

1   Open a document.
2   Go to **FILE → Print → Print Preview**.

The **Print Options** dialog box appears:

3   Select options for the preview.
4   Confirm with [**OK**].

As you can see from the dialog box we have selected the options Name, Description and Paragraph Numbers. This can be of great importance when working in a team. Also the page breaks are shown here and they are not on the screen.

The result can look like this:

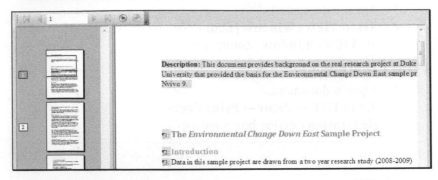

In the Print Preview window there are numerous possibilities to navigate, zoom, and change the view. The thumbnails can be hidden with **View → Thumbnails** which is a toggling function. Print all pages with **File → Print** or **[Ctrl] + [P]**.

Printing a Document

1　Open a document.
2　Go to **FILE → Print → Print...**
　　or **[Ctrl] + [P]**.
3　The **Print Options** dialog box (same as above) now shows. Select options for the printout.
4　Confirm with **[OK]**.

Printing with Coding Stripes

When you need to print a document with coding stripes (see page 192), you must first display the coding stripes on the screen. Then you need to select the option *Coding Stripes* in the **Print Options** dialog box:

The print options are: *Print on Same Page.*

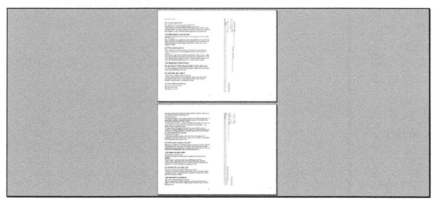

Or *Print on Adjacent Pages.*

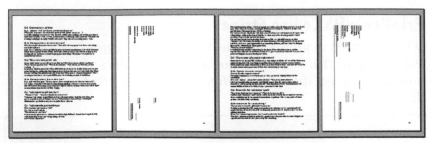

Page Setup

1. Open a document and open **Print Preview**.
2. Go to **LAYOUT** | **Page** | **Page Setup**.

alternatively

1. Open a document.
2. Open **FILE → Print → Print Preview**.
3. Go to **File → Page Setup...**

The **Page Setup** dialog box appears:

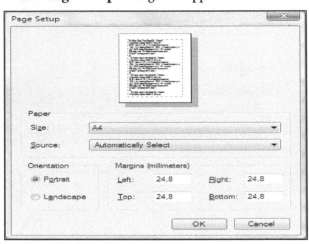

4. Decide the settings for paper size, orientation and margins, then [**OK**].

Tip: NVivo is powerful software for organizing and analyzing text documents, but it is weak as a standalone word processor. A best practice we recommend is creating a document in Word (or your preferref word processing software) and then importing the text into NVivo.

Tip: Make it a PDF!
In the event you find NVivo is mishandling your document formatting, try converting your text document to a PDF. NVivo is also a powerful tool for handling PDF files with special formatting, like multiple columns. What about if you want to import a PowerPoint presentation into NVivo? Make it a PDF!

Limitations in Editing Documents in NVivo

NVivo has certain limitations in creating advanced formatted documents.

Some of these limitations are:

- NVivo cannot merge two documents by any other means than copying/cutting and pasting text.
- It is difficult to format an image (change size, orientation, move).
- It is difficult to format a table.
- It is difficult to format a paragraph (hanging indent, first line different, line spacing).
- Copying from a Word document to NVivo loses some paragraph formatting.
- Footnotes and endnotes in a Word document are lost after importing to NVivo. Word footnotes can however be manually replaced by NVivo Annotations (see page 134).
- Headers and footers are lost after import to NVivo.
- Page numbers are lost after import to NVivo but may be replaced by Insert page field in Word.
- Bookmarks and Comments are lost after import to NVivo.
- Field codes do not exist in NVivo and these are converted to text after importing to NVivo.
- NVivo cannot apply several columns, except when used in a table. When a multi-column document is imported it is displayed on the screen as single column. The multi-column design is restored when such document is exported or printed.

Often it is preferable to create a document in Word and then import to NVivo. Simply because Word is a dedicated and advanced word processor.

Tip: Formatting your Word documents for NVivo:

1   Give your Word documents meaningful file-names. If you write an interview per document, it is advantageous if the file-name is the name of the interviewee (real name or a code name). After importing to NVivo, both the Source Item and the Case Node will be given this name. Put all interviews of same kind in the same folder, and consider the sort order. If you are using numbers in the file names then you should apply a similar series of names, with the same number of characters, like 001, 002, .. 011, 012, .. 101, 102, etc.

2   Use Word's paragraph styles to enable autocoding. For structured interviews you should create document templates with subject headings and paragraph styles.

3   Whenever needed you can use Find and Replace and create headings with approprate paragraph styles.

4   Divide the text into logical, appropriate paragraphs using the hard carriage return (ENTER on your keyboard). This facilitates the coding that can take place based on a keyword and the command 'Spread Coding to Surrounding Paragraph'. Remember triple-clicking!

6. HANDLING PDF SOURCES

Of particular interest to researchers who are conducting literature reviews, PDF documents will retain the original layout after import to NVivo and appear exactly as they were opened in Acrobat Reader. These PDFs can be coded, linked and searched as any other Source Item. One limitation is that PDF text cannot be edited nor can hyperlinks be created. Hyperlinks made in the original PDF, however, will function normally in NVivo.

Apart from bibliographic data with PDF articles downloaded from EndNote, new to NVivo 10 and 11, web pages and Evernote files can now be imported into NVivo as PDF sources. This new feature allows web pages and Evernote files to be organized, coded and queried the same as any imported .PDF file (See Chapters 15, 18 and 19).

Importing PDF Files

1   Go to **DATA | Import | PDFs**
    Default folder is **Internals**.
    Go to 5.

alternatively

1   Click on **[Sources]** in Area 1.
2   Select the **Internals** folder in Area 2 or its subfolder.
3   Go to **DATA | Import | PDFs**.
    Go to 5.

alternatively

3   Click on any empty space in Area 3.
4   Right-click and select **Import → Import PDFs...**
    or **[Ctrl] + [Shift] + [I]**.

alternatively

3   Drag and drop your file's icon from an outside folder into Area 3.
    Go to 5.

In each case, the **Import Internals** dialog box is shown:

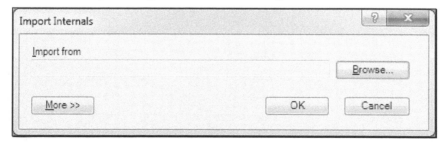

5   The **[Browse]** button gives access to a file-browser and you can select one or several PDFs for a batch import.
6   When the PDFs have been selected, confirm with **[OK]**.

The [**More**>>] button offers several options:

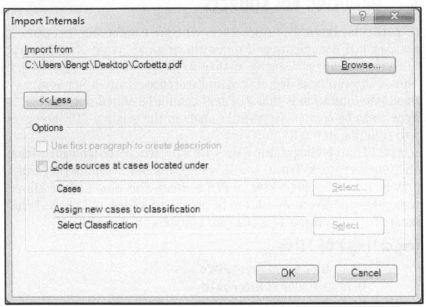

Use first paragraph to create descriptions: Not for PDF-items.

Code sources at cases located under: Each Source Item will be coded at a Case with the same name as the imported PDF file and located in a folder or under a parent Case that has been selected. Also you must assign the Cases to a Classification when importing (see Chapter 11, Classifications).

7   Confirm the import with [**OK**].

When only one PDF has been selected the **PDF Properties** dialog box appears:

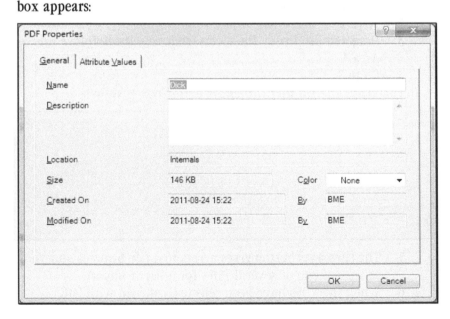

This dialog box will make it possible to modify the name of the PDF item and optionally add a description.

8   Confirm with [**OK**].

Opening a PDF Item

1   Click on [**Sources**] in Area 1.
2   Select the **Internals** folder in Area 2 or its subfolder.
3   Select the PDF in Area 3 that you want to open.
4   Go to **HOME | Item | Open → Open PDF**
or right-click and select **Open PDF...**
or double-click on the PDF in Area 3
or [**Ctrl**] + [**Shift**] + [**O**].

Please note, that you can only open one PDF at a time, but several PDFs can stay open simultaneously.

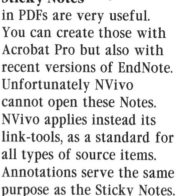

Sticky Notes in PDFs are very useful. You can create those with Acrobat Pro but also with recent versions of EndNote. Unfortunately NVivo cannot open these Notes. NVivo applies instead its link-tools, as a standard for all types of source items. Annotations serve the same purpose as the Sticky Notes.

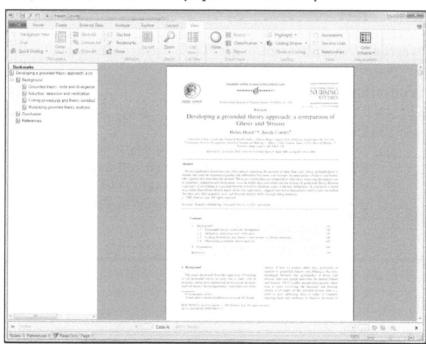

In this view you can code, link (See Also links, Annotations, Memo links) and search and query as with any other Source Item.

Selection Tools for PDF Items

There are two different selection tools for PDFs, Text or Region. Text Selection Mode is used for selecting any text in the PDF and is made as for any other selections within a Source Item. Selection Mode Text is default and is always active each time you open a PDF item.

Scanned text documents will not inherently allow selectable text; ensure you use software like Adobe Acrobat to recognize scanned text (OCR, Optical Character Recognition) so text selection is possible in NVivo.

Region Selection Mode is used when you need to select an image, a table or any graph that is in the PDF document. When you need to select an image, a table or any graph:

1   Open a PDF Source Item.
2   Go to **HOME | Editing | PDF Selection → Region**
    or point at the PDF right-click and select **Selection Mode → Region**.
3   With the mouse-pointer (which is now a cross) you define two diagonal corners of any rectangular area. Any text within such area will be interpreted as image not text.

To return to Selection Mode Text:

1   Go to **HOME | Editing | PDF Selection → Region**
    or point at the PDF, right-click and select **Selection Mode → Text**.

Selections made can now be used when coding and linking. Only hyperlinks cannot be created in a PDF Source Item. See page 194 on how a Node that codes a PDF item is shown.

Exporting a PDF Item

Like most NVivo items, PDF sources can also be exported:

1   Click on [**Sources**] in Area 1.
2   Select the **Internals** folder in Area 2 or its subfolder.
3   Select the PDF or PDFs in Area 3 that you want to export.
4   Go to **DATA | Export | Export → Export PDF...**
    or right-click and select **Export | Export PDF...**
    or [**Ctrl**] + [**Shift**] + [**E**].

Tip: Working with PDF text documents. NVivo's functionality to work with PDF text documents can be a dream come true for researchers working on literature reviews. While many academic articles can be downloaded as functional PDF text documents, book chapters or other types of print material must often be scanned by researchers themselves. We recommend Adobe Acrobat Pro or ABBYY FineReader as software that will take scanned documents and recognize their text (a process called OCR, Optical Character Recognition).

The **Export Options** dialog box appears:

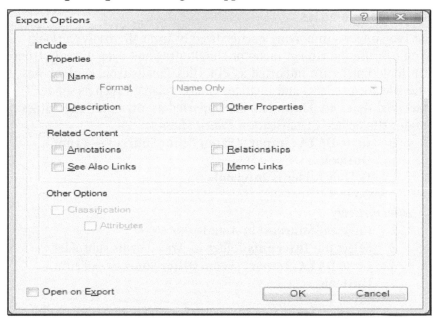

5   Select the options that you want. Confirm with **[OK]**.
6   Decide file name, file location, and file type. Possible file types are: .PDF and .HTML. The PDF file format is only available when none of the above options have been selected. Finally confirm with **[Save]**.

Please note, that any coding made on such items cannot be transferred when the Source Item is exported.

Tip: Using Word documents instead of PDFs. In our experience it is easier to work with Word files (.doc or .docx) than working with PDFs in NVivo. While it is not always possible to save your PDF files as Word documents, recent versions of Adobe Acrobat (X or XI) allow for PDF files to easily be saved as fully formatted Word files. Furthermore, Microsoft Word 2013 will allow for PDF files to be opened and saved as fully formatted Word files. *Also when you scan documents solely with the purpose of importing them to NVivo then create them as Word documents, which is the preferred file type.*

Importing emails

NVivo supports importing emails directly from Microsoft Outlook. You can use the ribbon menu or simply drag and drop directly from Outlook. Emails are imported as PDF files. Emails from Outlook has the file format .MSG and includes email metadata such as sender, received date, etc. These data are imported as attributes and values under the Source Classification *Email Message*.

1   Go to **DATA | Import | From Other Sources → From Outlook...**

     Default folder is **Internals**.

     Go to 5.

alternatively

1   Click on **[Sources]** in Area 1.

2   Select the **Internals** folder in Area 2 or its subfolder.

3   Go to **DATA | Import | From Other Sources → From Outlook...**

     Go to 5.

alternatively

3   Click on any empty space in Area 3.

4   Right-click and select **Import → Import from Outlook...** or **[Ctrl]** + **[Shift]** + **[I]**.

alternatively

4   Drag and drop your file's icon from an outside folder into Area 3.

     Go to 5.

In each case, the **Import Internals** dialog box is shown:

5   The **[Browse]** button gives access to a file-browser and you can select one or several emails for a batch import.

6   When the emails have been selected, confirm with **[OK]**.

When you want to import an attachment to an email open the email in Outlook and drag the attachment to Area 3 of the chosen source folder. Depending on the attached file type the **Properties** dialog will open.

7. HANDLING AUDIO- AND VIDEO-SOURCES - ONLY FOR PRO & PLUS

So far, we have mainly focused on text data, but NVivo has a variety of useful functions for researchers interested in working with audio and video data. NVivo provides two primary functions for handling audio and video source data. First, audio and video data can be imported into NVivo as a data source, which can be organized, coded and queried similar to text source data. But second, and perhaps more importantly for some researchers, NVivo contains a full functioning transcription utility for importing, creating, and exporting text transcripts. Instead of outsourcing transcription to third-party vendors or spending funds on specialized transcription software, NVivo gives researchers a very useful option for transcribing their own audio and video files within the software.

NVivo 11 can import the following audio formats: .MP3, .M4A, .WAV, and .WMA and the following video formats: .MPG, .MPEG, .MPE, .MP4, .MOV, .QT, .3GP, .MTS, and .M2TS. Several of these media formats are new to NVivo 11 to allow users to import more media content form their smart phones. Media files less than 40 MB can be imported and embedded in you NVivo project.

Files larger than 40 MB must be stored as external files. Importantly, external files can be handled the same way as an audio or video embedded item. NVivo contains an on-board audio and video player for external files, so even though a large video file may not be embedded in your project, you can still view, transcribe, code, and query the file using the NVivo player. But remember, if you open your NVivo project on another computer the external file references will no longer work, unless you assemble copies of those files in identically named file folders on the new computer you are using.

Even the not embedded media items are located under the **Internals** folder or its subfolders as they are managed in all respects as if they were embedded.

The threshold value for audio and video files that can be stored as external files can be reduced for all new projects with **FILE → Options...**, select the **Audio/Video** tab, section **Default for new projects** (see page 46). To adjust values for the current project, use **FILE → Info → Project Properties...**, select the **Audio/Video** tab, section **Settings** (see page 61). To adjust for the current Audio/Video item, go to **Audio/Video Properties** dialog box, the **Audio/Video** tab (see page 102).

When you need to view all items that are not embedded go to [**Folders**] in Area 1, select **Search Folders** and subfolder **All Sources Not Embedded** in Area 2.

Importing Media Files

Importing media files follows a similar, simple protocol as importing text files or PDFs:

    1   Go to **DATA | Import | Audios/Videos**
         Default folder is **Internals**.
         Go to 5.

alternatively

    1   Click [**Sources**] in Area 1.
    2   Select the **Internals** folder in Area 2 or its subfolder.
    3   Go to **DATA | Import | Audios/Videos**.
         Go to 5.

alternatively

    3   Click on any empty space in Area 3.
    4   Right-click and select **Import → Import Audios.../Import Videos...**
         or [**Ctrl**] + [**Shift**] + [**I**].

alternatively

    3   Drag and drop your file's icon from an outside folder into Area 3.
         Go to 5.

The **Import Internals** dialog box appears:

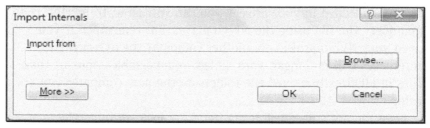

    5   The [**Browse...**] button gives access to a file browser and you can select one or several media files for a batch import.
    6   When the file or files have been chosen, confirm with [**Open**].

Importing media files is sometimes not possible caused by the absence in your computer of an uptodate device called *Codec*. Often the problem is solved by upgrading with an appropriate Codec package. If so contact us for assistance.

The [**More** >>] button lets you select more options:

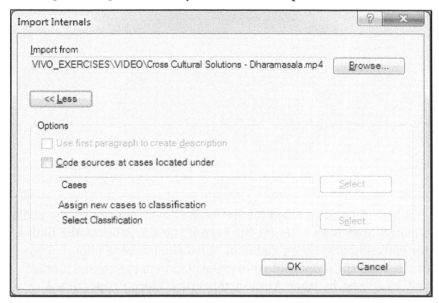

Use first paragraph to create descriptions. Not applicable for the import of media files.

Code sources at cases located under. Each Source Item will be coded at a Case with the same name as the imported file and located under in a folder or under a parent Case that has been selected. Also you must assign the Cases to a Classification when importing (see Chapter 11, Classifications).

7   Confirm the import with [**OK**].

When only one media file is imported the **Audio Properties/Video Properties** dialog box is shown:

This dialog box will make it possible to modify the name of the item and optionally add a description.

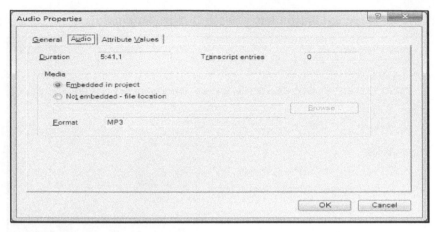

When the **Audio/Video** tab has been chosen you can let the audio file be stored as an external file even if the size is below the limit for embedding. After an audio- or video file has been imported you can change the properties from embedded item to external storage and vice versa by using **Audio Properties/Video Properties**. An embedded item cannot exceed 40 MB.

    8   Confirm with [**OK**].

At times you may need to move an external media file. When an external file has been moved the media item must be updated through NVivo. Go to **HOME | Item | Properties → Update Media file Location** or right-click and select **Update File Location** and select the external file's new location. From there, NVivo will find the correct media file.

Creating a New Media Item

Instead of importing an audio or video item, a new media item can also be created:

    1   Go to **CREATE | Sources | Audio/Video**.
        Default folder is **Internals**.
        Go to 5.

alternatively

    1   Click [**Sources**] in Area 1.
    2   Select the **Internals** folder in Area 2 or its subfolder.
    3   Go to **CREATE | Sources | Audio/Video**.
        Go to 5.

alternatively

    3   Click on any empty space in Area 3.
    4   Right-click and select **New Internal → New Audio.../New Video...**
        or [**Ctrl**] + [**Shift**] + [**N**].

The **New Audio/New Video** dialog box appears:

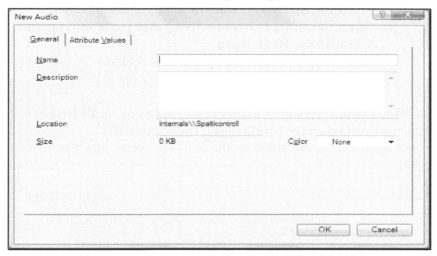

5 Type name (compulsory) and a description (optional), then
[**OK**].

When you create a new media item it initially has no media file
or transcript. Instead these pieces of information can be imported
separately. From the open media item, click the **Edit Mode** link and
go to **MEDIA | Import | Media Content** or **MEDIA | Import |
Transcript Rows** (see page 108). From here, select the required
contents.

Here is a typical list view in Area 3 of some audio and video items:

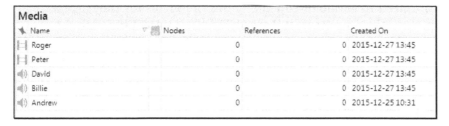

Opening a Media Item

Now that you've created and imported some media items you'll want
to open them to access their data. Crucially, when handling media
items you will have access to the **MEDIA** ribbon, one of NVivo's
context-dependent ribbons:

1   Click [**Sources**] in Area 1.
2   Select the **Internals** folder in Area 2 or its subfolder.
3   Select the media in item in Area 3 that you want to open.
4   Go to **HOME | Item | Open**
     or right-click and select **Open Audio/Video...**
     or double-click on the media item in Area 3
     or [**Ctrl**] + [**Shift**] + [**O**].

Please note, NVivo only allows you to open one media item at a time, but several items can stay open simultaneously.

An open audio item, showing the waveform, may look like this:

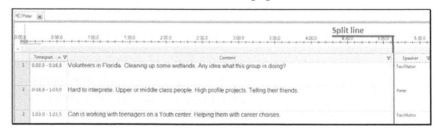

Provided a soundcard and speakers are connected to the computer you can now play and analyze the audio item.

Creating Custom Transcript Fields

When you import transcripts, see page 108, then the transcript file may have defined the Custom Transcript Fields. Otherwise, if you have defined those fields with **Application Options**, the **Audio/Video** tab, page 46, then all new projects will have them. If you need to define or edit the Transcript Fields for the current project, then use **Project Properties**, the **Audio/Video** tab, see page 61.

A practical arrangement is to use **MEDIA | Display | Split Panes** which separates the default fields from the Custom Transcript Fields. This makes it easier to adjust the column widths. This example is with hidden waveform as described on page 106.

Play Modes

NVivo offers three Play Modes for working with media items, with each having a special function relating to transcription. *Normal*

Mode simply plays your media item; *Synchronize Mode* plays your media item while scrolling through the corresponding rows of your transcript; and *Transcribe Mode* creates a new time interval each time you play your media item, and ends that interval when you stop.

Go to **MEDIA | Playback | Playmode** to view or change playmode options.

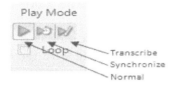

Playmode *Normal*
When a media item is opened the play mode is always *Normal*.
1   Go to **MEDIA | Playback | Play/Pause**
    or **[F4]**.

Only the selected section will be played if there is a selection along the timeline. The selection disappears when you click outside the selection.
1   Go to **MEDIA | Playback | Stop**
    or **[F8]**.

Rewind, Fast Forward etc.
1   Go to **MEDIA | Playback | Go to Start**.
2   Go to **MEDIA | Playback | Rewind**.
3   Go to **MEDIA | Playback | Fast Forward**.
4   Go to **MEDIA | Playback | Go to End**.
5   Go to **MEDIA | Playback | Skip Back**.
    or **[F9]**
6   Go to **MEDIA | Playback | Skip Forward**
    or **[F10]**

The *Skip* interval is determined by the setting under **FILE → Options**, the **Audio/Video** tab (see page 46).

Volume and Speed
1   Go to **MEDIA | Playback | Volume**. This slider also allows mute.
2   Go to **MEDIA | Playback | Play Speed**. There are fixed positions and continuous slider.

Play Mode Synchronized
You can play any media item synchronized so the transcription text row is highlighted and always visible (by automatic scrolling).
1   Go to **MEDIA | Playback | Play Mode → Synchronize**.
2   Play.

Play Mode *Transcribe*

You can link audio timeline intervals with rows of text (e.g., written comments, direct transcripts or translations). In NVivo, the practice of linking time segments of audio or video with rows of text is called *transcription*. While *transcription* can be used to create verbatim transcripts of your audio files, some researchers find it faster to write short-hand transcripts.

Transcription requires several steps. First, you need to define an interval that will correspond with the row of the text. Next, the audio timeline interval and the text row need to be linked. From there, you have a transcript ready to code and link.

1   Go to **MEDIA | Playback | Play Mode → Transcribe**.
2   Play.

Timeline intervals can be defined in a number of ways, such as by selecting portions of the timeline with your mouse when audio is paused, or by using keyboard commands to mark the start and end of an interval while audio is playing (our preferred method!). See page 107.

Selecting a Time Interval in Play Mode Normal

NVivo acts like a simple audio file player when in Normal Play Mode. There ar*e two ways* to select a time interval that *can be used for* coding or for creating a transcription row. Please note that these methods will work in *any* Play Mode:

1   Use the left mouse button to define the start of an interval, then hold the button, drag along the timeline, and release the button at the end of the interval.

alternatively

1   Play the media item, possibly at low speed, see above.
2   Determine the start of an interval by going to **MEDIA | Selection | Start Selection** or [**F11**].
3   Determine the end of an interval by going to **MEDIA | Selection | Stop Selection** or [**F12**].

The result is a selection (a blue frame) along the timeline. Now you can code or link from this selection. To proceed with creating the next selection you need to click outside the previous selection. Retaining the current selection will limit the play interval.

Creating a Transcript Row from a Time Interval in Normal Play Mode

Once you have selected a time interval, there are several methods to create a new row. Please note that these methods will work in *any* Play Mode:

1 Make a selection along the timeline.
2 Go to **LAYOUT | Rows and Columns | Insert → Insert Row**
   or right-click and select **Insert Row**
   or **[Ctrl] + [Ins]**.

The result is a transcript row corresponding to the selected time interval called *Timespan*, with the textbox in the column called *Content*:

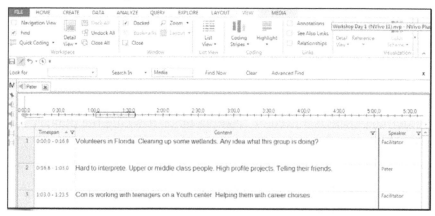

Should you need to adjust a timespan you can do as follows:

1 Select a transcript row by clicking in the row item number (the leftmost column). The corresponding timespan along the timeline is then marked with a purple guiding line.
2 Make a new modified selection along the timeline.
3 Go to **MEDIA | Selection | Assign Timespan to Rows**
   or right-click and select **Assign Timespan to Rows**.

As an alternative you can also modify the timespan directly in the transcript row by typing a new start time and a new stop time. From there you can then make a new selection along the timeline

1 Select a transcript row by clicking in the row item number (the leftmost column).
2 Go to **MEDIA | Selection | Select Media from Transcript**.

Creating a Transcript with Transcribe Mode

As experienced NVivo users and trainers, we believe that Transcribe Mode is the best method for researchers who are using media files to create verbatim transcripts, real-time summaries, or notes on extra-linguistic cues or vocal intonation. Transcribe Mode allows you, using basic keyboard shortcuts, to quickly and easily generate text to accompany your media data.

1   Go to **MEDIA | Playback | Play Mode → Transcribe.**.

2   Play and determine start of an interval by going to
     MEDIA | Playback | Start/Pause
     or [**F4**].

3   Determine end of an interval by going to
     MEDIA | Playback | Stop
     or [**F8**].

While transcribing you can pause the audio if you need time to finish writing. We recommend going to **FILE → Options**, the **Audio/Video** tab and turning on the setting *Skip back on play in transcribe mode*. This will automatically rewind an interval you have created back to its beginning after you pause your transcription.

At any time you can also create the beginning of a new interval with [**F11**] and then end it with [**F12**]. You will also get a new transcript row but you need to pause with a separate command.

Merging Transcript Rows

Sometimes there is a need of cleaning up or reducing the number of transcript rows by merging several rows:

1   Open a media item in edit mode.

2   Select two or more transcript rows by holding down the [**Ctrl**] key and left-clicking in the item number column of the transcript rows.

3   Go to **LAYOUT | Rows & Columns | Merge Rows**.

The merged row now covers the timespan from the first to the last selected timeslots.

Importing Transcripts

In the event your transcripts are existing text files on your computer (perhaps you are fortunate enough to be using a transcription service for your project), it is possible to import text material as a transcript for its original audio file. NVivo allows you to correspond your transcript text with the audio file by using either Timestamps, Paragraphs, or Tables. The file format of your imported text file needs to be .DOC, .DOCX, .RTF, or .TXT.

The *Timestamp* Style format:

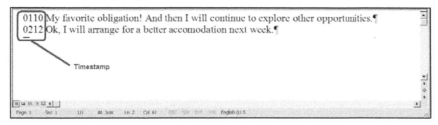

The *Paragraph* Style format:

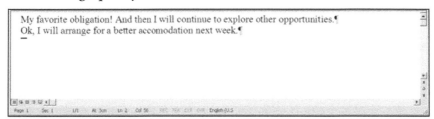

The *Table* Style format:

Timespan	Content	Speaker	
0110	My favorite obligation! And then I will continue to explore other opportunities.	Ruth	
0212	Ok, I will arrange for a better accomodation next week.	Edgar	
¶			

To import a transcript file:

1   Open the media item in edit mode.

2   Go to **MEDIA | Import | Transcript Rows**.

The **Import Transcript Entries** dialog box appears:

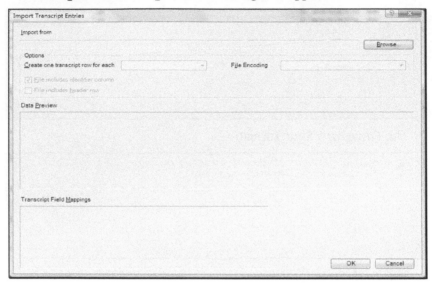

3   The **[Browse...]** button gives access to a file browser and you can select the file you want to import.

4   Once a file is selected at *Options, Create one transcript row for each* you need to select an alternative that corresponds to the appropriate style format.

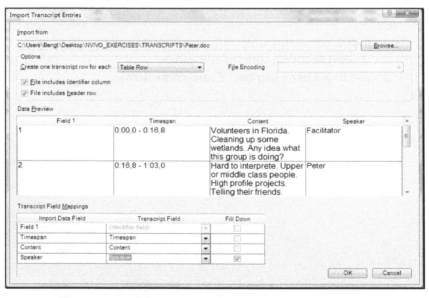

5   When Data Preview displays a correct image of the transcript then you need to set the Transcript Field Mappings so that imported data are mapped to the proper columns in the media item.

6   Confirm with **[OK]**.

Note, when more columns are included in the imported file these columns are also created in NVivo:

Transcript Display Options

Transcript rows can also be hidden:

1 Go to **MEDIA | Display | Transcript →
   Hide**.

This is a toggling function.

You may also hide/unhide the video player in a video item:

1 Go to **MEDIA | Display | Video Player**.

This is a toggling function.

For video items you may also want to display the transcript rows below the media timeline and the video player:

1 Open a video item.

2 Go to **MEDIA | Display | Transcript →
   Bottom**.

> **Tip:** Are you already working with a transcription service? Try **TranscribeMe!** Right-click in Area 4 and select **Purchase Transcript** or go to **DATA | Transcription | Purchase Transcript**. You can logg in, follow the instructions and receive a quotation for this service.

Coding a Media Item

With your newly created time intervals or transcript rows, you may want to begin coding data to correspond with project Nodes (Chapter 10, Introducing Nodes). Coding a media item can be done in two ways:

1. Coding the transcript row or words in the transcript text
2. Coding a timeslot along the timeline

These coding principles are the same for media items as for any text material: select a text or an interval that to code and then select the Node or Nodes at which you will be coding.

If you want to code a whole transcript row, select the row by clicking the item number column, then right-click and select the Node or Nodes that you want to code to.

If you want to code a certain timeslot along the timeline, make a selection and then select the Node or Nodes, see Chapter 10, Introducing Nodes and Chapter 12, Coding.

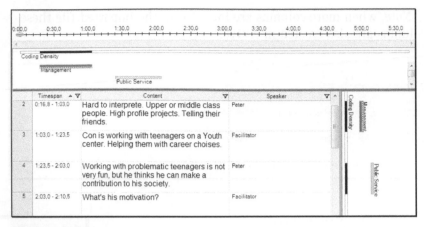

Shadow Coding

Shadow Coding is a special feature related to coding of media items. Shadow coding means that when a text or a row in a transcript has been coded the corresponding interval of the timeline displays the coding faintly, like a shadow. Shadow coding can only be shown with coding stripes turned on (see page 192). Coding stripes are filled colored lines and shadow coding stripes are the same color, but lighter – hence the name shadow coding.

The media item above is coded at the Nodes *Management* and *Public Service*. Both the transcript row and the timeslot are coded at the Node *Management*. Therefore the item has 'double' coding stripes. The Node *Public Service* is only coded at the transcript row. Shadow coding has no use other than being a visual aid when studying coding stripes. Shadow coding can be switched on and off with **VIEW | Coding | Coding Stripes → Shadow Coding**.

Working with the Timeline

Sometimes there is a need of selecting a timespan from an existing transcript:

1 Open a media item with transcript rows.
2 Select a transcript row.
3 Go to **MEDIA | Select | Select Media from Transcript**.

Now there is an exact selection and you can play, code or link from this selection.

Playing an interval from a transcript row:

1 Open a media item with transcript rows.
2 Select a transcript row.
3 Go to **MEDIA | Selection | Play Transcript Media**.

Only the selected interval will be played.

When you open a Node that codes both a row and a timeslot then click on a coding stripe, open the **Audio** tab and it looks like this. Playing from here only plays the coded timeslot(s).

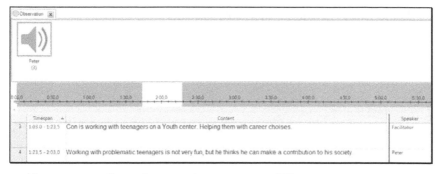

About autocoding of transcripts, see page 181.

Linking from a Media Item

An audio item can be linked (Memo Links, See Also Links and Annotations) in the same manner as any other NVivo item. However, hyperlinks cannot be created from an audio item. Links can be created from a selected timespan or from the transcript.

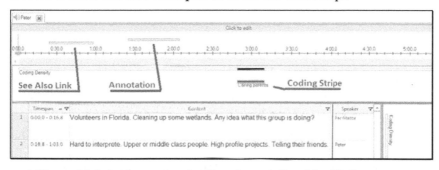

A Memo Link is shown in the list view. A See Also Link or an Annotation that refers to a timespan are shown above the timeline as a filled pink line and a filled blue line respectively. Coding stripes are shown below the timeline, see Chapter 9, Memos, Links, and Annotations.

Exporting a Media Item

Like any Source Item in NVivo, media items can be exported:

1 Click [**Sources**] in Area 1.
2 Select the **Internals** folder in Area 2 or its subfolder.
3 Select the media item or items in Area 3 that you want to export.
4 Go to **DATA | Export | Items**
or right-click and select **Export →**
Export Audio(Video)/Transcript...
or [**Ctrl**] + [**Shift**] + [**E**].

The **Export Options** dialog box appears:

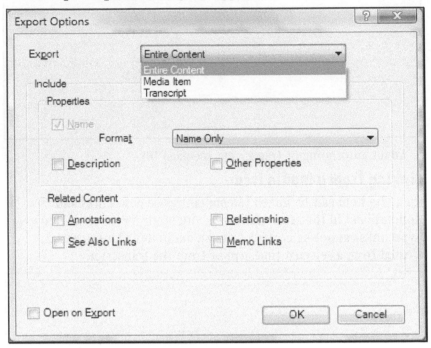

5 Select applicable options for the export of the media file, the transcript, or both. Confirm with [**OK**].

6 Decide the file path, file type (*.HTM, *.HTML) and filename, confirm with [**Save**].

When you select *Entire Content* the result is a web page and the media file and other supporting files are stored in a folder called 'Filename_files'. If you also select the option *Open on Export* then the web browser opens and the result is shown instantly.

- ◆ -

A media item can also be printed with the normal command **FILE → Print → Print** or [**Ctrl**] + [**P**]. A transcript and its coding stripes can similarly be printed.

8. HANDLING PICTURE SOURCES – ONLY FOR PRO & PLUS

In the same way that NVivo associates media sources with timespans which correspond to text (e.g., transcription rows), handling pictures in NVivo is about defining a Region of the picture which then can be associated with a written note, called a Picture Log. Both a Region and a Picture Log can be coded and linked. NVivo 11 can import the following picture formats: .BMP, .GIF, .JPG, .JPEG, .TIF and .TIFF.

Importing Picture Files

NVivo can easily import a number of the most common image types. Plenty of free online image converter websites exist in the event you find you possess an image file that is a different format than NVivo accepts:

1   Go to **DATA | Import | Pictures**.
      Default folder is **Internals**.
      Go to 5.

alternatively

1   Click [**Sources**] in Area 1.
2   Select the **Internals** folder in Area 2 or its subfolder.
3   Go to **DATA | Import | Pictures**.
      Go to 5.

alternatively

3   Click on any empty space in Area 3.
4   Right-click and select **Import → Import Pictures...**
      or [**Ctrl**] + [**Shift**] + [**I**].

alternatively

3   Drag and drop your file's icons from an outside folder into Area 3.
      Go to 5.

The **Import Internals** dialog box appears:

5   The [**Browse...**] button gives access to a file browser and you can select one or several picture files for import.
6   When the picture files have been selected, confirm with [**Open**].

The [**More** >>] button offers several options:

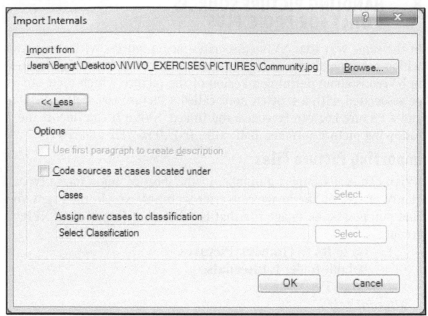

Use first paragraph to create descriptions. Not applicable for picture files.

Code sources at cases located under. Each Source Item will be coded at a Case with the same name as the imported file and located in a folder or under a parent Case that has been selected. Also you must assign the Cases to a Classification when importing (see Chapter 11, Classifications).

7   Confirm the import with [**OK**].

When only *one* picture file has been imported the **Picture Properties** dialog box appears:

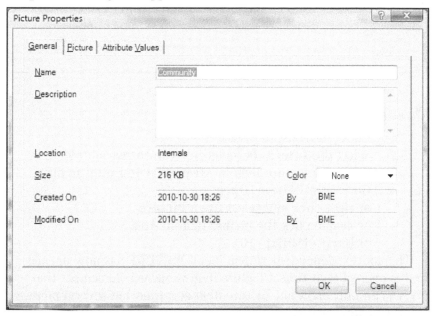

This dialog box makes it possible to modify the name of the item and optionally add a description. The **Picture** tab gives access to details and data from the imported picture:

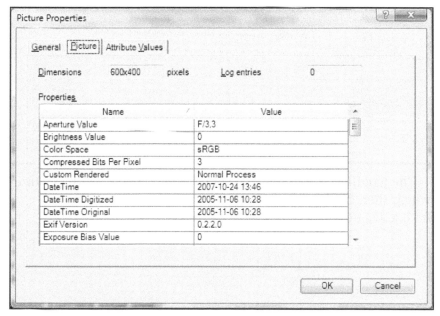

8   Confirm with [**OK**].

Here is a typical list view in Area 3 of some picture items:

Internals							
Name	Nodes	References	Created On	Created By	Modified On	Modified By	
Volunteers -	0	0	2015-12-27 17:1	BME	2015-12-27 17:15	BME	
Doctor Abro	0	0	2015-12-27 17:1	BME	2015-12-27 17:15	BME	
Community	0	0	2015-12-27 17:1	BME	2015-12-27 17:15	BME	

Opening a Picture Item

1 Click [**Sources**] in Area 1.
2 Select the **Internals** folder in Area 2 or its subfolder.
3 Select the picture item in Area 3 that you want to open.
4 Go to **HOME** | **Item** | **Open**
  or right-click and select **Open Picture...**
  or double-click the picture item in Area 3
  or [**Ctrl**] + [**Shift**] + [**O**].

The context dependent ribbon menu **PICTURE** has now opened and is opened each time a Picture item is opened. Remember that NVivo can only open one picture item at a time, but several picture items can stay open simultaneously.

An open picture item can look like this:

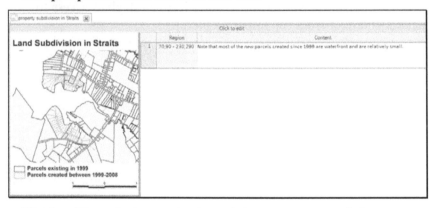

The handling of pictures is about defining a Region of the picture which then can be associated with a written note, a Picture Log. Both a Region and a Picture Log can be coded and linked.

Selecting a Region and Creating a Picture Log

1 Select a corner of the Region with the left mouse button,
then drag the mouse pointer to the opposite corner and
release the button.

2 Go to **LAYOUT** | **Rows & Columns** | **Insert → Row**
or [**Ctrl**] + [**Ins**].

The result can appear like this and the Picture Log can be typed in
the cell below the column head Content:

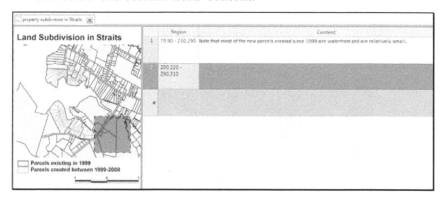

Sometimes you may need to redefine a Region and a Picture Log:

1 Select the row of the Picture Log that you wish to redefine.
When selecting a Row the corresponding Region is
highlighted.

2 Select a new Region (redefine a highlighted area).

3 Go to **PICTURE** | **Selection** | **Assign Region to Rows**.

alternatively

3 Right-click and select **Assign Region to Rows**.

In this way you adjust both a Region and a Row of the Picture
Log.

As an alternative you can use a Row from which you can select a
new Region:

1 Select a Row of the Picture Log. Corresponding region will
be highlighted.

2 Go to **PICTURE** | **Selection** | **Select Region from Log**.

alternatively

2 Right-click and select **Select Region from Log**.

You can also hide the Picture Log:

1   Go to **PICTURE | Display | Log**.

This is a toggling function and a Picture item with a hidden
Picture Log appears like this:

Editing Pictures

NVivo offers some basic functions for easy editing of picture items.
The following functions are menu options after a picture item has
been opened:

   PICTURE | Adjust | Rotate → Right 90°
   PICTURE | Adjust | Rotate → Left 90°
   PICTURE | Adjust | Compress
   PICTURE | Adjust | Brightness & Contrast

Adjusting Region Shading

A shaded region can be created from coding (yellow), by a See Also link (pink) or by an Annotation (blue). Sometimes this colored shading can disturb the view of a region. Therefore an option to adjust or close the shading is available:

PICTURE | Display →

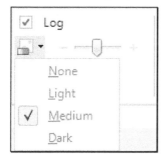

There are certain fixed values and also a slider to set the appropriate shading.

Coding a Picture Item

You can code a Picture Log, a selected text element or a Region of a picture item. The act of coding is in principle the same way you would code other elements of your NVivo project. In short you select data to be coded and then you select the Node or Nodes that the data will be coded at, see Chapter 10, Introducing Nodes and Chapter 12, Coding.

If you need to code a row of the picture log, select the row by clicking the leftmost column of the row, right-clicking and selecting a Node or Nodes.

If instead (or in addition) you need to code a Region, select the Region and select a Node or Nodes as usual.

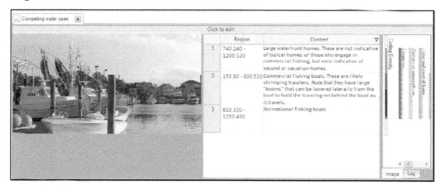

Coding stripes for a picture item are always shown in a window to the left and in a position leveled with the region. Coding stripes from a coded region are colored and filled while coding stripes from a coded picture log are lighter colored. (Same look as Shadow coding stripes.)

The above example shows a picture item that has been coded at the Node *Waterfront.* Both the region and the picture log have been directly coded and therefore 'double' coding stripes are shown.

We would also like to show when the Node *Warefront* has been opened. After having clicked the **Picture** tab to the right you will see both the coded region of the picture and the corresponding Picture Log.

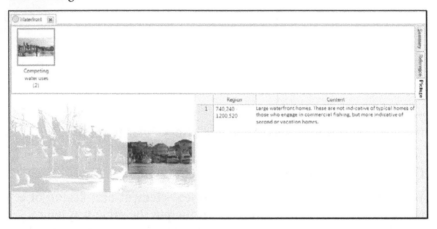

Linking from a Picture Item

A picture item can be linked (Memo Links, See Also Links and Annotations) in the same manner as any other NVivo item. However, hyperlinks cannot be created from a picture item. Links can be created from a selected region or from the Picture log. A Memo Link is not shown elsewhere than in the list view. See Also Links or Annotations are shown as pink and blue frames respectively:

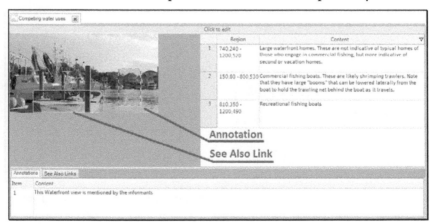

See also Chapter 9, Memos, Links, and Annotations.

Exporting a Picture Item

1   Click [**Sources**] in Area 1.
2   Select the **Internals** folder in Area 2 or its subfolder.
3   Select the picture item or items in Area 3 that you want to export.
4   Go to **DATA | Export | Items**
    or right-click and select **Export Picture/Log...**
    or [**Ctrl**] + [**Shift**] + [**E**].

The **Export Options** dialog box appears:

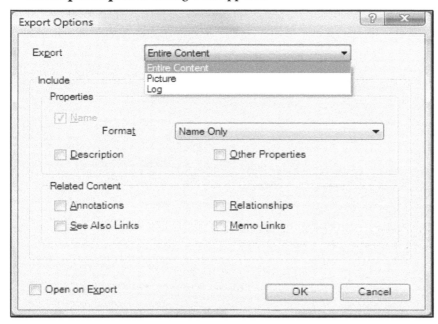

5   Select applicable options, which allows for the export of the picture file, the picture log or both. Confirm with [**OK**].
6   Decide file name, file location, and file type, confirm with [**Save**].

When you select *Entire Content* the result is a web page with the picture file in a folder called 'Filename_files'. Your web browser will open and the result is instantly shown if you also check the option *Open on Export.*

- ♦ -

A picture item can also be printed with the normal command **FILE → Print → Print** or [**Ctrl**] + [**P**]. The picture, and optionally the transcript and the coding stripes can be printed.

123

9.   MEMOS, LINKS, AND ANNOTATIONS

Memos, Memo Links, See Also Links, Hyperlinks and Annotations are NVivo tools that allow you to create connections and track your ideas across your data. While similar in function, each of these four tools operates differently, with Memos and Memo Links being closely related.

Exploring Links in the List View

Memo Links, See Also Links, and Annotations (but not Hyperlinks) can be opened and viewed in List View in Area 3 like any other Project Item.

1   Click [**Folders**] in Area 1.
2   Select any of the following folders in Area 2:
    Memo Links
    See Also Links
    Annotations

Next you will see the selected list of links as items in Area 3.

Right-clicking a **Memo Link** item in Area 3 will open a menu with the options: Open Linked Item, Open Linked Memo and Delete Memo Link. Exporting and printing the whole list of items are also available options.

Double-clicking a **See Also Link** in Area 3 opens the **See Also Link Properties** dialog box. Right-clicking on such item will open a menu with the options: Open From Item, Open To Item, Edit See Also Link... and Delete. Exporting and printing the whole list of items are also available options.

Double-clicking an **Annotation** item in Area 3 opens the source and its Annotation in Area 4. Right-clicking on an Annotation will open a menu with the options: Open Source and Delete. Exporting and printing the whole list of items are also available options.

Memos

Memos are a type of source that allows you to record research insights in a source document that can be linked to another item in your project. Any Source or Node can have one Memo linked to it, called a Memo Link. For example, Memos can be notes, instructions or field notes that have been created outside NVivo. A memo cannot be linked to another memo with a Memo Link.

Importing a Memo

As with other Project Items you can import them or create them with NVivo. The following file formats can be imported as memos: .DOC, .DOCX, .RTF, and .TXT.

   1   Go to **DATA | Import | Memos**.

       Default folder is **Memos**.

       Go to 5.

alternatively

   1   Click [**Sources**] in Area 1.

   2   Select the **Memos** folder in Area 2 or its subfolder.

   3   Go to **DATA | Import | Memos**.

       Go to 5.

alternatively

   3   Click on any empty space in Area 3.

   4   Right-click and select **Import Memos...**

       or [**Ctrl**] + [**Shift**] + [**I**].

alternatively

   3   Drag and drop your file's icon from an outside folder into Area 3.

       Go to 5.

The **Import Memos** dialog box appears:

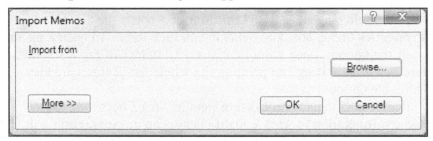

   4   The [**Browse...**] button gives access to a file browser and you can select one or several documents for a batch import.

   5   When the documents have been selected, confirm with [**Open**].

The [**More** >>] button gives access to several options:

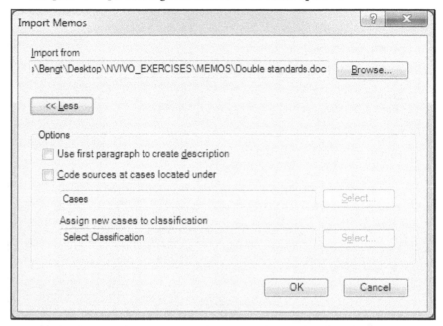

Use first paragraph to create description: NVivo copies the first paragraph of the document and pastes it into the description text box.

Code sources at cases located under: Each Source Item will be coded at a Case with the same name as the imported file and located in a folder or under a parent Case that has been selected. Also you must assign the Cases to a Classification when importing (see Chapter 11, Classifications).

    6   Confirm the import with [**OK**].

Creating a Memo

    1   Go to **CREATE | Sources | Memo**.
        Default folder is **Memos**.
        Go to 5.

alternatively

    1   Click [**Sources**] in Area 1.
    2   Select the **Memos** folder in Area 2 or its subfolder.
    3   Go to **CREATE | Sources | Memo**.
        Go to 5.

alternatively

    3   Click on any empty space in Area 3.
    4   Right-click and select **New Memo...**
        or [**Ctrl**] + [**Shift**] + [**N**].

The **New Memo** dialog box appears:

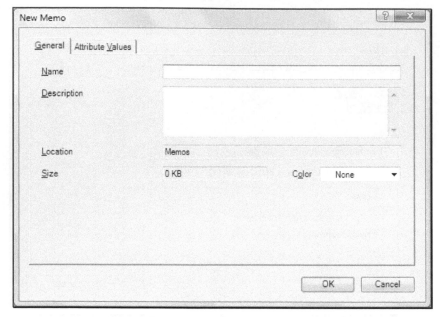

5   Type a name (compulsory) and a description (optional), then [**OK**].

Here is a typical list view in Area 3 of some memos:

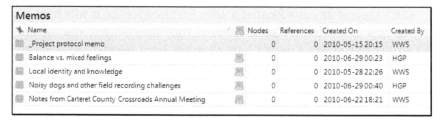

Opening a Memo

1   Click [**Sources**] in Area 1.
2   Select the **Memos** folder in Area 2 or its subfolder.
3   Select a memo in Area 3 that you want to open.
4   Go to **HOME | Item | Open**
     or right-click and select **Open Memo...**
     or double-click on the memo in Area 3
     or [**Ctrl**] + [**Shift**] + [**O**].

Please note, you can only open one memo at a time, but several memos can stay open.

Creating a Memo Link

Memo Links truly distinguish Memos from other types of NVivo sources. Memo Links are an optional component of Memos.

1   In the list view, Area 3, select the item from which you want to create a Memo Link. You cannot create a Memo Link to a memo that is already linked.

2   Go to **ANALYZE | Links → Memo Link → Link to Existing Memo...**

    or right-click and select **Memo Link → Link to Existing Memo...**

The **Select Project Item** dialog box is shown. Only unlinked memos can be selected, linked memos are dimmed.

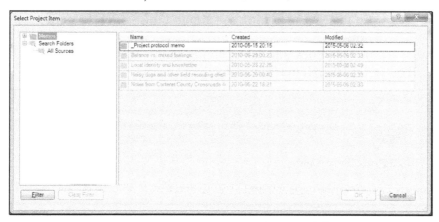

3   Select the memo that you want to link to and confirm with **[OK]**.

The Memo Link is shown in the list view in Area 3 with one icon for the memo and one icon for the linked item.

Creating a Memo Link and a New Memo Simultaneously

NVivo makes it easy to create a Memo Link and a new Memo simultaneously:

1   In the list view, Area 3, select the item from which you want to create a Memo Link and a new Memo.

2   Go to **ANALYZE | Links → Memo Link → Link to New Memo...**

    or right-click and select **Memo Link → Link to New Memo...**

    or **[Ctrl] + [Shift] + [K]**.

The **New Memo** dialog box is shown and you continue according to page 128.

Opening a Linked Memo

A Memo can be opened as outlined above, but a linked Memo can also be in the event where a Memo Link is in place.

1. In the list view, Area 3, select the item from which you want to open a Linked Memo.
2. Go to **ANALYZE | Links → Memo Link → Open Linked Memo**

   or right-click and select **Memo Link → Open Linked Memo**

   or **[Ctrl] + [Shift] + [M]**.

Deleting a Memo Link

1. In the list view, Area 3, select the item from which you want to delete a Memo Link.
2. Go to **ANALYZE | Links → Memo Link → Delete Memo Link**

   or right-click and select **Memo Link → Delete Memo Link**.

The **Delete Confirmation** dialog box appears:

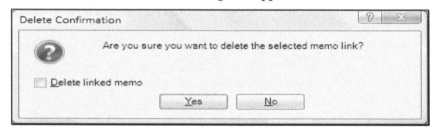

3. If you select *Delete linked memo* then also the Memo will be deleted, otherwise only the Memo Link will be deleted. Confirm with **[Yes]**.

Exporting a Memo

As mentioned, you may wish at some point to export a Memo you wrote inside NVivo but now need to email to a collaborator.

1. Click **[Sources]** in Area 1.
2. Select the **Internals** folder in Area 2 or its subfolder.
3. Select the document(s) Area 3 that you want to export.
4. Go to **DATA | Export | Items**

   or right-click and select **Export → Export <Item>**

   or **[Ctrl] + [Shift] + [E]**.

The **Export Options** dialog box appears:

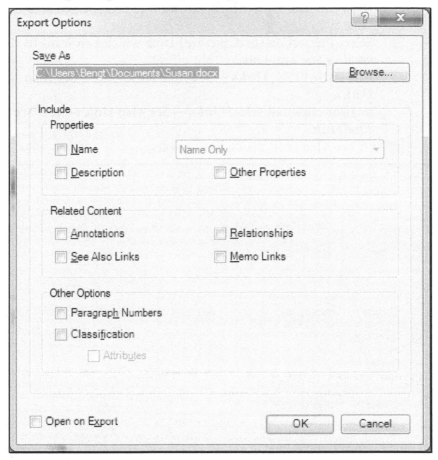

5   Select the options that you want. Confirm with **[OK]**.
6   Decide file name, file location, and file type. (.DOCX, .DOC, .RTF, .TXT, .PDF, or .HTML. Confirm with **[Save]**.

Remember, coding made on text items cannot be transferred when a Memo is exported.

See Also Links

See Also Links literally create connection points between different items from your NVivo project. See Also Links are links from a selection (text, picture region, or audio segment) in an item to another item or a certain selection from another item. Multiple See Also Links can be linked to the same item, unlike Memo Links which are a one-to-one relationship between a Memo and its attendant NVivo item.

Creating a See Also Link to Another Item

1. Open the item from which you want to create a See Also Link.
2. Select the section (text, picture) from which you want to create a See Also Link.
3. Go to **ANALYZE | Links → See Also Link → New See Also Link...**
or right-click and select **Links → See Also Link → New See Also Link...**

The **New See Also Link** dialog box appears:

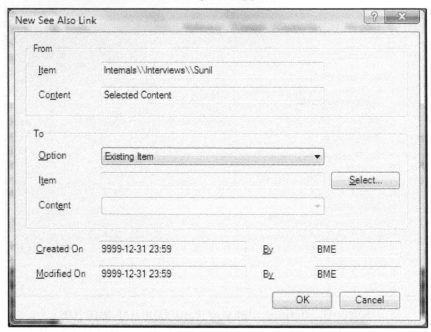

Under the **Option** drop down list, you can select what type of Project Item you will link. An item will be created if you select an option starting with New then. If you select the option Existing Item you go to the [**Select...**] button and use the **Select Project Item** dialog box to select an item to link to. When the item has been selected the link goes to the entire target item.

4. Confirm with [**OK**].

For example, in this Source Item the See Also Links are indicated as a pink colored highlighting:

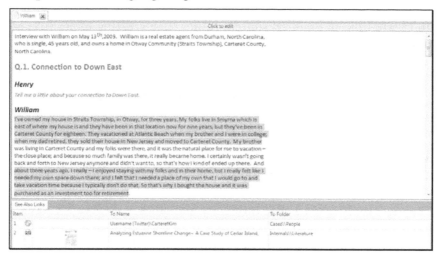

Creating a See Also Link to a Selection of Another Item

1   Open the target item that you want to link to.
2   Select the section (text, image) that you want to link to.
3   Copy with for example [**Ctrl**] + [**C**].
4   Open the item from which you want to create a See Also Link.
5   Select the area (text, image) that you want to link from.
6   Go to **HOME | Clipboard | Paste → Paste As See Also Link**.

Opening a See Also Link

1   Position the cursor on the See Also Link or select the entire link.
2   Go to **ANALYZE | Links | Se Also Links → Open To Item** or right-click and select **Links → Open To Item**.

The target item will open and if you have used the option *Selected Content* the selected area will be shown highlighted otherwise not.

Hiding or Unhiding See Also Links

You can view all the See Also Links from a certain item in a window below the open item. The links are shown as a list of items. Clicking on an item opens the link. Right-clicking and selecting **Open To Item...** also opens the link.

1   Open the item that has one or several See Also Links.
2   Go to **VIEW | Links | See Also Links**.

This is a toggling function for hiding or unhiding the See Also Link window.

Opening a Linked External Source

Provided the See Also Link leads to an external item, you are able to open that external source (file or web site) directly. You may wish to create links to external sources rather than creating hyperlinks as you may reduce unnecessary modifications to the external sources.

1   Position the cursor on the See Also Link or select the entire link.

2   Go to **ANALYZE | Links | See Also Links → Open Linked External File**

    or right-click and select **Links → Open Linked External File**.

Deleting a See Also Link

1   Position the cursor on the See Also Link or select the entire link.

2   Go to **ANALYZE | Links | See Also Link → Delete See Also Link**

    or right-click and select **Links → See Also Link → Delete See Also Link.**

3   Confirm with [**Yes**].

Annotations

Annotations and See Also Links are similar but different. When you create an Annotation, the Annotations tab appears at the bottom of a Source or Node at a point of your choosing. An Annotation could be a quick note, a reference or an idea. Unlike Memos, which can only link to entire sources, Annotations link to specific segments of your data (e.g., text from a focus group transcript, or a segment of time from a video source). An Annotation in NVivo shares similarities with a footnote in Word, especially because annotations are numbered within each Project Item. Annotations cannot be coded.

Creating an Annotation

1   Open a Source Item or a Node.

2   Select the text or other section area that you want to link to an Annotation.

3   Go to **ANALYZE | Annotation → New Annotation...**
    or right-click and select **Links → Annotation → New Annotation**.

A new window will open where the annotation can be typed. The linked area is then shown highlighted in blue.

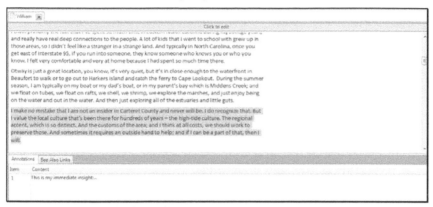

Hiding or Unhiding Annotations

When an NVivo item contains Annotations, you have the option of toggling the Annotations tab on or off.

1. Open the Project Item that contains Annotations.
2. Go to **VIEW | Links | Annotations**.

This is a toggling function and is valid separately for each item.

Deleting an Annotation

1. Position the cursor on the link to an Annotation.
2. Go to **ANALYZE | Annotation | Delete Annotation** or right-click and select **Links → Annotation → Delete Annotation**.
3. Confirm with [**Yes**].

Hyperlinks

NVivo can create links to external sources in two ways:

- Hyperlinks from a Source Item.
- External items (see page 74).

Creating Hyperlinks

1. Select a section (text or image) in a Source Item while in Edit mode.
2. Go to **ANALYZE | Links | Hyperlink → New Hyperlink...** or right-click and select **Links → Hyperlink → New Hyperlink...**

The **New Hyperlink** dialog box appears:

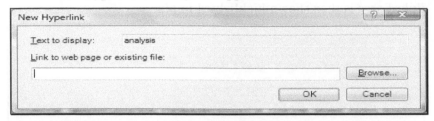

3   Paste a complete URL or use [**Browse...**] to find the target file in your computer or in your local network.

4   Confirm with [**OK**].

A Hyperlink is blue and underlined.

Opening a Hyperlink

The following three methods will open a Hyperlink:

1   Position the cursor on the link.

2   Go to **ANALYZE | Links | Hyperlink → Open Hyperlink**.

alternatively

1   Point at the link and the pointer becomes an arrow.

2   Right-click and select **Links → Hyperlink → Open Hyperlink**.

alternatively

1   Hold down the [**Ctrl**] key.

2   Click on the link.

This latter command will sometimes cause the external file (depending on the file type) to open as a minimized window. If so then either repeat this command or click on the Windows toolbar.

Deleting a Hyperlink

1   Position the cursor on the hyperlink while in Edit mode.

2   Go to **ANALYZE | Links | Hyperlink → Delete Hyperlink**.

alternatively

1   Point at the link in a Source Item while in Edit mode with the mouse pointer which will then become an arrow.

2   Right-click and select **Links → Hyperlink → Delete Hyperlink**.

The **Delete Hyperlink** dialog box appears:

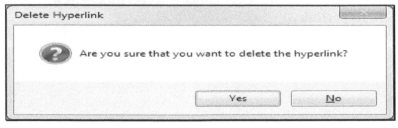

3   Confirm with [**Yes**].

10. INTRODUCING NODES

By definition, a Node is a connecting point. In NVivo 11, Nodes are the primary tool for organizing and classifying source data. You can think of a Node as a 'container' of source material. Nodes can represent abstract concepts, such as topics, themes, and ideas. Nodes can also represent tangible concepts, such as people, places, and things. Remember, Nodes can represent anything you would find useful to organize and classify elements of your project. Some researchers know very early what kind of Nodes they will need to organize and categorize your data. You can create Nodes before you start to work with your source material. Other researchers may need to brainstorm organizational categories, concepts and structures 'on the fly' as they work through their source material. The way you work with Nodes varies largely depending on the methods used, the research situation and your personality.

Early on in any project, a good idea is to identify a few Nodes that you think will be useful. These early Nodes can be coded at as you work through your data for the first time. These early Nodes can be moved, merged, renamed, redefined or even deleted later on as your project develops.

NVivo also has developed a system for organizing and classifying both Source Items and Nodes, see Chapter 11, Classifications.

The terms *Parent Node*, *Child Node* and *Aggregate* are used when NVivo's Node system is described. A *Parent Node* is the next higher hierarchical Node in relation to its *Child Nodes*.

An *Aggregate*[1] means that a certain Node in any hierarchical level accumulates the logical sum of all its nearest Child Nodes. Each Node can at any point of time activate or deactivate the function Aggregate and with immediate effect. The Aggregate control is in the **New Node** dialog box or **Node Properties** dialog box.

Case Nodes and Theme Nodes

In our work, we find it useful to make a distinction between Theme Nodes and Case Nodes. Theme Nodes are containers based on themes, your ideas and insights about your project. Case Nodes are containers based on cases, the tangible elements of your project, like your participants or research settings. Importantly, Nodes have the ability

---

[1] *Aggregate* has an imperfection in that the number of references is calculated as the arithmetic sum of the Child Nodes' references, which instead should be the logic sum as some references are overlapping.

to be labeled with customized meta-data called Node Classifications. A Case Node is understood as a member of a group of Nodes which are classified with Attributes and Values reflecting demographic or descriptive data. Case Nodes can be people (Interviewees), places or any group of items with similar properties.

A Theme Node therefore represents a theme or a topic common to the whole project. Theme Nodes are often represented by a Node hierarchy. The research design of many qualitative studies is often based on the intersection between Case Nodes and Theme Nodes. This is obvious for the design of Node Matrices (see page 214) and Framework Matrices (see page 253).

Interviews are often very important in a qualitative study. Therefore it is important ta have a basic understanding of how an interview preferably is represented in an NVivo project. It is easy to let the interview become a Source Item and the interview person becomes a Case Node. The document is the Source and the person is the Node. Demographic characteristics (e.g., gender, age, education etc.) are then applied to the Case Node in the form of Attributes and Values. See Chapter 11, Classifications.

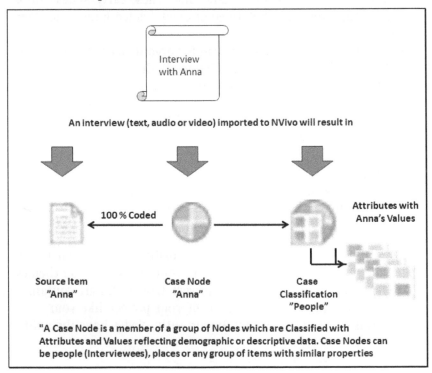

Creating a Node

Manually creating a new Node can be done in a number of ways.

    1   Go to **CREATE | Nodes | Node/Case**. Default folder is **Nodes**.
          Go to 5.

alternatively

    1   Click [**Nodes**] in Area 1.
    2   Select the **Nodes/Cases** folder in Area 2 or its subfolder.
    3   Go to **CREATE | Nodes | Node**. Go to 5.

alternatively

    3   Click on any empty space in Area 3.
    4   Right-click and select **New Node.../New Case** or **[Ctrl] + [Shift] + [N]**

The **New Node** dialog box appears:

> **Tip:** Some advice we offer coding newcomers is to record your thought processes in as much detail as possible when you are coding. The Description field of the **New Node** dialog box is an excellent place to capture why you have created that Node and how you think it relates to your coding hierarchy.

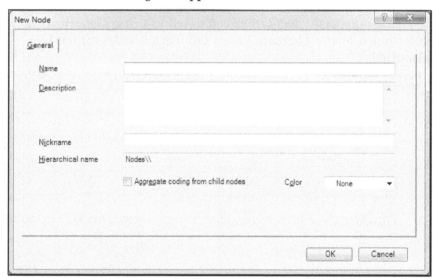

A new context dependent Ribbon menu, **NODE**, has now opened and is opened each time a Node is opened.

Alternatively, **New Case** dialog box appears:

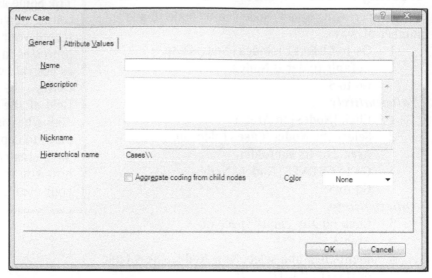

A new context dependent Ribbon menu, **CASE**, has now opened and is opened each time a Case is opened.

Please note, that Cases can be connected to a Case Classification, determined by the Attribute Values tab. Theme Nodes cannot be classified.

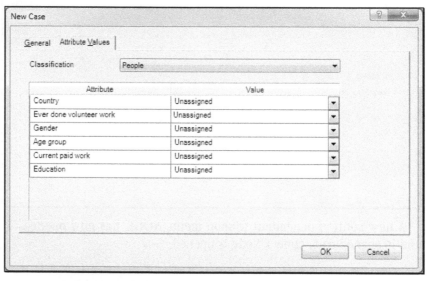

5   Type name (compulsory) and a description and a nickname (both optional), then **[OK]**.

Here is a typical list view in Area 3 of some Cases:

Cases			
↖ Name		Sources	References
⊞ Speakers		9	175
⊞ Focus Group Members		3	123
⊟ Interviewees		9	9
	Anna	1	1
	Bernadette	1	1
	Fredric	1	1
	Ken	1	1
	Mary	1	1
	Nick	1	1
	Phoebe	1	1
	Sunil	1	1
	Peter	0	0
	Grace	1	1

Building Hierarchical Nodes

As mentioned, Nodes can be organized hierarchically. As a result there are Node headings and subheadings in several levels of a coding hierarchy. Nodes can therefore form a sort of structured vocabulary, such as the MeSH (Medical Subject Headings) used by the Medline/PubMed article database. Cases can also be organized hierarchically if required.

> **Tip:** Nicknames are only for nodes. A practical use when nodenames are very long. Use simple abbreviations. Must be unique within the project. Useful for the **Find** function and when coding with the Quick Coding Bar.

Creating a Child Node

Assembling a Node hierarchy of Parent Nodes and Child Nodes is simple in NVivo:

1 Click [**Nodes**] in Area 1.
2 Select the **Nodes** folder in Area 2 or its subfolder.
3 Select the Node to which you want to create a Child Node.
4 Go to **CREATE | Nodes | Node**
   or right-click and select **New Node...**
   or [**Ctrl**] + [**Shift**] + [**N**].

The **New Node** dialog box now is shown.

5 Type a name (compulsory) and a description and a nickname (both optional), then [**OK**].

It is also possible to move Nodes within the list view, Area 3, with drag-and-drop or cut ([**Ctrl**] + [**X**]) and paste ([**Ctrl**] + [**V**]). When you drag one Node icon on top of another Node icon you create a child Node. You can also create a Child Node when you cut a Node, left-click a different Node, and then paste.

Here is a typical list view in Area 3 of some hierarchical Nodes:

Underlying items in the list can be opened or closed by clicking the + or – symbols, but also by using **VIEW | List View | List View→ Expand All (Selected) Nodes/ Collapse All (Selected) Nodes**. A useful function is showing Child Node Headers. When these headers are displayed you can modify the column widths. Apply **View | List VIEW | List View → Child Node Headers** (toggling).

These menu options are also available by right-clicking in Area 3: **Expand/Collapse**.

Merging Nodes

> **Tip:** If you select *Append linked memos* a new memo will be created with the same name as the new node. If all merged nodes have memos the new memo will append the contents from all its memos.

Any Node can be merged into an existing Node. Merging two Nodes simply combines the content of one Node into another.

1 Cut or copy one or more Node(s).
2 Select a target Node.
3 Go to **HOME | Clipboard | Merge → Merge Into Selected Node**
   or right-click and select **Merge Into Selected Node**
   or **[Ctrl] + [M]**.

In each case the **Merge Into Node** dialog box is shown:

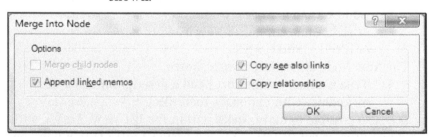

4 Select the applicable options, then click **[OK]**.

Alternatively, you can merge two (or more) Nodes into a new Node:

1   Cut or copy two or more Nodes.
2   Select the folder under which you want to place the new Node.
3   Go to **HOME | Clipboard | Merge → Merge Into New Node...** or right-click and select **Merge Into New Node...**

alternatively

3   Select the parent node under which you want to place the new Node.
4   Go to **HOME | Clipboard | Merge → Merge Into New Child Node** or right-click and select **Merge Into New Child Node...**

The **Merge Into Node** dialog box appears:

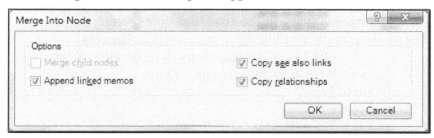

5   Select the applicable option(s), then click [**OK**].

The **New Node** dialog box appears:

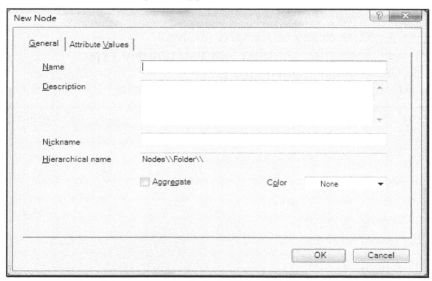

6   Type name (compulsory) and description and a nickname (optional), then [**OK**].

Relationships – Only for Pro & Plus

Relationships are Nodes that indicate that two Project Items (Source Items or Nodes) are related, such as the hypothesis *Poverty* **influences** *Public Health*. Data supporting that hypothesis could be coded at such relationship Node, which represents the relationship between the Nodes *Poverty* and *Public Health*.

Different relationship types are defined by the user and are stored under [**Classifications**] in the **Relationship Types** folder. Relationship Nodes are then created as associative, one way, or symmetrical (see below). The Relationships folder is not allowed to have subfolders and these Nodes cannot be arranged hierarchically. Classifications cannot be assigned to Relationships.

Creating a Relationship Type

Before creating relationships amongst your data, you must create some relationship types. In the above example (*Poverty* **influences** *Public Health*), the relationship type is titled **influences**.

1 Go to **CREATE | Classifications | Relationship Type**.
Default folder is **Relationship Types**.
Go to 5.

alternatively

1 Click [**Classifications**] in Area 1.
2 Select the **Relationship Types** folder in Area 2.
3 Go to **CREATE | Classifications | Relationship Type**.
Go to 5.

alternatively

3 Click on any empty space in Area 3.
4 Right-click and select **New Relationship Type...**
or [**Ctrl**] + [**Shift**] + [**N**].

The **New Relationship Type** dialog box appears:

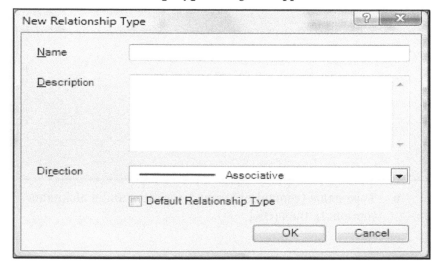

5   Select *Associative, One Way* or *Symmetrical* from the drop-down list at **Direction**.

6   Type a name (compulsory) and a description (optional), then [**OK**].

The list view with Relationship Types in Area 3, may look like this:

Relationship Types				
★ Default	Name		Direction	Created On
↻ ✓	Associated		———	2013-10-12 09:06
↻	Is best fried to		◄——►	2013-10-12 17:18
↻	Is married to		———	2013-10-12 17:17
↻	Loves		——►	2013-10-12 17:17

Creating a Relationship

Now that you have defined a relationship type, it's time to begin creating relationships between items in your NVivo project.

1   Go to **CREATE | Nodes | Relationships**.
     Default folder is **Relationships**.
     Go to 5.

alternatively

1   Click [**Nodes**] in Area 1.

2   Select the **Relationships** folder in Area 2.

3   Go to **CREATE | Nodes | Relationships**.
     Go to 5.

alternatively

3   Click on any empty space in Area 3.

4   Right-click and select **New Relationship...**
     or [**Ctrl**] + [**Shift**] + [**N**].

The **New Relationship** dialog box appears:

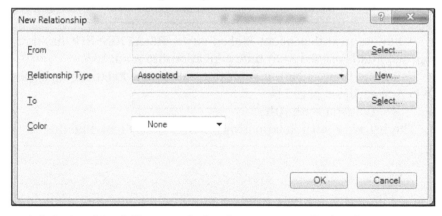

A Relationship defines a relation between two Project Items, Source Items or Nodes.

5   Use the [**Select...**] buttons to find the items that will be connected by this Node.

6   Select one From-item and one To-item. Confirm with [**OK**].
7   Select a Relationship Type with the drop-down list.

The **New Relationship** dialog box will then look like this to represent a much more concrete relationship: that *Anna* **is married to** *Raul*:

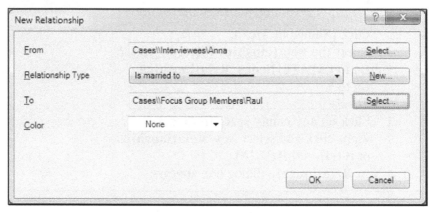

A new context dependent Ribbon menu, **RELATIONSHIP**, has now opened and is opened each time a Relationship is opened.

Using the {**New...**}-button you can create a new Relationship Type when needed, see page 144.

8   Confirm with [**OK**].

The list view with Relationships in Area 3 may look like this:

Using the Quick Coding Bar on Relationships

NVivo 11 has improved the Quick Coding bar to facilitate the creation of new Relationships and new Relationship Types. When you have found a section in your sources that verifies a relationship of some kind you select this text accordingly. Then with the Coding bar you first select Relationships in the **In** scroll bar:

Then you select a From Case and a To Case and a proper Relationship type. You can also as an alternative create new items by typing new names in the Coding bar and finally confirm with the Code button. The default direction will be *Associated* and can easily be changed later on.

Viewing a Relationship from a Related Item

1   Open an item in Area 3 that has a relationship.
2   Go to **View | Links → Relationships**
    which is a toggling function.

A new window will open and the relationship will show:

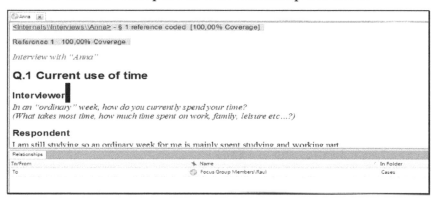

Exporting a Node

All Project Items (except folders) can be exported in various file formats:

1   Select the item(s) that you want to export, like a Node.
2   Go to **DATA | Export | Items...**
    or right-click and select **Export → <Item>**
    or **[Ctrl] + [Shift] + [E]**.

The **Export Options** dialog box appears:

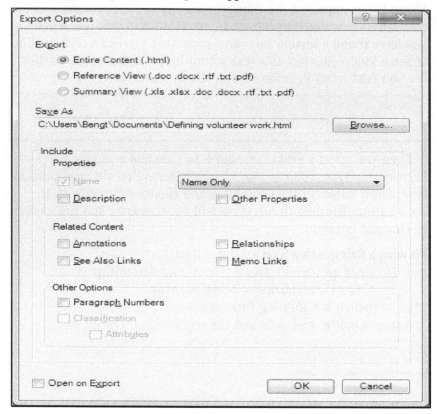

3   Select options, file name, location, and type, then [**OK**].

The option *Entire Content* creates a HTML-page with several files and folders that can be uploaded to a Web-server.

Converting a Relationship to a Node

By copying a Relationship and then pasting it into the Node or Case folder the result will be a new node with the same name as the Relationship.

The Folder Structure for Nodes

The project folder structure emphasizes on the important difference between Nodes (Theme Nodes), Cases (Case Nodes), Sentiments (see page 175), Relationships (see page 144) and Node Matrices (see page 214). The default folders in Area 2 are:

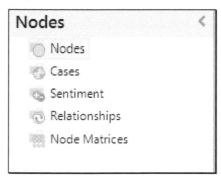

These folders and the names are not possible to delete, move or rename. The folder names are depending on the user interface language setting, see page 39. However, the user can create subfolders to the default folders **Nodes** and **Cases**.

11. CLASSIFICATIONS

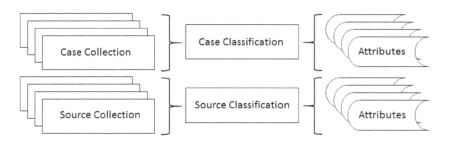

Case and Source Classifications

Nodes, Classifications and Attributes are related in the following way.

Source Items hold primary or secondary data. They can be text sources, media sources or picture sources.

Cases represent information that is generated from a certain source like an informant, a place, an organization or any other source that is subject to the current study.

Nodes (Theme Nodes) represent a topic, a phenomenon, an idea, a value, an opinion, a case, or any other abstraction or tangible object thought to be important for the current study. Theme nodes are not classified.

Attributes represent characteristics or properties of a Source Item or a Node which has or will have an impact when analyzing data. Each such attribute has a set of **Values**. Attributes and values hold the demographic data of the study. For example, if gender is your attribute, the possible values are male or female.

Classifications are defined by NVivo as a collective name for a certain set of Attributes that will be assigned to certain Source Items or Cases. Classifications are not applied on Theme Nodes.

Classifications therefore fall into two types: Node Classifications and Source Classifications. We will explore how to create Classifications, how they are associated with Source Items and Nodes and how individual values are handled. Attributes cannot be created without the existence of Classifications. This chapter presents examples of how to create a Case Classification, but the procedures are similar for Source Classifications.

151

Case Classifications

An example: You are part of a study looking at the experiences of pupils, teachers, politicians and schools. There are reasons to create individual Nodes for each of these four groups:

- Attributes for pupils could then be: Age, gender, grade, number of siblings, social class.
- Attributes for teachers could then be: Age, gender, education, number of years as teacher, school subject.
- Attributes for politicians could then be: Age, gender, political preference, number of years as politician, other profile.
- Attributes for schools could then be: Size, age, size of the community, political majority.

Each of these four groups needs its own set of attributes, with each attribute requiring its own set of values. Each such set of attributes will collectively form a Node Classification.

Source Classifications – Only for Pro & Plus

In NVivo, Classifications are also applied to Source Items with attributes and values. Source Classifications, for example, could be applied to certain interviews that may need attributes like the time of the interview for longitudinal studies, place and other conditions. Source Classifications can also be applied to research that is the result of a literature review, with attributes like journal name, type of study, keywords, publication date, name of authors etc.

Creating a Classification

Although NVivo includes some default Classifications (e.g., the Node Classification *Person* and the Source Classification *Reference*), it is possible to create your own custom Classifications:

1 Go to **CREATE | Classifications | Case Classification**.
 Default folder is **Node Classifications**.
 Go to 5.

alternatively

1 Click [**Classfications**] in Area 1.
2 Select the **Node Classifications** folder in Area 2.
3 Go to **CREATE | Classifications | Case Classification**.
 Go to 5.

alternatively

3 Click on any empty space in Area 3.
4 Right-click and select **New Classification...**
 or [**Ctrl**] + [**Shift**] + [**N**].

The **New Classification** dialog box appears:

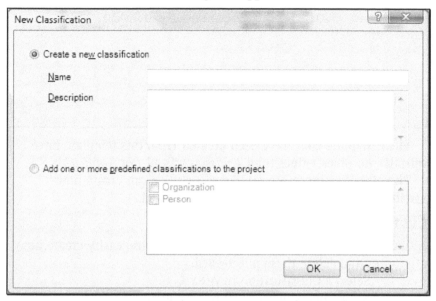

You can choose between creating your own new Classification or using one of NVivo's templates.

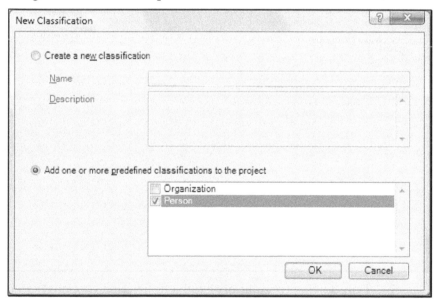

This example uses the template *Person*.

5   Click [**OK**].

The result is shown like this in Area 3:

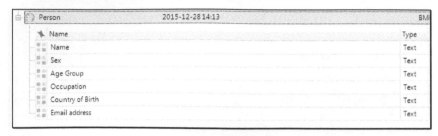

The attributes that have been created from this template have initially no other values than *Unassigned* and *Not Applicable*.

The classification can easily be edited. You can create new attributes and you can delete those not needed.

Customizing a Classification

A Classification can easily be edited. You can also easily create new attributes and delete those not needed.

1   Select a Classification in Area 3.

2   Right-click and select **New Attribute...**
     or **[Ctrl] + [Shift] + [N]**.

The **New Attribute** dialog box appears:

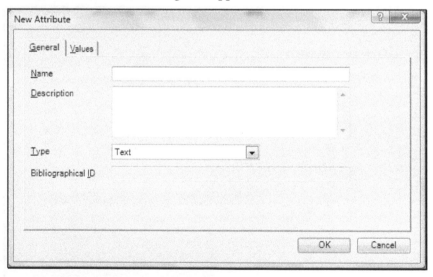

5   Type a name (compulsory) and a description (optional) and select the attribute type (Text, Integer, Decimal, Date/Time, Date, Time or Boolean), then **[OK]**.

The data type field indicates what kind of data will constitute an Attribute's Values. There are seven data types: **Text** data includes any text content (e.g., profession); **Integer** data includes a number without a decimal place; **Decimal** data includes a number with a decimal place; **Time** data is the time in hours, minutes and seconds; **Date/Time** data is a combination of the calendar date and time; and **Boolean** data are binary pairs (e.g., yes or no, 0 or 1).

You can also decide which values belong to the attribute. Use either the **New Attribute** dialog box or the **Attribute Properties** dialog box, under the **Values** tab:

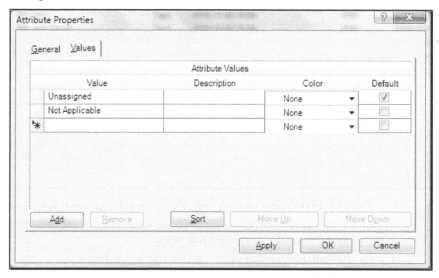

6   The [**Add**] button creates a text box in which you can type new values. Confirm with [**OK**]. To delete any value you need to select this value, then click [**Remove**] and if this value has been assigned to any case you will be asked to replace the value by an existing one.

Finally, you need to assign the Classification to a Case.

1   Select one or several Cases that shall be assigned a Classification.

2   Right-click and select **Classification** → <**Name of Classification**>.

Alternatively, if you only select *one* Case:

1   Select the Case that shall be assigned a Classification.

2   Right-click and select **Case Properties** or [**Ctrl**] + [**P**].

The **Case Properties** dialog box appears:

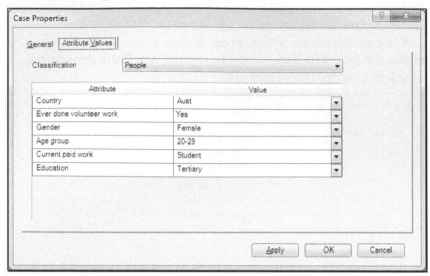

3   Use the **Attribute Values** tab. The **Classification** drop-
     down list will give you access to all Case Classifications in
     the project. Select your desired Node.
4   In the column *Value* you can use the drop-down list to set
     individual values to the current Case.
5   Confirm with [**OK**].

Working with the Classification Sheet

The overview of the attributes and values of Source Items or Cases is
called a Classification Sheet. This sheet is a matrix where rows are
Source Items or Cases and columns are Attributes. The cells contain
the values.

While creating a Classification allows you to establish the
Attributes and Values associated with classified items, the
application of that metadata is done through the Classification Sheet.
When a Classification Sheet is opened you can update values, along
with sorting and filtering data.

1   Go to **EXPLORE | Classification Sheets | Case
     Classification Sheets → <Name of Classification>**.

alternatively

1   Select a Classification in Area 3.
2   Right-click and select **Open Classification Sheet**
     or key command [**Ctrl**] + [**Shift**] + [**O**]
     or double-click.

alternatively

1   Select a classified Source Item or a classified Case in Area 3
2   Right-click and select **Open Classification Sheet**.

Below is a sample Classification Sheet. As you can see, each row is an item that has been classified with the Classification *Person*, each column is an Attribute, and each cell contains the attribute's attendant value:

People	A : Country	B : Ever done volunteer ...	C : Gender	D : Age group
1 : Annette	US	Yes	Female	40-49
2 : Annie	US	Yes	Female	20-29
3 : Dan	US	Yes	Male	60+
4 : Elaine	US	No	Female	30-39
5 : George	US	Yes	Male	60+
6 : Jin	US	Yes	Male	20-29
7 : Jose	US	Yes	Male	20-29
8 : Marie	US	Yes	Female	30-39
9 : Olivia	US	Yes	Female	50-59
10 : Raul	US	No	Male	30-39
11 : Roberta	US	No	Female	30-39
12 : Rosa	US	Yes	Female	40-49

Once you have your Classification Sheet open, there are a number of options for editing, structuring, viewing and occluding aspects of your data.

Editing the Classification Sheet

Once you point at a cell in the Classification sheet there will be right side arrow in the cell. Clicking at the arrow lets you select any of the available values or overtype any value and a new value will be created. However, you cannot delete any value here.

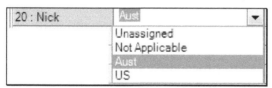

Hiding/Unhiding Row Numbers (Toggling Function)
1 Open a **Classification Sheet**.
2 Go to **LAYOUT | Show/Hide | Row IDs**
or right-click and select **Row → Row IDs**.

Hiding Rows
1 Open a **Classification Sheet**.
2 Select one row or several rows that you want to hide.
3 Go to **LAYOUT | Show/Hide | Hide Row**
or right-click and select **Row → Hide Row**.

Hiding/Unhiding Rows with Filters

1. Open a **Classification Sheet**.
2. Click the 'funnel' in any column head
   or select a column and go to **LAYOUT | Sort & Filter | Filter
   → Filter Row**.

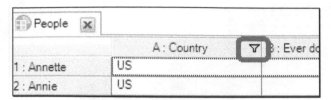

The **Classification Filter Options** dialog box appears:

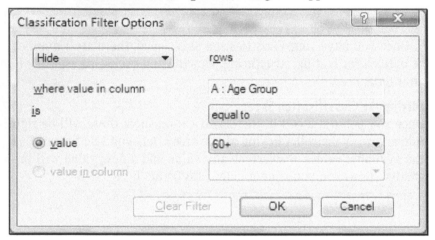

3. Select value and operator for hiding or unhiding. Confirm
   with [**OK**]. When a filter has been applied the funnel
   symbol turns *red*.

To reset a filter select [**Clear Filter**] in the **Classification Filter
Options** dialog box.

Unhiding Rows

1. Open a **Classification Sheet**.
2. Select one row on each side of the hidden row that you
   want to unhide.
3. Go to **LAYOUT | Show/Hide | Unhide Row**
   or right-click and select **Row → Unhide Row**.

Unhiding All Rows

1. Open a **Classification Sheet**.
2. Go to **LAYOUT | Sort & Filter | Filter → Clear All Row
   Filters**
   or right-click and select **Row → Clear All Row Filters**.

Hiding /Unhiding Column Letter /Toggling Function)
1   Open a **Classification Sheet**.
2   Go to **Layout | Show/Hide | Column IDs**
    or right-click and select **Column → Column IDs**.

Hiding Columns
1   Open a **Classification Sheet**.
2   Select one column or several columns that you want o hide.
3   Go to **LAYOUT | Show/Hide | Hide Column**
    or right-click and select **Column → Hide Column**.

Unhiding Columns
1   Open a **Classification Sheet**.
2   Select a column on each side of the hidden column that you
    want to unhide.
3   Go to **LAYOUT | Show/Hide | Unhide Column**
    or right-click and select **Column → Unhide Column**.

Unhiding All Columns
1   Open a **Classification Sheet**.
2   Go to **LAYOUT | Sort & Filter | Filter → Clear All Column
    Filters**
    or right-click and select **Column → Clear All Column
    Filters**.

Transposing the Classification Sheet (Toggling Function)
Transposing means that rows and columns switch places.
1   Open a **Classification Sheet**.
2   Go to **LAYOUT | Transpose**
    or right-click and select **Transpose**.

Moving a Column Left or Right
1   Open a **Classification Sheet**.
2   Select the column or columns that you want to move. If
    you want to move more than one column they need to be
    adjacent.
3   Go to **LAYOUT | Rows & Columns | Column → Move
    Left/Move Right**.

Resetting the Classification Sheet
1   Open a **Classification Sheet**.
2   Go to **LAYOUT | Tools | Reset Settings**
    or right-click and select **Reset Settings**.

Exporting Classification Sheets

A Classification Sheet can be exported as a tab delimited text-file or an Excel spreadsheet:

1. Select the Classification Sheet in Area 3 that you want to export.
2. Go to **DATA | Export → Export Classification Sheets...**

The **Export Classification Sheets** dialog box appears:

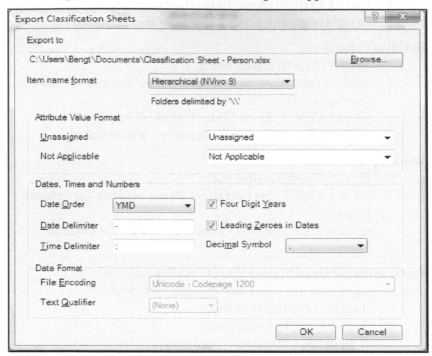

With [**Browse...**] you can decide name, file path and file format.

3. Confirm with [**OK**].

Importing a Classification Sheet

You can import a Classification Sheet as a tab-delimited text-file or an Excel spreadsheet. All Nodes, Attributes and Values are created from the imported file if they do not exist already.

1. Go to **DATA | Import | Import Classification Sheets** or click [**Classifications**] in Area 1, click on any empty space in Area 3, right-click and select **Import Classification Sheets...**

Tip: An easy way to convert an Excel worksheet to text is:
1. Select the whole worksheet
2. Copy
3. Open Notepad
4. Paste into Notepad
5. Save with a new name

160

The **Import Classification Sheets Wizard** – **Step 1** appears:

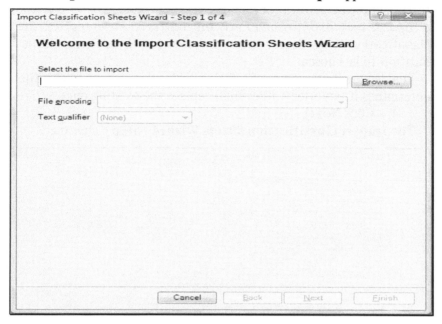

2   With [**Browse...**] you can find the file that you want to import.

3   Click [**Next**].

The **Import Classification Sheets Wizard** – **Step 2** appears:

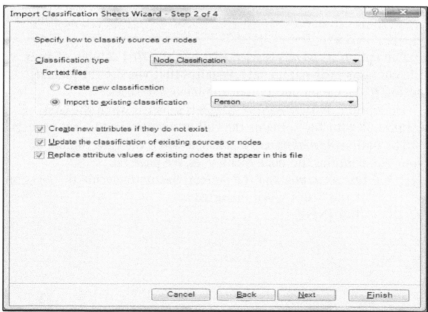

Here you decide if you want to create a new classification or use an existing one.

Create new attributes if they do not exist creates new attributes for the chosen classification.

Update the classification of existing sources or Nodes replaces the classification of the Source Items or Nodes that already exist in the location to be chosen.

Replace attribute values of existing Nodes that appear in this file determines if imported values shall replace the existing ones.

4   Click **Next**].

The **Import Classification Sheets Wizard – Step 3** appears:

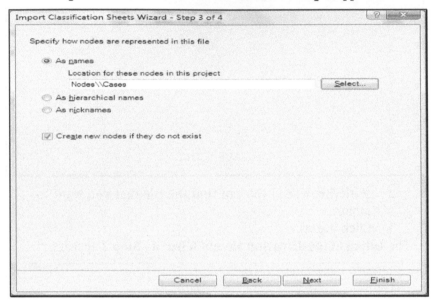

The option *As names* is selected when the first column of your file contains node names only. Requires that you use the [**Select**]-button to decide the location of the imported Nodes.

The option *As hierarchical names* is selected when the first column of your file contains the full hierarchical name, see page 23.

The option *As nicknames* is selected when the first column of your file contains the node nicknames, see page 141.

5   Use *As names* and the [**Select**]-button to decide the location of the Nodes when imported.

6   Click [**Next**].

The **Import Classification Sheets Wizard – Step 4** appears:

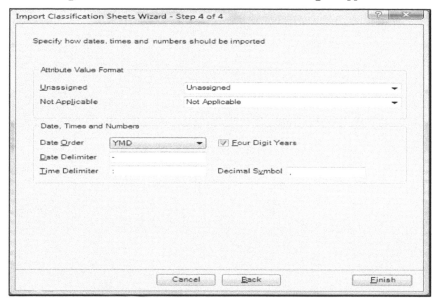

7   Decide the formats of unassigned values, dates, times and numbers.

8   Confirm with **[Finish]**.

The result, a Classification Sheet in NVivo, looks like this:

14 : Anna	Aust	Yes	Female	20-29
15 : Bernadette	Aust	Yes	Female	60+
16 : Fredric	Aust	Yes	Male	30-39
17 : Grace	Aust	Yes	Female	20-29
18 : Ken	Aust	Yes	Male	50-59
19 : Mary	Aust	Yes	Female	60+
20 : Nick	Aust	Yes	Male	30-39
21 : Peter	Aust	No	Male	30-39
22 : Phoebe	Aust	Yes	Female	30-39
23 : Sunil	Aust	Yes	Male	20-29

The Classification itself with its attributes can be displayed Area 3:

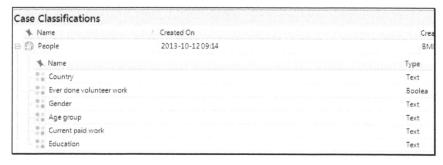

163

12. CODING

Coding is the act of assigning a portion of your source material to one of your Nodes. Coding can be carried out in two ways: *Manual Coding* (or just C*oding*) is conducted by the NVivo user; *Autocoding* is conducted by the NVivo software responding to pre-determined elements of source material.

The item being coded can be any piece of data, even something as small as a single word from a document or single frame from a video. However, the contents of a Descriptions or in Annotations cannot be coded. Nodes are the set of conceptual terms or case information that you will code to. One usually says that you are *coding* a certain source element at a certain Node.

As arguably the most important function of qualitative data analysis software, NVivo offers a variety of methods for coding data:
- The Quick Coding Bar
- Drag-and-drop
- Right-click/Menus/Keyboard Commands
- Autocoding by various principles
- Range coding
- In Vivo coding
- Coding by Query

Here follows some basic definitions used both in the NVivo commands and in our instructions:

Code implies that the entire content of a Source Item(s) or a selection is coded to a new or existing node.

Code to Recent Nodes implies that the entire content of a Source Item(s) or a selection is coded to any of the listed nodes.

Code at Current Nodes implies that you code a selection at the Node or the Nodes that were used most recently.

Code In Vivo implies that a selection creates a Node in the **Nodes** folder with the same name as the selected text (max 256 characters).

Create As implies that the entire content of a Source Item(s) is created as a Set, Node or one or several Cases.

The Quick Coding Bar

The Quick Coding Bar can be moved around on the screen or be positioned in the lower part of Area 4. You can toggle hiding/unhiding and docked/floating by going to **VIEW | Workspace | Quick Coding** and the options **Hide, Docked** and **Floating**. Ideally, you will find the **Quick Coding Bar** useful enough to keep open each time you use NVivo – we do!

The **Quick Coding Bar** is active as long as a selection has been made in a Source Item or in a Node.

The drop-down list at **In** has four options: *Nodes, Cases, Relationships* and *Nicknames*. The first time in a new work session you normally select *Nodes* and then click on the first [...] button that now displays the **Select Location** dialog box. From here you can select among Node folders and parent Nodes.

We have explained Nodes and Relationships in this book, but Nicknames deserve some attention here. Nicknames are an opportunity for you to create 'shortcuts' to your most popular Nodes. For example, giving your 5 most popular Nodes nicknames allows you to efficiently access them from the **Quick Coding Bar** without needing to browse through your coding hierarchy. Nicknames can also be useful for creating shortened versions of Nodes with long names.

After selecting your Nodes, Cases, Relationships, or Nickname, proceed to the drop-down list at **Code At**. This list contains all Nodes at the selected location in alphabetic order. You can also use the second [...] button that opens the **Select Project Items** dialog box thus giving access to all Nodes. You can select more than one Node to code at. You can also create a new Node by typing its name in the **Code At** text box at. The location of this new Node is determined by the setting in the left textbox **In**. Command **[Ctrl]** + **[Q]** positions the cursor in the right text box **Code At**, which will auto-complete Node names based on your typing – another shortcut.

The **Code At** drop-down also list saves the names of the last nine Nodes used during an ongoing work session. You find this list below a divider and in the order they were last used.

After you have selected your Nodes, the **Quick Coding Bar** can perform the following functions:

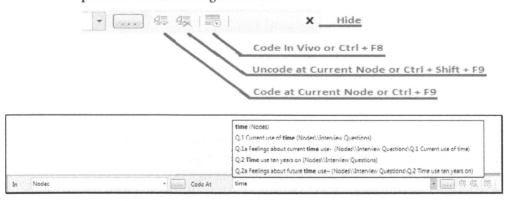

As soon as you type the node name in the text box possible alternatives will show and you can easily select the right node.

Drag-and-Drop Coding

Drag-and-drop coding is probably the fastest and easiest coding method. Using this method and a customized screen is, according to us, the best way to code your data.

1 Click [**Sources**] in Area 1.

2 Select the folder in Area 2 with the Source Item that you want to code.

3 Open the Source Item in Area 3 that you want to code.

4 Select the text or image that you want to code.

5 Click [**Nodes**] in Area 1 and select the folder with the Nodes that you want to code to.

6 With the left mouse button pressed, drag the selection from the Source Item to the Node that you want to code to.

Use Right Detail View to fully optimize your screen location. This view allows you to drag source data easily into a Node.

Go to **VIEW** | **Workspace** | **Detail View** → **Right** (see page 50)

Go to **VIEW** | **Workspace** → Uncheck **Navigation View**

You can apply this technique when you need to create a new node. You simply drag your selection at a space below the list of Nodes or Cases and the field turns blue. As soon as you release the mouse button the **New Node** dialog box appears and you need to decide the node name, location and possibly a description.

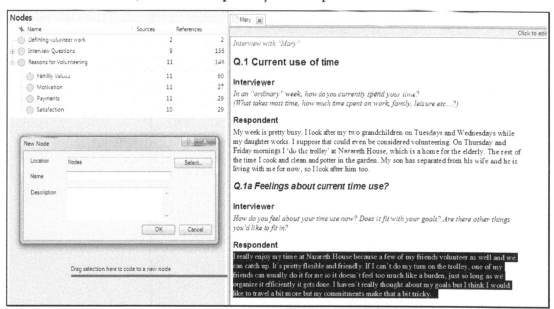

Confirm with [**OK**].

Menus, Right-Click, or Keyboard Commands

While we prefer drag-and-drop coding, you will no doubt find yourselves in situations where you need to code using another method.

Coding a Source Item

1 Click **[Sources]** in Area 1.
2 Select the folder in Area 2 with the Source Item that you want to code.
3 Select the Source Item or Items in Area 3 that you want to code.
4 Go to **ANALYZE | Coding | Code → Code [Ctrl] + [F2]**

alternatively

4 Right-click and select
   Code [Ctrl] + [F2]
   Code to Recent Nodes <select>

And this is the new **Select Code Items** dialog box:

In this dialog box you can select one or several existing nodes to code to. Note that the top text box offers a search function and can easiiy be used for searching among existing nodes. When you select

[**New Node**] the result, depending on what location you highlight, may look like the example at the arrow above.

Finally, type a name in the text box and confirm with [**OK**]. If you want to add a description then select the new node in the List View, right-click and select **Node Properties** or [**Ctrl**] + [**Shift**] + [**P**].

An alternative that will give you the same result (New Node) is when you select a source, right-click and select **Create As → Create As Node**.

Coding Source Items to Cases

This function can be used when several Source Items need to be converted to Cases. For example, you can create a list of Cases if you have recently imported a number of interview transcripts. .

1   Click [**Sources**] in Area 1.
2   Select the folder in Area 2 with the Source Item that you want to code.
3   Select the Source Item or Items in Area 3 that you want to create as Cases.
4   Right-click and select **Create As → Create As Cases...**

The selected sources will be coded at a new Case or Cases and the **Select Location** dialog box will let you decide in what folder or under what parent Case the new Cases will be located. One Case for each selected source will be created with the same name as the sources. The **Select Location** dialog box also makes it possible that you allocate one of the existing Case Classifications to the new Case or Cases.

Coding a Selection from a Source Item

While Case Nodes will often pertain to entire source files, though not always, Theme Nodes often involve selections from a Source Item:

1   Click [**Sources**] in Area 1.
2   Select the folder in Area 2 with the Source Item that you want to code.
3   Open the Source Item in Area 3 that you want to code.
4   Select the text or the section that you want to code.
5   Go to **ANALYZE | Coding | Code → Code**   [**Ctrl** + [**F2**]

The new **Select Code Items** dialog box will open and you can choose a new or existing node or nodes to code to.

alternatively

5   Right-click and select
     Code   [**Ctrl** + [**F2**]
     Code to Recent Nodes <select>
     Code In Vivo   [**Ctrl**] + [**F8**]

Uncoding a Source Item

As qualitative data coding is often an iterative process, sources may need to be uncoded.

    1   Click [**Sources**] in Area 1.
    2   Select the folder in Area 2 with the source that you want to uncode.
    3   Select the Source Item or items in Area 3 that you want to uncode.
    4   Go to **ANALYZE** | **Uncoding** | **Uncode**   **[Ctrl]** + **[Shift]** + **[F2]**

alternatively

    4   Right-click and select
        Uncode   **[Ctrl]** + **[Shift]** + **[F2]**
        Uncode from Recent Nodes <select>

From the **Select Project Items** dialog box you select the node or nodes you want to uncode from.

Uncoding a Selection from a Source Item

    1   Click [**Sources**] in Area 1.
    2   Select the folder in Area 2 with the Source Item that you want to uncode.
    3   Open the Source Item in Area 3 that you want to uncode.
    4   Select the text or the section that you want to uncode.
    5   Go to **ANALYZE** | **Uncoding** | **Uncode**   **[Ctrl]** + **[Shift]** + **[F2]**

alternatively

    5   Right-click and select
        Uncode   **[Ctrl]** + **[Shift]** + **[F2]**
        (With the **Select Project Items** dialog box you can select the node(s) you want to uncode from.)
        Uncode from Recent Nodes <select>

Uncoding a Selection from a Node

    1   Click [**Nodes**] in Area 1.
    2   Select the folder in Area 2 with the Node that you want to uncode.
    3   Open the Node in Area 3 that you want to uncode.
    4   Select the text or the section that you want to uncode.
    5   Right-click and select
        Uncode   **[Ctrl]** + **[Shift]** + **[F2]**
        (With the **Select Project Items** dialog box you can select the node(s) you will uncode from.)
        Uncode from Recent Nodes <select>
        Uncode from this Node   **[Ctrl]** + **[Shift]** + **[F3]**
        (When you select all, **[Ctrl]** + **[A],** in an open node and apply **Uncode from this Node** then the whole node will be uncoded but remain with zero coding.)

Uncoding Intersecting Content

Uncode content in one node that intersects with content in another node.

1. Click [**Nodes**] in Area 1.
2. Select the folder in Area 2 with the Node that you want to uncode.
3. Select the node(s) in Area 3 that you want to uncode
4. Go to **ANALYZE | Uncoding | Uncode Intersecting Content**

The Select source project items dialog box appears.

5. Select the node(s) that you want to uncode from.
6. Click [**OK**].

The Codebook

A long awaited function is the new Codebook for exporting a list of all nodes (not Cases) in any selected node folder. The export format is Word (.docx) or Excel (.xlsx) and the default location is My Documents.

1. Go to **DATA | Export | Codebook**.

In case there are no subfolders in the Nodes folder then the Codebook opens directly.

If here are subfolders then this dialog box opens and you can select the appropriate folder or folders. Confirm with [**OK**]:

Note, that the number of sources and references is an option here.

The Codebook now opens directly and may look like this (.docx):

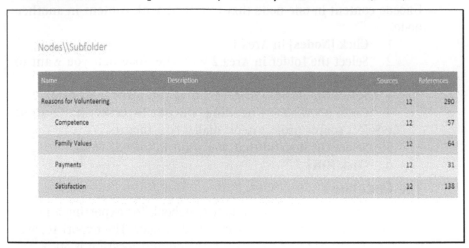

The layout allows the Description in the middle column and for future updates many of us are requesting an *Aggregate* mark and an indication of a linked *Memo* when existing.

Autocoding – By Themes - Only for Plus

This function is depending on the current Text content language that is decided at Project Properties, see page 56.

NVivo will analyze your source items or nodes to find frequent themes. Such themes are grouped in nodes and are sorted after occurrence.

1   Click **[Sources]** or **[Nodes]** in Area 1.
2   Select folder in Area 2 with source items or nodes that you want to autocode.
3   Select source items or nodes in Area 3 that you want to autocode.
4   Go to **ANALYZE | Coding | Auto Code**
or right-click and select **Auto Code...**

The Auto Code Wizard – Step 1 appears:

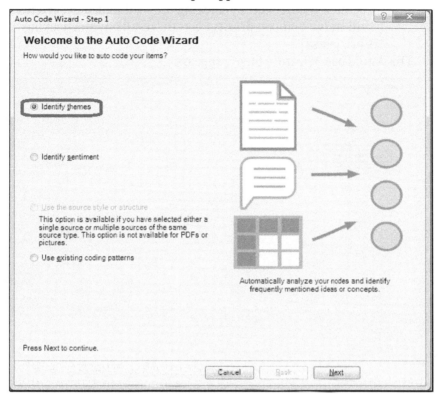

5   Select *Identify themes* and click [**Next**].

The Auto Code Wizard – Step 2 appears:

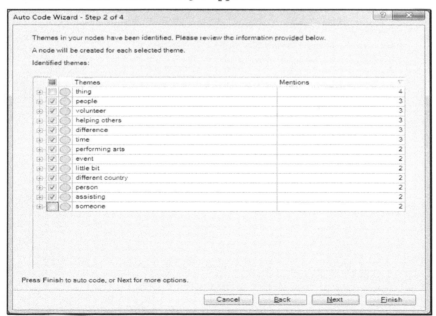

6 NVivo has found a number of words or phrases with repeated occurrence. By clicking on + a detailed occurrence will show. You can deselect certain results by unchecking. Click [**Next**].

The Auto Code Wizard – Step 3 appears:

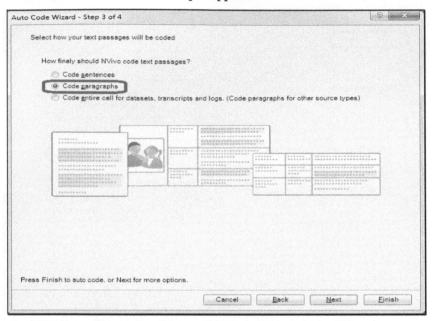

7 We select *Code paragraphs* and click [**Next**].

The Auto Code Wizard – Step 4 appears:

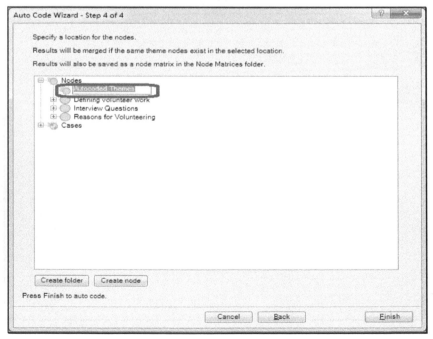

8 NVivo suggest location for the new nodes. You can modify with the [**Create folder**]- and [**Create node**]-buttons. Click [**Finish**].

The result is twofold: a node matrix located at **Nodes\\Node Matrices**\\:

	A : assisting	B : difference	C : different country	D : event	E : helping others	F : little bit
1 : Internals\\Focus Groups\\NonVols	0	0	0	0	0	0
2 : Internals\\Focus Groups\\Vols 01	0	0	0	1	0	1
3 : Internals\\Focus Groups\\Vols 02	0	0	0	0	0	0
4 : Internals\\Interviews\\Anna	1	2	0	0	1	0
5 : Internals\\Interviews\\Bernadette	0	0	0	0	0	0
6 : Internals\\Interviews\\Fredric	0	0	0	0	1	0
7 : Internals\\Interviews\\Grace	0	0	0	0	0	0
8 : Internals\\Interviews\\Ken	1	1	1	0	1	1
9 : Internals\\Interviews\\Nick	0	0	0	0	0	0
10 : Internals\\Interviews\\Phoebe	0	0	0	0	0	0
11 : Internals\\Interviews\\Sunil	0	0	0	0	0	0

..and a node hierarchy located at **Nodes\\Nodes\\Autocoded themes**\\:

Autocoded Themes

Name	Sources	References
assisting		2
difference		2
different country		1
event		1
helping others		3
little bit		2
people		2
performing arts		1
person		2
time		2
volunteer		2

The difference between these two results is important: The node matrix cannot be edited but the hierarchical node tree can be used for continued coding or other modifications.

Autocoding – By Sentiments – Only for Plus

This feature is language dependent and can only work for the language set in Project Properties, Text content language, page 56.

NVivo analyzes your source items or nodes to find grounds for sentiments in words or phrases. The result is nodes named **Positive** or **Negative** with child nodes named **Very** and **Moderately** respectively. These nodes are included in the project template and are therefore permanent and cannot be changed, moved or renamed. They can however be used for any type of supplementary or manual coding.

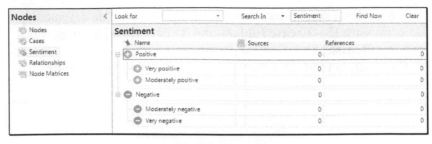

1   Click **[Sources]** or **[Nodes]** in Area 1.
2   Select a folder in Area 2 with source items or nodes that you want to autocode.
3   Select the source items or nodes in Area 3 that you want to autocode.
4   Go to **ANALYZE | Coding | Auto Code**
     or right-click and select **Auto Code...**

The Auto Code Wizard – Step 1 appears:

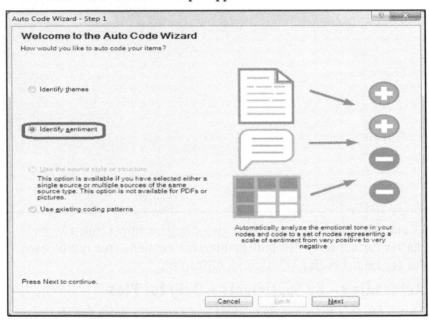

5   Select *Identify sentiment* and click **[Next]**.

The Auto Code Wizard – Step 2 appears:

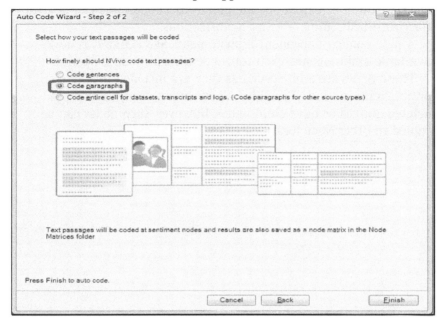

6   We select *Code paragraphs* and click [**Finish**].
The result is twofold, a node matrix located under **Nodes\\Node Matrices**:

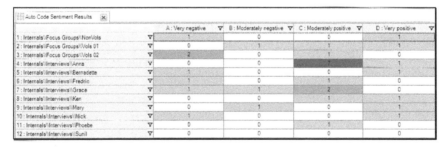

	A : Very negative	B : Moderately negative	C : Moderately positive	D : Very positive
1 : Internals\\Focus Groups\\NonVols	1	0	0	1
2 : Internals\\Focus Groups\\Vols 01	0	1	1	1
3 : Internals\\Focus Groups\\Vols 02	2	0	1	0
4 : Internals\\Interviews\\Anna	0	0	7	1
5 : Internals\\Interviews\\Bernadette	1	0	0	1
6 : Internals\\Interviews\\Fredric	1	0	1	0
7 : Internals\\Interviews\\Grace	1	1	2	0
8 : Internals\\Interviews\\Ken	0	0	1	1
9 : Internals\\Interviews\\Mary	0	1	0	1
10 : Internals\\Interviews\\Nick	1	0	0	1
11 : Internals\\Interviews\\Phoebe	0	0	1	0
12 : Internals\\Interviews\\Sunil	0	0	0	0

..and a node hierarchy located under **Nodes\\Sentiment**:

Sentiment		
Name	Sources	References
Positive	11	21
Very positive	7	7
Moderately positive	7	14
Negative	8	10
Moderately negative	3	3
Very negative	6	7

The difference between these two results is important: The node matrix cannot be edited but the hierarchical node tree can be used for continued coding or other modifications.

A new context dependent Ribbon menu, **SENTIMENT**, is now available and is opened each time a Sentiment Node is opened.

These nodes are a bit special as they are included in NVivo's project template for NVivo Plus. They cannot change names, be deleted, moved or have child nodes. However, such nodes can be copied to other Node locations.

Autocoding – By Structures

This feature is not language dependent as it is based on the use of paragraph styles (Heading 1, Heading 2, etc.) to create a hierarchical Node structure. The feature is only applicable to source items and not to nodes. Autocoding by structures codes the text under each heading under the name of the heading. If several documents are being auto coded at the same time or separately and they have the same structure of styles and headings then common

> **Did you know?** Our website has custom autocoding Word templates to help structure your research data: www.formkunskap.com

Nodes are created automatically. A practical usage of this feature is when you apply a custom Word template with an established style set as a questionnaire for interviews. Autocoding can be applied to properly structured interview transcripts to, for example, code Source Item contents according to Case Nodes upon import:

1   Click [**Sources**] in Area 1.
2   Select the folder in Area 2 with the source items that you want to autocode.
3   Select the Source Item or items in Area 3 that you want to autocode.
4   Go to **ANALYZE | Code | Auto Code** or right-click and select **Auto Code...**

The **Auto Code Wizard – Step 1** appears:

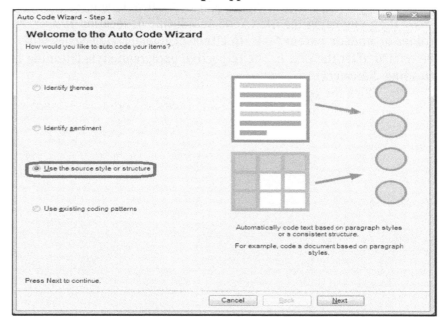

5   Select *Use source style or structure* and click [**Next**].

The Auto Code Wizard – Step 2 appears:

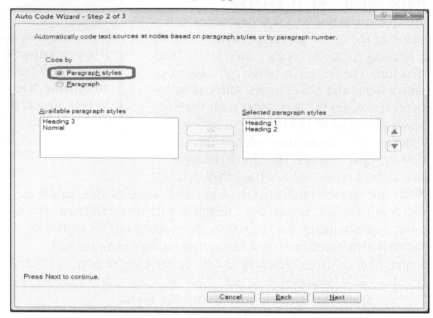

First, you need to decide which paragraph template should become the base for the new Node structure. NVivo will find all existing paragraph style templates in any Word document. The templates are selected with the [>>] button and are then transferred to the right textbox. The option *Existing Node* allows you to select the parent Node under which the new Nodes will be located. If you select *New Node* then you name the new Node and decide its location in a folder or under a parent Node. In either case underlying Nodes will be named after the text in the respective paragraph style (Heading 1, Heading 2 etcetera).

2   Click [**Next**].

The Auto Code Wizard – Step 3 appears:

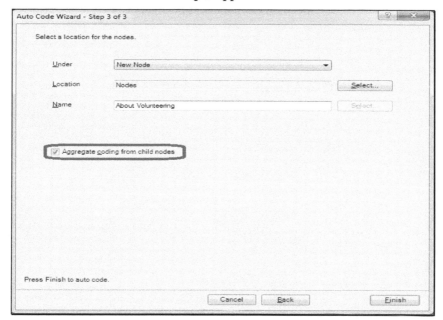

3   Decide location for the new nodes. If you select *New Node*
     you have to give the parent node a new name. Checking
     Aggregate makes the whole new node tree aggregated.
     Finally click [**Finish**].

- ♦ -

It is also possible to auto code transcripts of audio- or video-items.
Suppose that we have an audio item and a transcript with two
optional columns, Speaker and Organization:

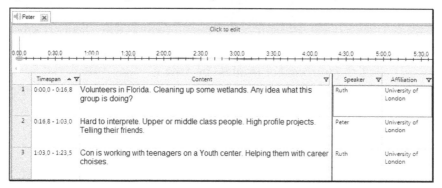

If you select **Code by** *Transcript Fields* autocoding such item will
be based on these optional columns which will then create new
Nodes named after the column contents:

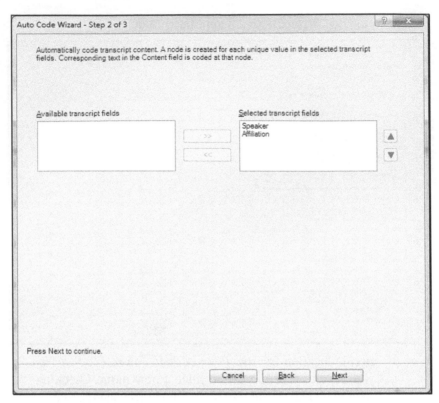

In this example *University of London* will become a Parent Node to the Child Nodes *Ruth* and *Edgar*. The content in the column Content will then be the coded text.

Autocoding – By Patterns – Only for Plus

This feature is not language dependent as it uses its own project data as input for the analysis. This method is based on selected nodes which you then use for coding more source items or nodes applying frequent words found in the nodes that form the pattern.

1   Click **[Sources]** or **[Nodes]** in Area 1.
2   Select folder in Area 2 with the source items or nodes you want to autocode.
3   Select the source item(s) in Area 3 you want to autocode.
4   Go to **ANALYZE | Coding | Auto Code**
     or right-click and select **Auto Code...**

The **Auto Code Wizard – Step 1** appears:

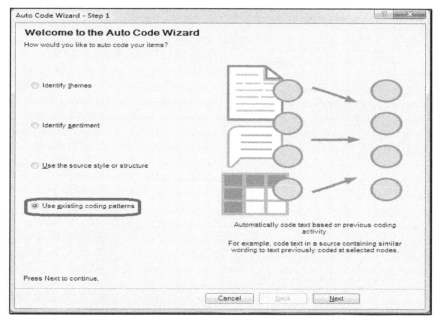

5 Select *Use existing coding patterns* and click [**Next**].
The Auto Code Wizard – Step 2 appears:

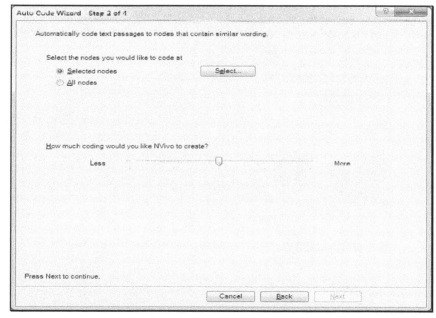

6 With the [**Select...**]-button you select the nodes with pattern for your autocoding. The slider **How much...** is used to specify more or less coding based on the occurrence of relvant words in the pattern nodes. Click [**Next**].

The Auto Code Wizard – Step 3 appears:

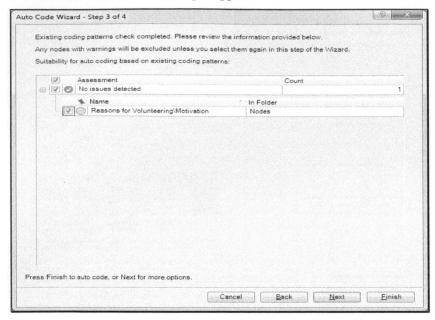

7   This is the result of the autocoding and you can accept or uncheck each separate node. Click [**Next**].

The Auto Code Wizard – Step 4 appears:

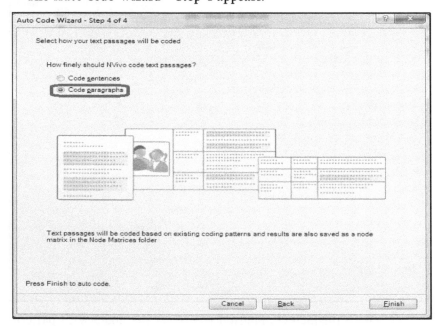

8   We choose *Code paragraphs* and click [**Finish**].

The result is twofold, a new node matrix located at **Nodes\\Node Matrices\\:**

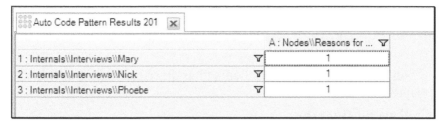

..and the autocoded source items:

The reason in this case that these source items are coded at 3 nodes is that the node, its aggregated parent node and the node matrix are summarized.

Range Coding

Range coding is another principle for a rational coding of certain items. The basis for range coding is the paragraph number in a document, the row number in a transcript or picture log or the timespan in an audio- or video item.

The available options depend on the type of item that has been selected for range coding. The command is **ANALYZE|Coding|Range Code** and in this case only existing Nodes can be used to code at.

Range Code			? X
Code	Paragraphs ▼		
	Enter paragraph numbers and/or paragraph ranges separated by commas. For example: 1,3,5-12		
Code at			Select...
		Code	Clear	Close

The coding takes place when you click **[Code]**.

In Vivo Coding

In Vivo coding is an established term used within qualitative research long before dedicated software existed. In Vivo coding creates a new Node from the selection of text and then, using the *In Vivo* command, the selected text (max 256 characters) will become the Node name. The new

> **Tips:** Use In Vivo Coding like this: Select a Heading in your Source Item with a text that will become the Node name. Apply In Vivo Coding. Continue coding at this Node with the Quick Coding bar.

Node's location is always in the **Nodes** folder. Node name and location can be changed later.

1   Select the text you want to NVivo code.
2   Go to **ANALYZE** | **Coding** | **Code In Vivo**
      or right-click and select **Code In Vivo**
      or [**Ctrl**] + [**F8**].

You can also use the Quick Coding bar described earlier in this chapter.

Coding by Queries

Queries can be instructed to save the result. The saved result is a Node and is instantly created when the query is run, see Chapter 13, Queries.

Visualizing your Coding

Opening a Node

1   Click [**Nodes**] in Area 1.
2   Select the **Nodes** folder in Area 2 or its subfolder.
3   Select the Node in Area 3 that you want to open.
4   Go to **HOME** | **Item** | **Open** → **Open Node**
      or right-click and select **Open Node...**
      or double-click the Node in Area 3
      or [**Ctrl**] + [**Shift**] + [**O**].

Each open Node is displayed in Area 4 and could therefore be docked or undocked. These windows always have a certain number of view mode tabs on its right side. If the Node has only been used to code text then the view mode tabs are: *Summary, Reference* and *Text*.

The *Reference* view mode is the default, automatically selected each time a Node is opened:

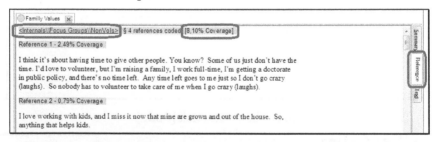

The link with the name of the Source Item opens in Area 4. You can also point at or select a section, go to **HOME** | **Item** | **Open** → **Open Referenced Source** or right-click and select **Open Referenced Source**. When a Source Item is opened via a Node like this the coding at the current Node is highlighted.

References coded are coded segments (like a text-segment) of a source item.

Coverage means that the Node or a resu... to a certain percentage of the whole Sourc... measured in number of characters.

Hiding/Unhiding Reference to Source Items

1 Open a Node.
2 Go to **VIEW | Detail View | Node -**
3 Uncheck *Sources, References* or *Co...*

The option *Sources* hides the reference t... sections and its coverage.

The option *References* hides information... and its coverage.

The option *Coverage* hides information a... Source Items and its coded sections.

The presentation can be modified in mar... **| Detail View | Node → Coding Context, Coding By Users, Coding Information, Coding Excerpt** and **Node Text**.

The *Summary* view mode displays all coded Source Items as a list of shortcuts. Each such shortcut can be opened with a double-click and the coded section is highlighted:

The *Text* view mode displays all coded text Source Items as thumbnails in the upper part of Area 4. Clicking on a thumbnail displays the coded section of that Source Item. Double-clicking the thumbnail opens the whole Source Item and the coded sections are highlighted:

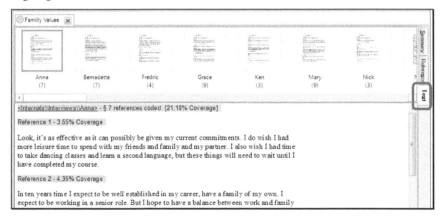

The *Audio* view mode provides a visual interface to easily listen to segments of coded audio:

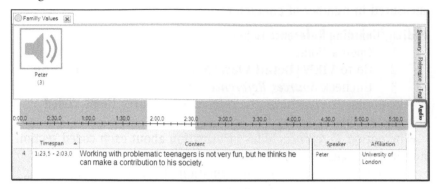

The *Video* view mode provides a visual interface to easily view segments of coded video:

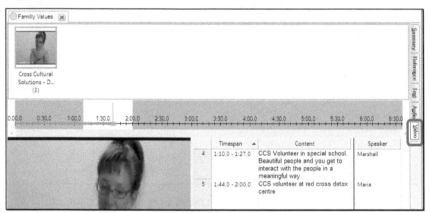

The *Picture* View mode provides an interface to view regions of coded image sources:

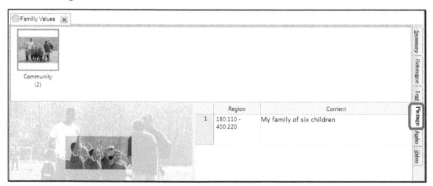

The *Dataset* view mode displays sections of coded dataset sources:

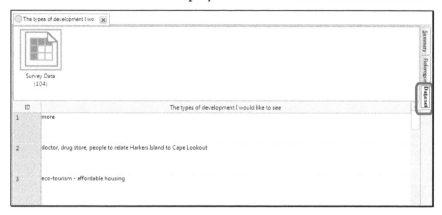

Viewing Coding Excerpt

1   Open a Node.
2   Go to **VIEW** | **Detail View** | **Node → Coding Excerpt**.
3   Select *None, Start* or *All.*

The option *None*:

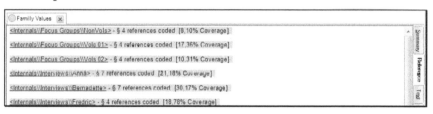

The option *Start*:

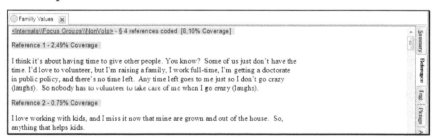

The option *All* is the default and has been shown above.

Viewing Coding Context

1   Open a Node.
2   Select the text or section that you want to show in its context.
3   Go to **VIEW** | **Detail View** | **Node → Coding Context** or right-click and select **Coding Context**.
4   Select *None, Narrow, Broad, Custom...* or *Entire Source.*

Example using the option *Broad* for a node coding a text source item:

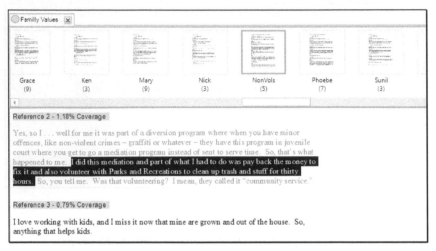

Example using the option *Broad* for a node coding an Audio source. Playback is possible for the interval including the context.

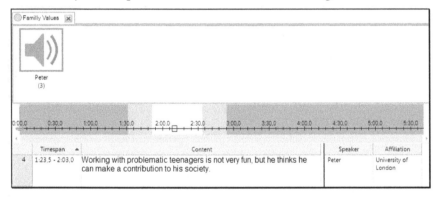

Example using the option *Narrow* for a node coding a Picture source.

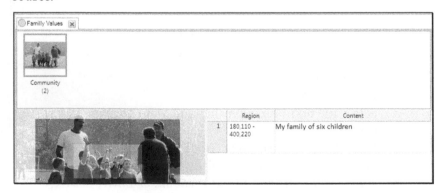

Highlighting Coding

The coded text or section in a Source Item can be highlighted in brownish color. Settings made are individual to Project Items and are temporarily saved during a work session, but are reset to none when a project is closed.

1   Go to **VIEW** | **Coding** | **Highlight**.
There are several options:

None	Highlighting is off.
Coding for All Nodes	Highlights all Nodes that the Item is coded at.
Coding For Selected Items...	Opens Select Project Items showing current Nodes, other Nodes are dimmed.
Matches For Query	Highlights the words used by Text Search Queries.
Modify Select Items...	Opens Select Project Items and you can modify selection of Nodes.

Coding Stripes

The open document, memo, or Node can be made to show the current coding as colored vertical stripes in a separate right hand window. Coding stripes are shown in Read-Only mode or in Edit mode. Using the Refresh link on top of the window recovers colors and functions of the stripes.

1   Go to **VIEW** | **Coding** | **Coding Stripes**
There are several options:

None	Coding Stripes are off.
Nodes Recently Coding	Shows the Nodes that are recently coded at.
Selected Items...	Is active when coding stripes have been selected.
All Nodes Coded	Shows all Nodes that the Item is coded at.
Nodes Most Coding	Shows the Nodes that are most coded at.
Nodes Least Coding	Shows the Nodes that are least coded at.
Coding Density Only	Shows only the Coding Density Bar and no Nodes.
Modify Selected Items...	Opens Select Project Items showing current Nodes, other Nodes are dimmed.
Show Items Last Selected	Shows the Nodes that were last opened.
Number of Stripes...	Selects the number of stripes (7 - 200).

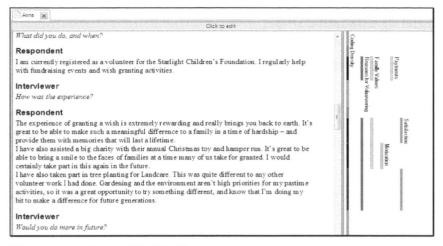

What can you do with Coding Stripes?

When you point and right-click at a certain coding stripe the following options will show: **Highlight Coding, Open Node..., Uncode, Hide Stripe, Show Sub-Stripes, Hide Sub-Stripes** and **Refresh**.

A click on the coding stripe highlights the coded area and double-click opens the Node.

By pointing at a coding stripe the Node name is shown. By pointing at the Coding Density Bar all Node names are shown that are coded at near the pointer.

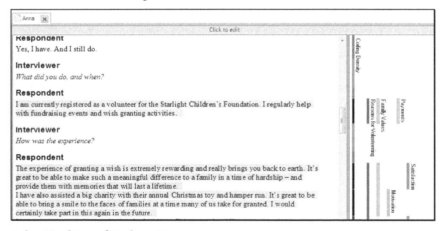

Color Marking of Coding Stripes

The colors of the coding stripes are automatically selected by NVivo. You can also use a custom color scheme, see page 25.

    1   Show coding stripes using any of the above options.

    2   Go to **VIEW | Visualization | Color Scheme → Item Colors**.

Nodes without individual colors will be shown without any color.

Printing with Coding Stripes

See Chapter 5, section Printing with Coding Stripes (page 89).

Viewing a Node that Codes a PDF Source Item

The PDF Source

A coded PDF showing coding stripes can for example look like this (the content of bookmark panel depends on the original PDF and can be hidden or unhidden by going to **VIEW | Window | Bookmarks**):

When you need to code a complete PDF document with any of the commands '**Code Sources at** <Node>' or '**Create As Node**' or '**Create As Case Nodes**' the number of references in that Node is calculated like this:

All text is one reference and each page is a region.

Exploring the Node

A Node that codes a PDF item will show the PDF in the Summary tab, in the Reference tab and in the specific PDF tab as follows:

The **Summary** tab will show the PDF as any other shortcut in the list of coded items.

The **Reference** tab will show coded text as plain text and coded region as coordinates:

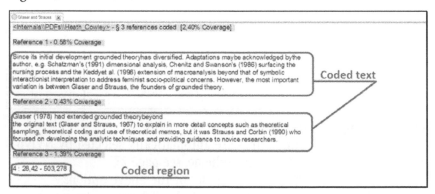

The **PDF** tab will show coded text or region as clear windows in the original PDF layout. Only coded pages with show:

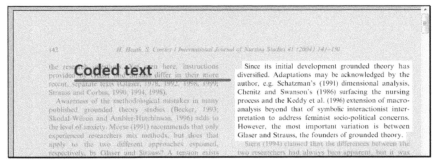

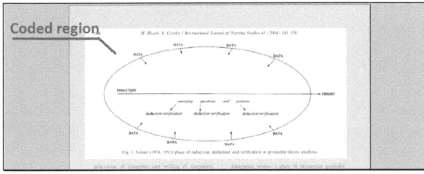

13. QUERIES

This chapter is about how to create and run various kinds of queries. In our experience, new NVivo users are sometimes intimidated by Queries – many types exist and using them effectively can take some practice. Remember, although not every query type will be right for project, every query type requires similar elements of foundational input. You will find queries increasingly simple once you read this chapter and learn the key features of a Query.

NVivo 11 also includes a very useful Query Wizard, **QUERY | Create | Query Wizard**. This tool is a well-constructed graphical means for helping researchers find what type of Query to use. For our purposes, we recommend understanding and practicing each Query individually. The Query Wizard provides a false sense of security for new users. But the beauty of Queries will reveal itself when you practice time and again how to use each distinct method.

When you create a query, you first decide whether it will become a new NVivo item within the Queries folder (Area 1). The option *Add to Project* is available in the dialog boxes **New <Type> Query** and **<Type> Query Properties**. Add to Project lets you type a name of the query and it will be saved for future use. The saved queries respond the same as other NVivo items – they can be copied, pasted, and moved into folders. Query items open into query dialog boxes where you can adjust the settings of each query. Importantly, you will need to **Run** a query before you will see any search results; queries can be created without being **Run**.

You can construct simple queries that find certain items or text elements. You can also construct complex queries that combine search words and Nodes or that combine several Nodes. The results of queries based on search words and Nodes can generate new Nodes, sets or data visualizations like Word Clouds, or both. You can also merge query results with existing Nodes.

NVivo offers seven different query types, Text Search Queries, Coding Queries, Matrix Coding Queries, Word Frequency Queries, Compound Queries, Group Queries, and Coding Comparison Queries, which we discuss in Chapter 23, Collaborating with NVivo. Saving a query, editing a query, moving a query to another folder, deleting a query and previewing or saving results are dealt with in the next chapter, Common Query Features.

The Query Wizard

For beginners who are not yet experienced of using queries the Query Wizard can be of help to decide which type of query to apply.

1   Go to **QUERY | Create | Query Wizard**

The **Query Wizard** appears and the four options display the clarifying graphs as follows:

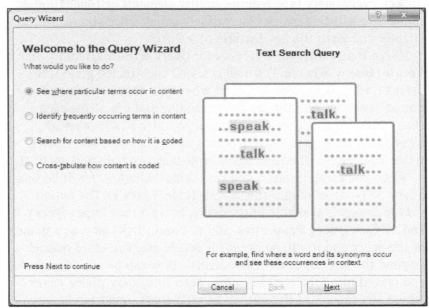

The above option will create a **Text Search Query**.

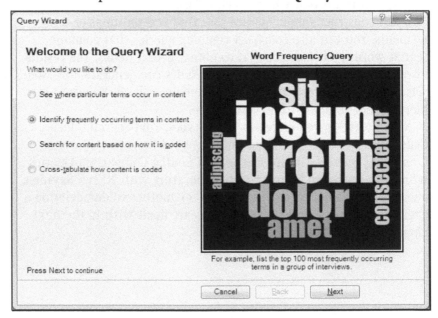

The above option will create a **Word Frequency Query**.

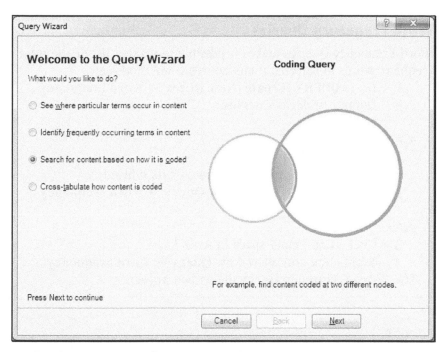

The above option will create a **Coding Query**.

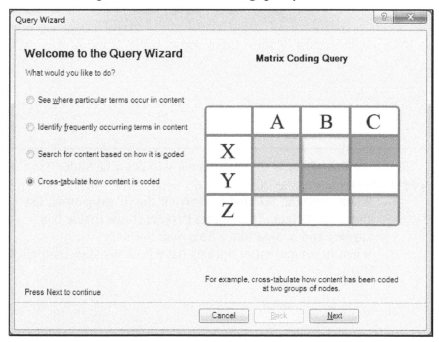

The above option will create a **Matrix Coding Query**.

Word Frequency Queries

Word Frequency Queries makes it possible to make a list of the most frequent words in selected items: Source Items, Nodes etc.

1   Go to **QUERY | Create | New Query → Word Frequency...**
Default folder is **Queries**.
Go to 5.

alternatively

1   Click **[Queries]** in Area 1.
2   Select **Queries** folder in Area 2 or its subfolder.
3   Go to **QUERY | Create | New Query → Word Frequency...**
Go to 5.

alternatively

3   Click at an empty space in Area 3.
4   Right-click and select **New Query → Word Frequency...**

The **Word Frequency Query** dialog box appears:

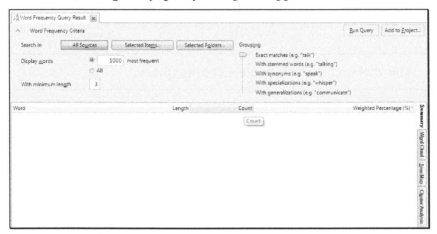

The **Grouping** slider is the same as we will describe under **Text Search Queries** (see page 205).

5   When choosing *Selected Items* from the **Of** drop-down list and then **[Select...]** the **Select Project Items** dialog box appears and is used like a Text Search Query.
6   When items and other options have been decided, then click **[Run]**.

The result may look like this, with the *Summary* tab open by default:

Word	Length	Count	Weighted Percentage (%)
theory	6	446	1.40
grounded	8	348	1.10
time	4	325	1.02
work	4	306	0.96
volunteer	9	300	0.94
like	4	239	0.75
research	8	202	0.64
people	6	186	0.59
interviewer	11	183	0.58
respondent	10	175	0.55
one	3	165	0.52
think	5	164	0.52

Select *one* word (it is not possible to select more than one), right-click and the following options appear:

- *Open Node Preview* (or double-click or key command [**Ctrl**] + [**Shift**] + [**O**]) opens like any Node with search words and synonyms highlighted with Narrow Coding Context (5 words).
- *Run Text Search Query*
  The **Text Search Query** dialog box is shown with the search words and synonyms transferred to the search criteria. The options Selected Items is inherited from the **Word Frequency Query** dialog box. The dialog box can be edited before you run it. See also page 203 on what you can do with Text Search Queries.
- *Export List...*
- *Print List...*
- *Create As Node...*
  Creates a Node with the search words and synonyms and a Narrow Coding Context (5 words). The Context Setting is retained in the Nodes folder or its subfolder during the ongoing work session.
- *Add to Stop Words List*[2]

---

[2] Alternatively: Go to **QUERY** | **Actions** | **Add to Stop Words List**

Word Clouds

The *Word Cloud* tab displays a custom tag cloud based on your query:

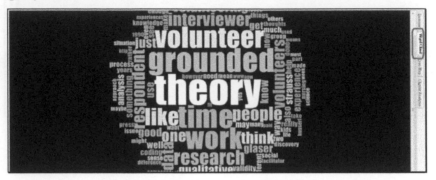

The Tag Cloud tab displays up to 100 words. The size of the words reflects their frequency. Words are sorted alphabetically and include stemmed words and synonyms if the Word Frequency Query is set accordingly. Click on a word and a Text Search Query is created and runs with results displayed as a Node preview.

Tree Maps

The *Tree Map* tab displays a custom tree map based on your query:

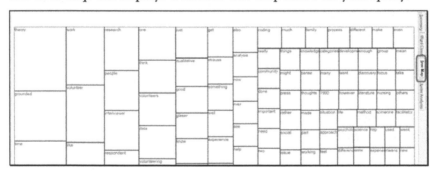

The Tree Map tab displays up to 100 words. The size of the area of each element reflects the frequency of the word. Click on a word and a Text Search Query is created and run with the results displayed as a Node preview. For more on Hierarchy Charts and Tree Maps, see page 342.

Cluster Analysis

The *Cluster Analysis* tab displays a custom cluster analysis based on your query:

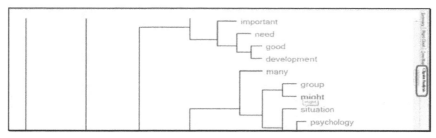

The Cluster Analysis tab displays up to 100 words. Words that co-occur are clustered together. When this tab has been selected the Ribbon menu **CLUSTER ANALYSIS** is shown and you can choose between 2D Cluster Map, 3D Cluster Map, Horizontal Dendrogram, Vertical Dendrogram or Circle Graph. With **CLUSTER ANALYSIS | Options | Select Data** you can choose the metric coefficient. Checking **CLUSTER ANALYSIS | Options → Word Frequency** when viewing 2D or 3D Cluster Maps lets you present the size of symbols reflecting its occurrence. The Cluster map applies a certain color for each cluster in each type of cluster diagram. In order to study the clustering structure you can vary the number of cluster as any number between 1 and 20 (10 is default) in each type of cluster diagram by going to **CLUSTER ANALYSIS | Options → Clusters**.

Tag Clouds, Tree Maps, and Cluster Analysis can also be used like this: Select a word in the graph, right-click and the menu is similar to the one explained on page 201. Only the Cluster Analysis has two unique alternatives: Copy (the whole graph) and Select Data (Pearson, Jaccard's or Sørensen's coefficients).

For more on Cluster Analysis, see page 348.

Text Search Queries

Text Search Queries search for certain words or phrases among items:

1   Go to **QUERY | Create | New Query → Text Search...**
    Default folder is **Queries**.
    Go to 5.

alternatively

1   Click [**Queries**] in Area 1.
2   Select **Queries** folder in Area 2 or its subfolder
3   Go to **QUERY | Create | New Query → Text Search...**
    Go to 5.

alternatively

3   Click on an empty space in Area 3.
4   Right-click and select **New Query → Text Search...**

The **Text Search Query** dialog box appears:

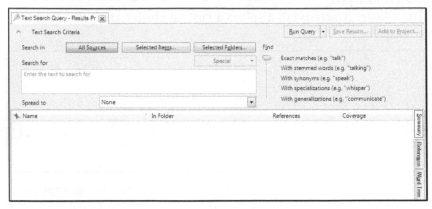

5   Type the search word or the search criteria in the **Search for** text box, for example 'motivation OR reason'. Move the slider **Find** over the option *Including stemmed words*, this way the query searches words with same stem as the typed search words. (English, French, German, Portuguese and Spanish only).

6   Use the options at **Spread to**: Coding References, Narrow Context, Broad Context, Custom Context or Entire Source.

When several words are typed in a sequence, e.g. ADAM EVE, the search is made as an OR-combination and when the words are surrounded by quotes, "ADAM EVA", an exact phrase search is run.

The slider **Find** has five options:

Position	Result	Example
Exact match	Exact matches only	sport
With stemmed words	Exact matches Words with the same stem	sport, sporting
With synonyms	Exact matches Words with same stem Synonyms[3] (words with a very close meaning)	sport, sporting, play, fun
With specializations	Exact matches Words with same stem Synonyms[1] (words with a very close meaning) Specializations (words with a more specialized meaning)	sport, sporting, play, fun, running, basketball
With generalizations	Exact matches Words with same stem Synonyms[3] (words with a very close meaning) Specializations (words with a more specialized meaning—a 'type of') Generalizations (words with a more general meaning)	sport, sporting, play, fun, running, basketball, recreation, business

All settings work for NVivo's text content languages. The text content language options are available when you go to **FILE → Info → Project Properties,** the **General** tab: *Text Content Language* (see page 55). If this setting is made for *Other* then only 'Exact match' can be used but can be combined with the conventional operators under [**Special**] which offers the following optional search functions:

Option	Example	Comment
Wildcard ?	ADAM?	? represents *one* arbitrary character
Wildcard *	EVA*	* represents *any number* of arbitrary characters
AND	ADAM AND EVA	Both words must be found
OR[4]	ADAM OR EVA	Either word must be found
NOT	ADAM NOT EVA	Adam is found where Eve is not found
Required	+ADAM EVA	Adam is required but Eve is also found
Prohibit	-EVA ADAM	Adam is found where Eve is not found
Fuzzy	ADAM~	Finds words of similar spelling
Near...	"ADAM EVA"~3	Adam and Eve are found within 3 words from each other
Relevance...	ADAM^2EVA	Adam is 2 times as relevant as Eve is

7   Confirm with [**Run Query**].

---

[3] Each content language has its own built-in, non-editable synonym list.

[4] The operator OR can be replaced by space like 'ADAM EVA'.

The format of the result depends on the settings made under the **Query Options** tab in the **Text Search Query** dialog box (see page 232).

After you run a Text Search Query, the *Preview Only* option displays a list of shortcuts in Area 4 and can look like this. These shortcuts contain the search results within a given Source Item. The Summary tab is default:

The list of shortcuts can easily be sorted by clicking on the column head. When you double-click on such shortcut the item will open and the search words are highlighted:

Creating a Set

You might find it useful to combine results from your search into a Set:

1. Select the shortcuts that you want to create as a set.
2. Go to **CREATE | Collections | Set → Create As Set...**
   or right-click and select **Create As → Create As Set...**
3. Type a name of the new set and confirm with [**OK**].

alternatively, if you already have a set:

1. Select the shortcuts that you want to add to a set.
2. Go to **CREATE | Collections | Set → Add To Set...**
   or right-click and select **Add To Set...**
3. Select Set in the **Select Set** dialog box.
4. Confirm with [**OK**].

Creating a Node

You can also combine results from your search into a new Node:

1 Select the shortcuts that you want to create as a Node.

2 Right-click and select **Code Sources → Code Sources At Existing Nodes** (selected sources will be coded at one or several Nodes)
or **Code Sources → Code Sources At New Node** (selected sources will be coded at one new Node)
or **Create As → Create As Node** (selected shortcuts will become one new Node)
or **Create As → Create As Cases** (one new Case per item will be created)

3 In the **Select Location** dialog box you must determine where the new Node or Nodes shall be located.

4 Type a name for the new Node. When Case Nodes are created they will inherit the names of the sources. The **Select Location** dialog box makes it optional that you allocate one of the existing Node Classifications to the new Case Node(s). Confirm with [**OK**].

Saving Search Results

1 Select the shortcuts that you want to create as a Node.

2 Right click and select **Store Query Results** (all shortcuts will be merged into one new Node)
or right-click and select **Store Selected Query Results** (selected shortcuts will be merged into one new Node)

The **Store Query Results** dialog box is shown.

3 Determine the name and location of the new Node.

The *Reference* view mode displays 5 words on each side of the search word (Coding Context) and otherwise the view options are the same as for an open Node (see Chapter 12, section Visualizing your Coding, page 186):

The *Text* view mode is also identical as for an open Node (see page 187):

Word Trees

The *Word Tree* view mode is a feature for Text Search Queries that visualizes how a word occurs within a corpus of sentences. This is one of our favorite NVivo visualizations. Remember, to generate a Word Tree you need to ensure query options set for *Preview* and that Spread Coding is off:

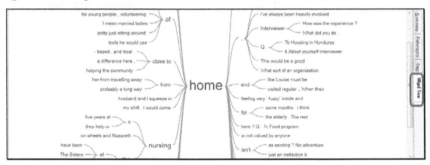

A new context dependent Ribbon menu, **WORD TREE**, now appears and there you can find a list called **Root Term**. This list is sorted by frequency, and displays words resulting from the placement of the **Finding matches** slider. Each selected Root Term creates a new Word Tree. You can also decide the number of words (Context Words) that surrounds a Root Term.

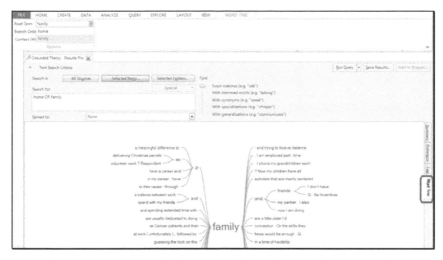

Finally, you can also click any word of the Word Tree and the whole branch will be highlighted. Double-clicking a selected branch opens a Node preview. Clicking the root term will highlight all branches of the Word Tree. You can also select a branch, right-click and the following menu appears: Run Text Search Query (similar to double-clicking the branch), Export Word Tree, Print and Copy. A full Word Tree can also be exported as a low-resolution image. Unfortunately, at present NVivo does not contain functionality for exporting high-resolution images. But we have requested this function and we are hopeful for the future.

Coding Queries

Coding Queries are advantageous when you have advanced your project's structure in such a way that you can acquire project insights via complex queries.

1   Go to **QUERY | Create | New Query → Coding...**
     Default folder is **Queries**.
     Go to 5.

alternatively

1   Click [**Queries**] in Area 1.
2   Select the **Queries** folder in Area 2 or its subfolder.
3   Go to **QUERY | Create | New Query → Coding...**
     Go to 5.

alternatively

3   Click at an empty space in Area 3.
4   Right-click and select **New Query → Coding...**

The **Coding Query – Results Preview** dialog box appears:

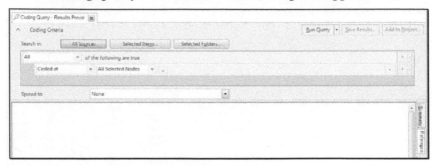

5   Each criteria row allows you to select *Coded at* or *Not Coded at* and *All Selected Nodes* or *Any Selected Node* or *Any Case Where* and then specify at the [...]-button.

To the right in the dialog box there is an option to add or delete rows and other options to modify the criterions:

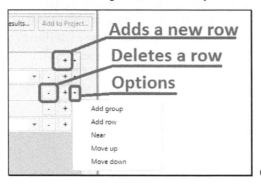
or

An example of a Coding Query. Observe, the operators All and Any corresponds to the well-known AND and OR.

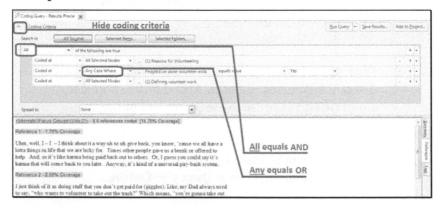

The [**Save Results...**]-button decides name and location of the node that is a result of the query. The **Store Query Results** dialog box is shown.

The [**Run Query**]-button runs the query as a preview unless you choose **Run Query → Run and Save Results** and the query is run followed by the **Store Query Results** dialog box. Observe that the default location in this box is the **Results** folder each time the query is re-run.

Compound Queries - Only for Pro & Plus

Compound Queries make it possible to create complex queries that can combine Node searches with text searches.

1   Go to **QUERY | Create | New Query → Compound...**
     Default folder is **Queries**.
     Go to 5.

alternatively

1   Click [**Queries**] in Area 1.
2   Select the **Queries** folder in Area 2 or its subfolder.
3   Go to **QUERY | Create | New Query → Compound...**
     Go to 5.

alternatively

3   Click at an empty space in Area 3.
4   Right-click and select **New Query → Compound...**

The **Compound Query** dialog box is shown. The query is divided into *Subquery 1* and *Subquery 2*. The operator[5] between them can be chosen among several options.

---

[5] See page 238 onward for explanations of the other operators on this drop-down list.

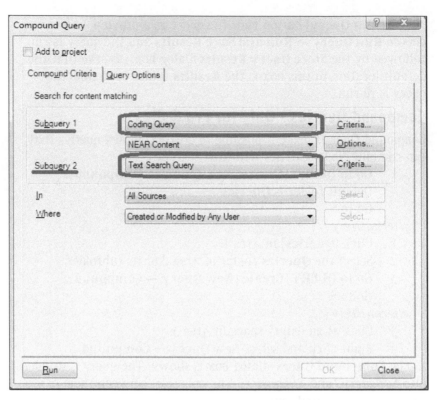

5   Choose *Coding Query* at **Subquery 1**.

6   The [**Criteria...**] button opens the **Subquery Properties**
      dialog box that is similar the **Coding Query** dialog box only
      that the option *Add To Project* and the **Query Options** tab
      are missing.

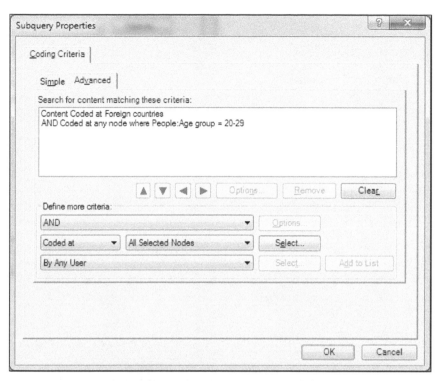

7   We use the **Advanced** tab and use the following criteria:
    The Node *Foreign countries* AND the *Age Group 20-29*. See
    the section about Coding Queries, page 209.

8   Click [**OK**].

9   In the **Compound Query** dialog box select the operator
    NEAR Content and with the [**Options...**] button you select
    Overlapping.

10 Choose *Text Search Query* at **Subquery 2**.

11 The [**Criteria...**] button opens the **Subquery Properties**
    dialog box, which is similar to the **Text Search Query**
    dialog box only the option *Add To Project* and the **Query
    Options** tab missing.

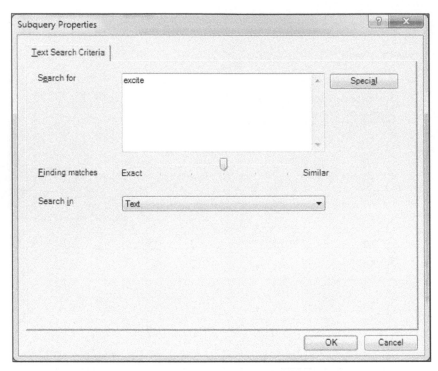

12 Type **excite** in the text box **Search for**, and pull the
    slider below two steps to the right which includes *Stemmed
    search* and synonyms.

The **Finding matches** slider is the same as described under **Text
Search Queries** (see page 205).

13 Click **[OK]**.

14 Click **[Run]** in the **Compound Query** dialog box.

The format of the results depends on the settings made under the
Query Options tab in the dialog box **Compound Query** (see page
232).

When you have run a Compound Query with *Preview Only* the
result looks like under Text Search Queries, page 206 and onwards,
with two exceptions: The Word Tree tab is not included and the
option **Store Selected Query Results** for selected shortcuts in
Summary view is also not included.

Matrix Coding Queries - Only for Pro & Plus

Matrix Coding Queries have been introduced to display how a set of
Nodes relates to another set of Nodes. The results are presented in
the form of a matrix or table.

Example: We want to explore how different age groups relate to certain selected themes represented by theme nodes.

1   Go to **QUERY** | **Create** | **New Query** → **Matrix Coding...**
    Default folder is **Queries**.
    Go to 5.

alternatively

1   Click [**Queries**] in Area 1.
2   Select the **Queries** folder in Area 2 or its subfolder.
3   Go to **QUERY** | **Create** | **New Query** → **Matrix Coding...**
    Go to 5.

alternatively

3   Click on an empty space in Area 3.
4   Right-click and select **New Query** → **Matrix Coding...**

The **Matrix Coding Query** dialog box appears:

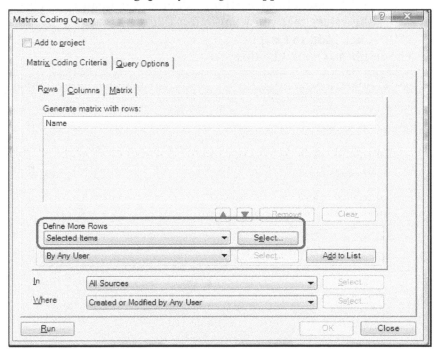

5   Select the **Matrix Coding Criteria** tab and then the **Rows** tab.
6   Choose *Selected Items* from the **Define More Rows** drop-down list.
7   Click [**Select...**].

The **Select Project Items** dialog box appears:

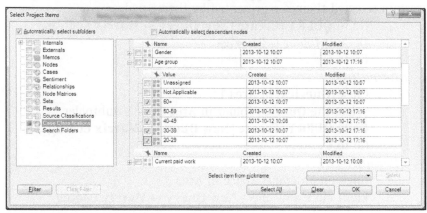

8   Select **Node Classifications\\People\Age Group** and check the values that you want to use. Click **[OK]**.

9   Click **[Add to List]**.

The result may look like this:

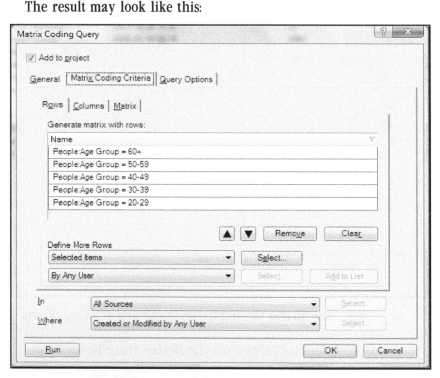

10 Select the **Matrix Coding Criteria** tab and then the **Columns** tab.

11 Choose *Selected Items* from the **Define More Columns** drop-down list.

12 Click **[Select...]**.

The **Select Project Items** dialog box appears:

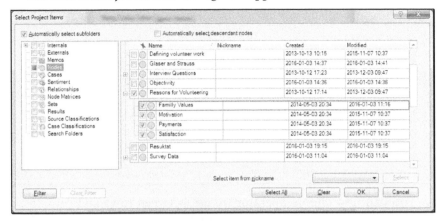

13 Select **Nodes\\Experience** and check the Nodes that you want to study. Click **[OK]**.

14 Click **[Add To List]** in the **Matrix Coding Query** dialog box. When you have defined the columns the result may be like this:

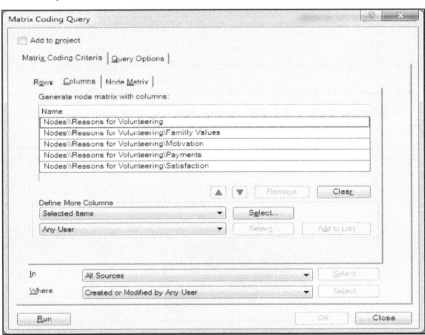

If there are Nodes that you would like to delete, select them and click **[Remove]**. The whole list is cleared with **[Clear]**. If you want to change the order then select a Node and use the arrow buttons to move up or down. You can also click on the column head, a toggling function.

15   Select the **Matrix Coding Criteria** tab and then the **Matrix** tab.

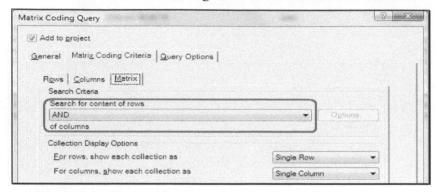

You can now choose operator[6] to use between rows and columns.

16   Click **[Run]** in the **Matrix Coding Query** dialog box.

The format of the result depends on the settings under the **Query Options** tab in the dialog box **Matrix Coding Query** (see page 230).

The option *Preview Only* displays the matrix in Area 4 and may look like this:

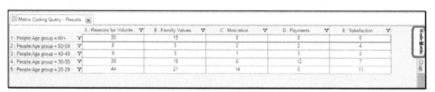

You can also show a Chart of this matrix. Click the *Chart* tab on the right side of the window:

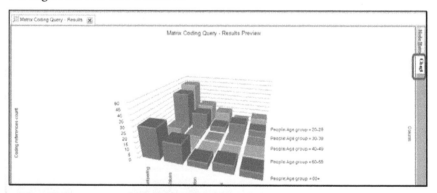

The ribbon menu **CHART** opens when the matrix is showing as a Chart. The Chart options allow adjusting formatting, zooming and rotating. By going to **CHART | Type** the following drop-down menu appears:

_____

[6] See page 238 onward for explanations of the other operators on this drop-down list.

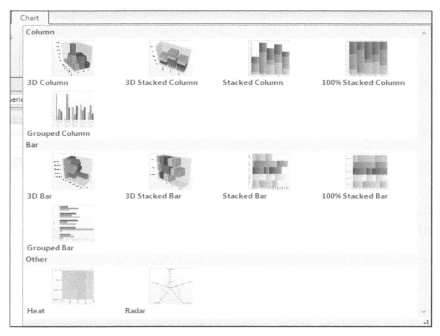

Here you can choose from various types of diagrams.

Opening a Cell

A matrix is a collection of cells. Each cell is a Node. You may need therefore to study each cell separately.

1 Open the matrix.
2 Select the cell you want to open.
3 Right-click and select **Open Matrix Cell**
  or double-click the cell.

The cell opens and can be analyzed as any other cell. This Node is an integral part of the matrix and if you want to save it as a new Node then select the whole Node in the *Reference* view mode and go to **ANALYZE | Coding | Code** or right-click and select **Code** or [**Ctrl**] + [**F2**].

Viewing Cell Content

There are several options to view cell content when cells are not opened.

1 Open the matrix.
2 Go to **View | Detail View | Matrix Cell Content → <select>**
  or right-click and select **Matrix Cell Content → <select>**
  any of the following options:

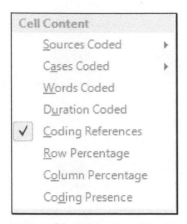

Hiding/Unhiding Row Numbers
1 Open the matrix.
2 Go to **LAYOUT | Show/Hide | Row IDs**
   or right-click and select **Row → Row Ids**.

Hiding Rows
1 Open the matrix.
2 Select one or more rows that you want to hide.
3 Go to **LAYOUT | Show/Hide | Hide Row**
   or right-click and select **Row → Hide Row**.

Hiding/Unhiding Rows with Filters
1 Open the matrix.
2 Click the 'funnel' in a certain column head
   or select a column and go to **LAYOUT | Sort & Filter | Filter
   → Filter Row**.

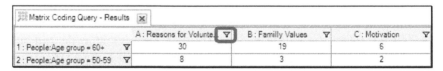

The **Matrix Filter Options** dialog box appears:

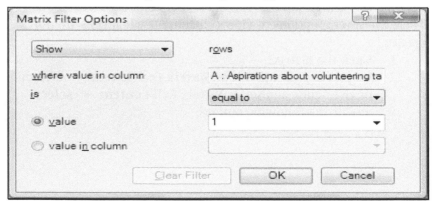

3   Select value and operator for hiding or unhiding. Confirm with **[OK]**. When a filter is applied the funnel turns *red*.

To clear a filter use **[Clear Filter]** in the **Matrix Filter Options** dialog box.

Unhiding Rows
1   Open the matrix.
2   Select one row on each side of the hidden row that you want to unhide.
3   Go to **LAYOUT** | **Show/Hide** | **Unhide Row**
     or right-click and select **Row → Unhide Row**.

Unhiding All Rows
1   Open the matrix.
2   Go to **LAYOUT** | **Sort & Filter** | **Filter → Clear All Row Filters**
     or right-click and select **Row → Clear All Row Filters**.

Hiding/Unhiding Column Letters
1   Open the matrix.
2   Go to **LAYOUT** | **Show/Hide** | **Column IDs**
     or right-click and select **Column → Column IDs**.

Hiding Columns
1   Open the matrix.
2   Select one or more columns that you want to hide.
3   Go to **LAYOUT** | **Show/Hide** | **Hide Column**
     or right-click and select **Column → Hide Column**.

Unhiding Columns
1   Open the matrix.
2   Select one column on each side of the hidden column that you want to unhide.
3   Go to **LAYOUT** | **Show/Hide** | **Unhide Column**
     or right-click and select **Column → Unhide Column**.

Unhiding All Columns
1   Open the matrix.
2   Go to **LAYOUT** | **Sort & Filter** | **Filter → Clear All Column Filters**
     or right-click and select **Column → Clear All Column Filters**.

Transposing the Matrix
Transposing means that rows and columns are changing places.
1   Open the matrix.
2   Go to **LAYOUT** | **Transpose**
     or right-click and select **Transpose.**

Moving a Column Left or Right
1. Open the matrix.
2. Select the column or columns that you want to move. If you want to move more than one column they need to be adjacent.
3. Go to **LAYOUT | Rows & Columns | Column → Move Left/Move Right**.

Resetting the Whole Matrix
1. Open the matrix.
2. Go to **LAYOUT | Tools | Reset Settings**
   or right-click and select **Reset Settings**.

Viewing the Cells Shaded or Colored
1. Open the matrix.
2. Go to **VIEW | Detail View | Matrix → Matrix Cell Shading → <select>**
   or right-click and select **Matrix Cell Shading → <select>**.

Exporting a Matrix
1. Open or select the matrix.
2. Go to **DATA | Export | Export Matrix...**
   or right-click and select **Export Matrix...**
   or **[Ctrl] + [Shift] + [E]**.

The **Save As** dialog box is shown and you can decide the file name and file location and create a text file or an Excel spreadsheet.

When you view a Chart you can export the image in the following formats: .JPG, .BMP or .GIF.

Converting a Matrix to Nodes
There are situations when you need to convert cells in a matrix to Nodes.
1. Open or select the matrix.
2. Copy by going to **HOME | Clipboard | Copy**
   or right-click and select **Copy**
   or **[Ctrl] + [C]**.
3. Click **[Nodes]** in Area 1.
4. Select the **Nodes** folder in Area 2 or its subfolder.
5. Go to **HOME | Clipboard | Paste → Paste**
   or right-click and select **Paste**
   or **[Ctrl] + [V]**.

The **Paste** dialog box appears:

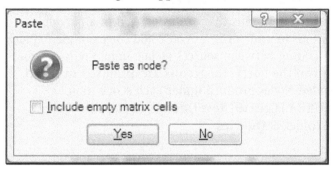

6   Confirm with [**Yes**].

The result is a hierarchical Node[7] where the Parent Node inherits the name of the matrix, called 'Matrix Parent'. The first generation Child Nodes are the rows, called 'Row Parents' and the grandchildren Nodes contain contents from each cell.

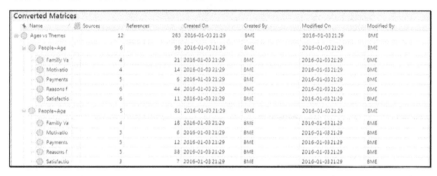

These Nodes can then be used for Cluster Analysis (see page 348).

---

[7] When *converting a Node Matrix* to Nodes then the "Matrix Parent" and the "Row Parents" are calculated with the *Aggregate* function. This method is giving the correct number of Sources but the number of references is suffering from the imperfection we mentioned on page 137.

Group Queries - Only for Pro & Plus

Use Group Queries to find items that are associated in a particular way with other items in your project. You could for example explore the difference in coding between sources (scope items) with a Group query. When you run the query, the results are displayed in Detail View with the coded Nodes grouped under each scope item.

    1   Go to **QUERY | Create | New Query → Group...**
          Default folder is **Queries**
          Go to 5.

alternatively

    1   Click on **[Queries]** in Area 1.
    2   Select the **Queries** folder in Area 2 or its subfolder
    3   Go to **QUERY | Create | New Query → Group...**
          Go to 5.

alternatively

    3   Click on any empty space in Area 3.
    4   Right-click and select **New Query → Group...**

In each case, the **Group Query** dialog box appears:

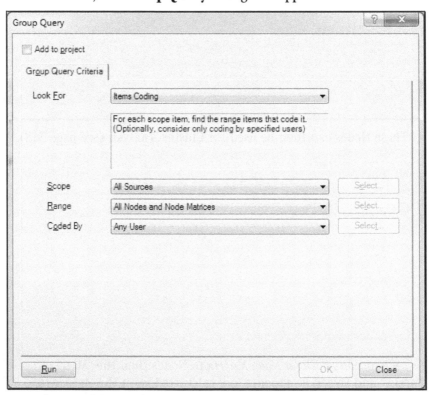

The **Look For:** drop-down list has the following options:

Items Coding	For each scope item, find the range items that code it. (Optionally, consider only coding by specific users)
Items Coded At	For each scope item, find the range items that it codes. (Optionally, consider only coding by specific users)
Items by Attribute Value	For each attribute value in the scope, find the items in the range that have that value assigned.
Relationships	For each scope item, find the items that it has a relationship of the selected direction/type with.
See Also Links	For each scope item, find the range items that it has s See Also link with.
Map Items	For each map in the scope, find the range items that appear in the map.
Maps	For each scope item, find the maps in the range that it appears in.

Depending on what options you select the **Scope** and **Range** drop-down lists offers corresponding alternatives.

Let's assume that you need to explore what Nodes two selected sources are coded at.

5 Select *Items Coding* from the **Look For** drop-down list.

6 Select *Selected Items* from the **Scope** drop-down list.

7 Click the [**Select**] button and from the **Select Project Items** dialog box select for example two Source Items (two interviews). Click [**OK**].

8 Select *Selected Folders* from the **Range** drop-down list.

9 Click the [**Select**] button and from the **Select Folders** dialog box select for example the **Theme Nodes** folder. Click [**OK**].

10 Finally click [**Run**] in the **Group Query** dialog box.

Group Query Results are displayed as an expandable list in Area 3. This list cannot be saved. The query, however, can be saved as any other queries, see Chapter 14, Common Query Features. When the saved query is run the expandable list appears again.

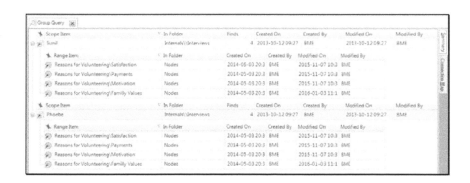

Selecting the **Connection Map** tab to the right the following graph is shown:

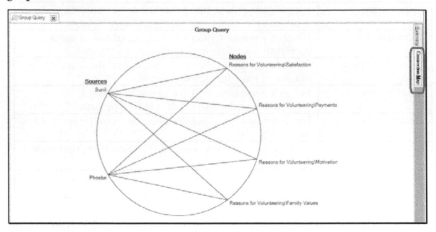

In a corresponding way you can select any scope item like Node(s), map(s), and then the range of its related items.

14. COMMON QUERY FEATURES

This chapter deals with the functions and features common to several types of queries. The Filter function which is described here is an example of a common query feature. One way to benefit from the filter function is letting the filter eliminate unwanted items. For example, you can use the filter to eliminate Nodes that were created later than last week.

The Filter Function

The [**Select...**] button is available in many dialog boxes when queries are created. This button always opens the **Select Project Items** dialog box:

Automatically select subfolders means that when a folder is selected in the left hand window all the underlying subfolders and items will be selected. Folders which cannot have subfolders (Nodes, Sets, and Results) will select all of the items therein.

Automatically select hierarchy means that when a certain item in the right hand window has been selected all underlying items are also selected.

The [**Filter**] button is always available at the bottom left corner of the **Select Project Items** dialog box and this button opens the **Advanced Find** dialog box:

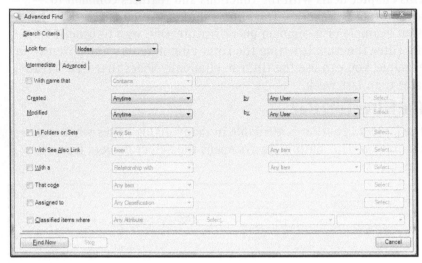

These are the same as the Advanced Find search functions (see page 308).

Saving a Query

As mentioned at the beginning of previous chapter, Queries made can be saved so that they can be run again at a later stage or be copied and edited for future needs.

The region from the upper right corner of the dialog for Text Search, Word Frequency and Coding Queries is:

1 Click [**Add to Project...**] and this dialog opens:

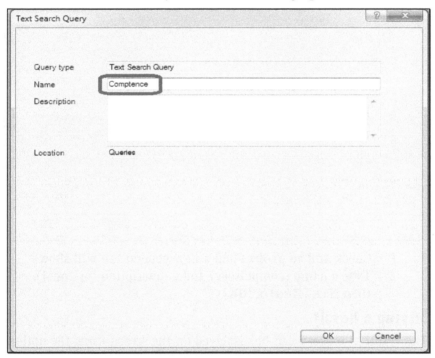

2 Type a name (compulsory) and a description (optional), then click [**OK**].

The dialog for Matrix Coding, Compound Coding, Coding Comparison and Group Queries is:

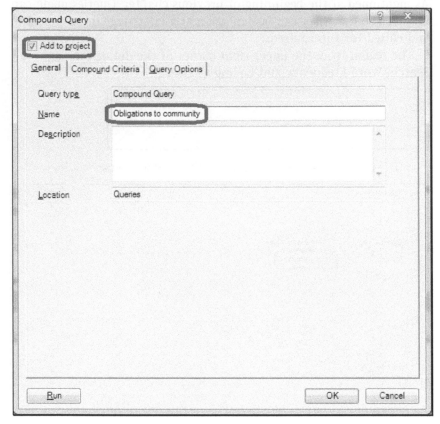

1 Check **Add to project** and a new general tab will show.
2 Type a name (compulsory) and a description (optional), then click **[Run]** or **[OK]**.

Saving a Result

The result of a query can be displayed on the screen using the option *Preview Only.* The result is shown in Area 4 but not saved.

Preview Only for Text Search Queries opens the Summary tab (see page 187).

Preview Only for Coding Queries and Compound Queries opens the Reference tab (see page 186).

Preview Only for Matrix Search Queries opens the Node Matrix tab (see page 218).

If you want to save the result as a Node there are a few options to choose from, for example *Create Results as New Node* or *Merge Result into Existing Node.*

The region from the upper right corner of the dialog for Text Search and Coding Queries is:

In order to save a result you must first both run and view the result as a preview using [**Run Query**] and then use [**Save Results...**] or using the **Run and Save Results** option under the [**Run Query**] button:

Next the **Store Query Results** dialog box will show:

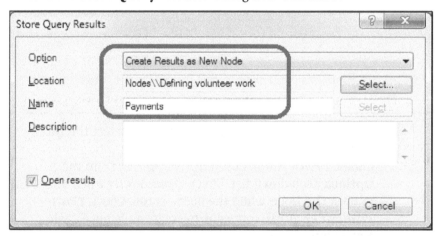

1 Choose *Create Results as New Node* from the **Options** drop-down list. Check *Open results* when you want open the Node when the query is run.
2 Accept default **Location** *Results*[8] or use [**Select**] and choose another location, for example the *Nodes* folder when you want to use this Node for future coding or else future editing.
3 Type a name (compulsory) and a description (optional), then [**OK**].

---

[8] Storing results in the *Results* folder means that the node cannot be edited nor can it be used for further coding or uncoding.

For Matrix Coding Queries and Compound Queries the dialog is:

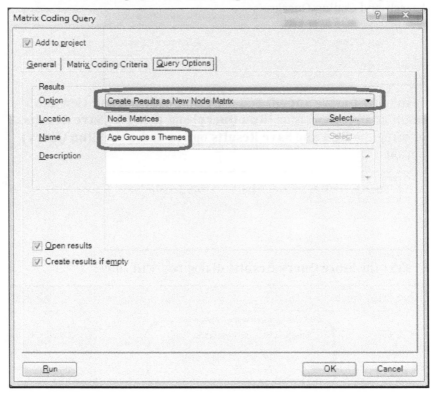

1   In the **Matrix Coding Query** dialog box select the **Query Options** tab.

2   Choose *Create Results as New Node Matrix* from the **Options** drop-down list. Check *Open results* when you want to open the Node when the query is run. Check *Create results if empty* if you want to create an 'empty' Node Matrix when zero result.

3   Accept **Location** *Results*[9] or choose another location, *Node Matrices*, with the **[Select]** button.

4   Type a name (compulsory) and a description (optional), then click **[Run]** or **[OK]**.

- ◆ -

Results from Word Frequency Queries, Coding Comparison Queries and Group Queries cannot be saved - only preview is possible. However, such results can always be displayed by running a saved query anew.

───────────────

[9] Storing results in the *Results* folder means that the node cannot be edited nor can it be used for further coding or uncoding.

Spread Coding

Spread Coding is a function that is used to widen the coding from a given result of a query. For instance a Text Search Query finds words and by spreading the coding the result can be set to code each surrounding paragraph where the words are found.

The **Spread Coding** drop-down list allows you to decide options for coding surround sections of data nearby your coded query result. The following options[10] are available for Text Search, Coding and Compound Queries:

- None
- Coding Reference (applicable when searching in Nodes)
- Narrow Context
- Broad Context
- Custom Context
- Entire Source

The dialog box for a Text Search Query or a Coding Query is:

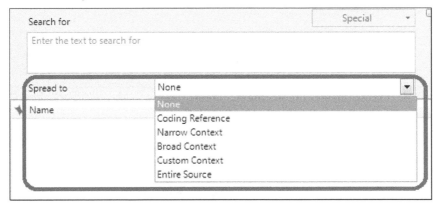

_____

[10] As alternatives to *Narrow* and *Broad* you may use *Custom* which can override these settings for any specific task.

The dialog box for a **Compound Query** is:

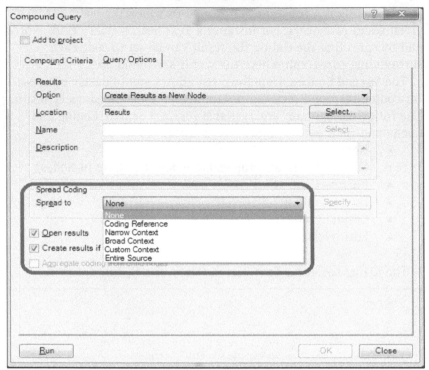

- ♦ -

Using **QUERY | Actions | Last Run Query** the
<...> **Query Properties** dialog box is shown again and you may
modify or edit the query. Each time a query is run it is also saved
provided such option has been selected. When editing a query you
can for example apply Surrounding Paragraphs at the **Spread Coding**
drop-down list.

About the Results Folder

The Results folder is the default folder where a result of query is saved. You can however modify **Query Properties** so that query results will be saved in any Node location. But there are some advantages to using the **Results** folder.

First, it is practical to see if the result is reasonable (before it is saved in its final location or made into a Node) or if the query needs immediate modification. Sometimes, when the query is not saved but the result is, the command **HOME | Item | Open → Open Linked Query Properties...**, or right-click and select **Linked Query Properties...** will allow you to open or modify the query.

Nodes in the Results folder cannot be edited or used for further coding or uncoding and commands like **Uncode from this Node** and **Spread Coding** are unavailable. After verifying your Node in the Results folder you should move the result to a location under Nodes, where it can be more fully analyzed.

When you run a Text Search Query that is saved in the Results folder Coding Context Narrow (5 words) is activated, but the Coding Context is reset as soon as the Node is moved to a location under Nodes. If you then should need Coding Context this feature can be activated with a separate command (see page 189).

Editing a Query

A saved query can be run anytime:

1   Click [**Queries**] in Area 1.
2   Select the **Queries** folder in Area 2 or its subfolder.
3   Select the query in Area 3 that you want to run.
4   Go to **QUERY | Create | Run Query**
     or right-click and select **Run Query...**

You can always optimize a saved query so that it fulfils your changing needs. Or you may wish to copy a query before editing:

1   Click [**Queries**] in Area 1.
2   Select the **Queries** folder in Area 2 or its subfolder.
3   Select the query in Area 3 that you want to edit.
4   Go to **HOME | Item | Properties**
     or right-click and select **Query Properties...**
     or [**Ctrl**] + [**Shift**] + [**P**].

One of the following dialog boxes is shown:

- **Text Search Query Properties**
- **Word Frequency Query Properties**
- **Coding Query Properties**
- **Matrix Coding Query Properties**
- **Compound Query Properties**
- **Coding Comparison Query Properties**
- **Group Query Properties**

The **Text Search Query Properties** dialog box is:

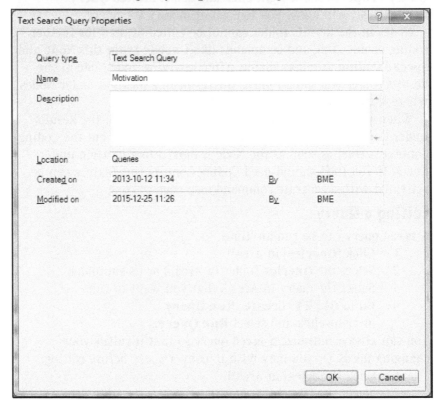

In this dialog box you cannot modify the criterion. You need to select the query, go to **HOME | Item | Open → Open Query...** or right-click and select **Open Query...** or key command **[Ctrl]** + **[Shift]** + **[O]**.

The **Matrix Coding Query Properties** dialog box, for example, has the same contents as the **Matrix Coding Query** dialog box. Here you can make your modifications.

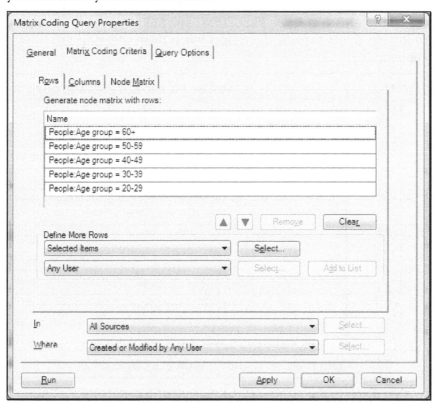

[**OK**] will carry out the modifications without running the query.

[**Apply**] will carry out the modifications without running the query again and the dialog box will remain shown so that more modifications can be made.

[**Run**] will carry through the modifications and run the query. If the option Create Results as a New Node under the **Query Options** tab has been selected then another Node will be created in the given folder. If you choose to let the results initially be located under the **Results** folder they can be moved later on.

The Operators

In the **Coding Query, Matrix Coding Query and Subquery Properties** dialog boxes there are drop-down lists with various operators: AND, OR, NEAR, PRECEDING and SURROUNDING. The following charts explain the results when these operators are applied.

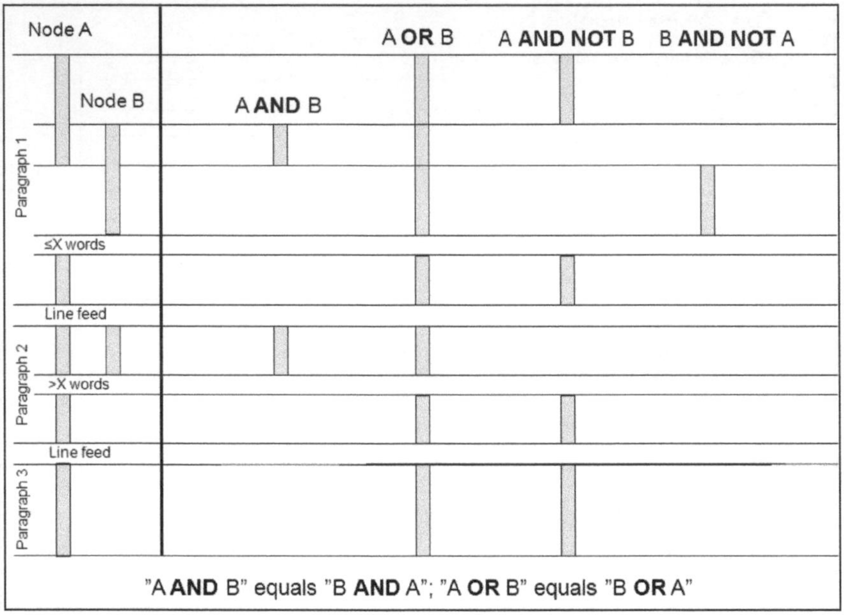

Node A		A OR B	A AND NOT B	B AND NOT A
	Node B	A AND B		

Paragraph 1 / ≤X words / Line feed / Paragraph 2 / >X words / Line feed / Paragraph 3

"A AND B" equals "B AND A"; "A OR B" equals "B OR A"

AND displays the elements of a document where both A and B have been coded.

OR displays the elements of a document where either A or B or both A and B have been coded.

AND NOT displays the elements of a document where A but not B have been coded.

```
Node A
    Node B
Paragraph 1
    ≤X words
    Line feed
Paragraph 2
    >X words
    Line feed
Paragraph 3
```

Column headers: Overlapping | Within X words | Within same paragraph | Within same coding reference*) | *) search in nodes only | Within same scope item**) | **) equal to "A OR B"; "B OR A"

"A **NEAR** B" equals "B **NEAR** A"

NEAR Content Overlapping displays the elements of a document where A and B are overlapping.

NEAR Content In Custom Context[11]. The **[Specify]** button allows you to select between Broad Context, Narrow Context or Custom Context.

For example:

- **NEAR Content Within X words** displays the elements of a document where A and B are within X words from each other.
- **NEAR Content In Surrounding Paragraph** displays the elements of a document where A and B are within same paragraph delimited by line feed.

NEAR Content In Same Scope Item displays the elements of a document where A and B are within the same document.

NEAR Content In Same Coding Reference displays the elements of a document where A and B are within the same Node.

---

[11] As alternatives to *Narrow* and *Broad* you may use *Custom* which can override these settings for any specific task.

Node A

Node B

Paragraph 1

Overlapping | Within X words | Within same paragraph | Within same coding reference*) | *) search in nodes only | Within same scope item

≤X words

Line feed

Paragraph 2

>X words

Line feed

Paragraph 3

"A **PRECEDING** B"

PRECEDING Context Overlapping displays the elements of a document where A and B overlap as long as A is coded earlier or from the same starting point as B.

PRECEDING Content In Custom Context[12]. The [**Specify**] button allows you to select between Broad Context, Narrow Context or Custom Context.

For Example:

- **PRECEDING Context Within X words** displays the elements of a document where A and B are within X words as long as A is coded earlier or from the same starting point as B.
- **PRECEDING Context In Surrounding Paragraph** displays the elements of a document where A and B are within the same paragraph delimited by line feed as long as A is coded earlier or from the same starting point as B.

PRECEDING Context In Same Scope Item displays the elements of a document where A and B are within same document as long as A is coded earlier or from the same starting point as B.

PRECEDING Context In Same Coding Reference displays the elements of a document where A and B are within same Node as long as A is coded earlier or from the same starting point as B.

---

[12] As alternatives to *Narrow* and *Broad* you may use *Custom* which can override these settings for any specific task.

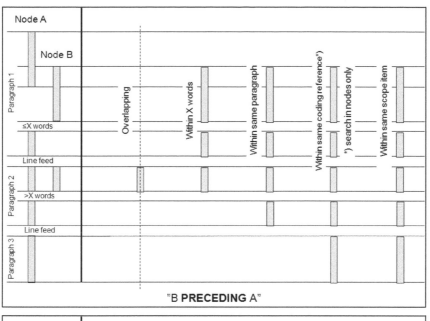

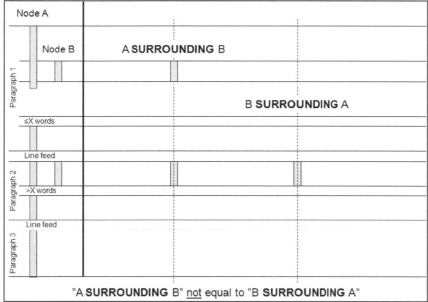

SURROUNDING Context displays the elements of a document where A overlaps B as long as A is coded earlier or from the same starting point as B and terminates later than or at the same point as B.

15. HANDLING BIBLIOGRAPHIC DATA

Along with source material that is gathered as project evidence, reference material (e.g., peer-reviewed academic research papers) often play a crucial role in grounding a qualitative research project. NVivo 11 also allows users to import reference material, including full-text documents, from common reference handling software like EndNote, RefWorks and Zotero. When imported, reference materials become Source Items and as a result they can be coded and analyzed the same way as other sources. For advanced analysis, we offer a method of using the Framework Matrices (see Chapter 16, About the Framework Method) to efficiently work with academic reference material, such as Literature Reviews. This chapter is about importing bibliographic data stored in certain selected reference handling software. The file formats that can be imported to NVivo are: .XML for EndNote and .RIS for RefWorks and Zotero .

In this chapter, we will use as an example importing data into NVivo from EndNote (the top reference handling software, in our opinion). The following two reference records will be exported from Endnote:

℧	Author	Year	Title	Journal	Ref Type	URL	Last Updated
℧	Cafazzo, J. ...	2009	Patient-perceived barriers to the ado...	Clinical jour...	Journal Arti...	http://www.ncbi.nlm...	2011-08-24
	Ritchie, L.; P...	2011	An exploration of nurses' perceptions...	Applied nur...	Journal Arti...	http://www.ncbi.nlm...	2011-08-24

The clip symbol indicates that one reference has a file attachment (typically a PDF full text article) and the other not.

On the next page, you will see a shot of a typical reference from EndNote. As you can see, each reference listing contains a wealth of meta-data about a single reference:

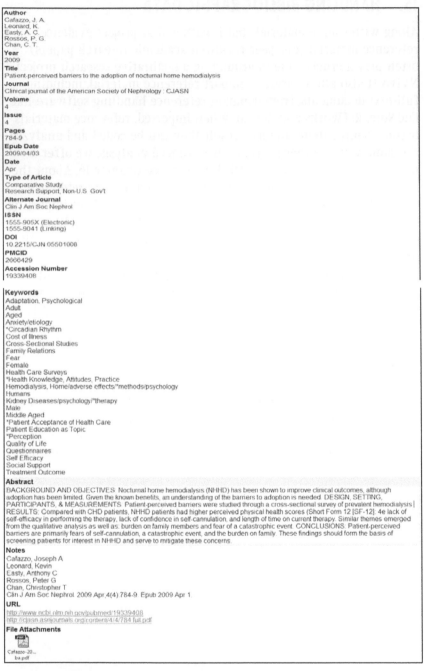

Author
Cafazzo, J. A.
Leonard, K.
Easty, A. C.
Rossos, P. G.
Chan, C. T.
Year
2009
Title
Patient-perceived barriers to the adoption of nocturnal home hemodialysis
Journal
Clinical journal of the American Society of Nephrology : CJASN
Volume
4
Issue
4
Pages
784-9
Epub Date
2009/04/03
Date
Apr
Type of Article
Comparative Study
Research Support, Non-U.S. Gov't
Alternate Journal
Clin J Am Soc Nephrol
ISSN
1555-905X (Electronic)
1555-9041 (Linking)
DOI
10.2215/CJN.05501008
PMCID
2666429
Accession Number
19339408

Keywords
Adaptation, Psychological
Adult
Aged
Anxiety/etiology
*Circadian Rhythm
Cost of Illness
Cross-Sectional Studies
Family Relations
Fear
Female
Health Care Surveys
*Health Knowledge, Attitudes, Practice
Hemodialysis, Home/adverse effects/*methods/psychology
Humans
Kidney Diseases/psychology/*therapy
Male
Middle Aged
*Patient Acceptance of Health Care
Patient Education as Topic
*Perception
Quality of Life
Questionnaires
Self Efficacy
Social Support
Treatment Outcome

Abstract
BACKGROUND AND OBJECTIVES: Nocturnal home hemodialysis (NHHD) has been shown to improve clinical outcomes, although adoption has been limited. Given the known benefits, an understanding of the barriers to adoption is needed. DESIGN, SETTING, PARTICIPANTS, & MEASUREMENTS: Patient-perceived barriers were studied through a cross-sectional survey of prevalent hemodialysis RESULTS: Compared with CHD patients, NHHD patients had higher perceived physical health scores (Short Form 12 [SF-12]: 4e lack of self-efficacy in performing the therapy, lack of confidence in self-cannulation, and length of time on current therapy. Similar themes emerged from the qualitative analysis as well as: burden on family members and fear of a catastrophic event. CONCLUSIONS: Patient-perceived barriers are primarily fears of self-cannulation, a catastrophic event, and the burden on family. These findings should form the basis of screening patients for interest in NHHD and serve to mitigate these concerns.

Notes
Cafazzo, Joseph A
Leonard, Kevin
Easty, Anthony C
Rossos, Peter G
Chan, Christopher T
Clin J Am Soc Nephrol 2009 Apr,4(4):784-9. Epub 2009 Apr 1.
URL
http://www.ncbi.nlm.nih.gov/pubmed/19339408
http://cjasn.asnjournals.org/content/4/4/784.full.pdf
File Attachments
Cafazzo-20...
ba.pdf

The communication between reference handling software and NVivo is in the form of an XML structured file. Reference handling software typically allows you to export a collection of citations. The export command from for example EndNote is **File → Export** and the file type must be set as XML. This creates you a file with all the above information including a file path to the PDF.

Importing Bibliographic Data

In NVivo go to **DATA | Import | From Other Sources → From EndNote...**. With the file browser you will find the XML-file you exported from your reference handling software. Click **[Open]**.

The **Import from EndNote** dialog box appears:

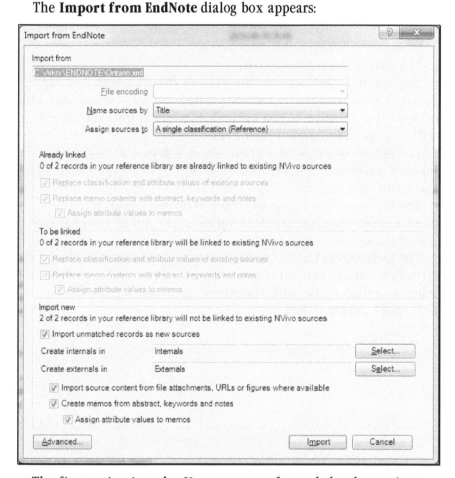

The first option is under **Name sources by** and the alternatives are: Title and Author and year.

The second option is to decide if you want one Source Classification for all your bibliographic data, Reference. Then there will be one attribute called Reference Type and the values will be Journal Article, Book, Conference Proceedings etc. If this is your preference then select
Assign sources to: *A single classification (Reference).*
If you instead prefer one Source Classification for each reference type then select
Assign sources to: *Different classifications based on record type.*

The next option is under the section **Import new** at the bottom of the screen. The first example is a reference with a linked PDF and the second example without PDF. The principle is that PDFs will be imported as Internal Source Items and other references will be imported as External Source Items.

Under the section **Import unmatched records as new sources** you need to define one location for Internal sources and one location for External sources. In our example we have created these two folders:

Internals\\Bibliographic Data and

Externals\\Bibliographic Data.

The option *Import source content from file attachments, URLs or figures where available* is necessary when you want to import a PDF or any other resource. If you uncheck this option then the record will be imported as an External item.

The option *Create memos from abstract, keywords and notes* is selected when each bibliographic item will have a linked memo with the mentioned content.

The option *Assign attribute values to memos* assigns same classification and same attribute values to the linked memo as the linked item.

The [**Advanced**] button makes it possible for some individual settings for the items that is about to be imported. This is useful when you need to import bibliographic data as an update to previously imported data.

The PDF Source Item

The internal PDF Source Item has the same look and layout as the original article and can now be coded, linked, searched and queried:

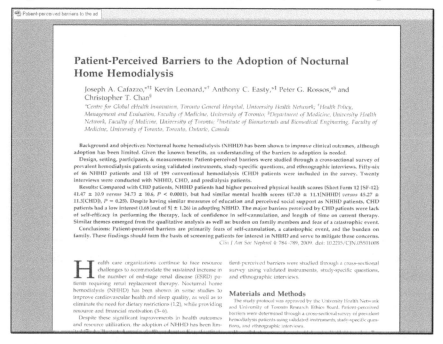

The **PDF Properties**, **General** tab, has now the following content imported through the XML file. The name of the PDF-item is the name of the EndNote file attachment, which can be set in EndNote to correspond to the title of the article. As you can see below, the abstract has been copied into the Description field of the PDF source:

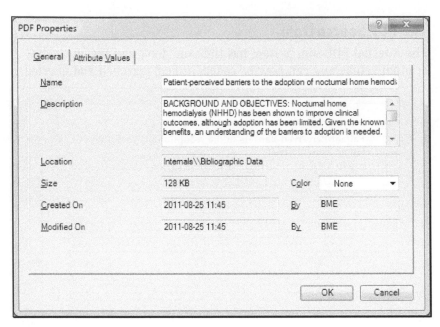

The **PDF Properties**, **Attribute Values** tab, has now the following content:

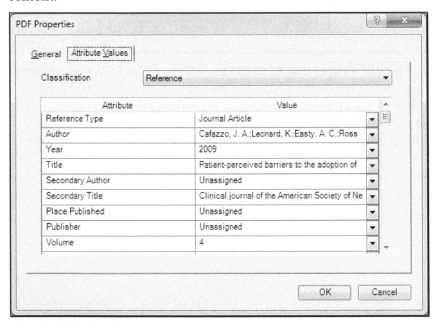

Author is one of the Attributes and the values are the list of author names for each Source Item.

Keywords is also an Attribute (not shown here) and its values are the whole list of keywords originating from this Source Item (see page 244).

The Linked Memo

If you elect to create a linked memo it will have the same name as the linked item. The memo is a normal text document and can be edited and otherwise handled as any Source Item. The content in our example is from the Abstract, Keywords and Notes fields of the original reference record. This is a useful feature because it allows you to search and code the abstract, which is not possible when the abstract is only located in the source description field.

The **Memo Properties**, **General** tab, has now the following content:

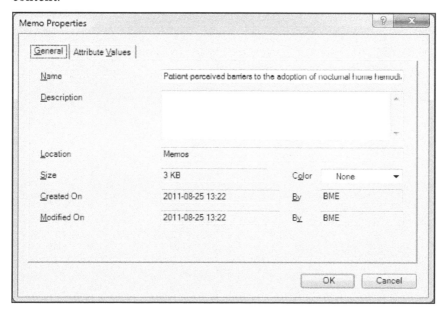

The **Memo Properties**, **Attribute Values** tab, has now the following content in a case where *Assign attribute values to memos* in the **Import from EndNote** dialog box has been checked:

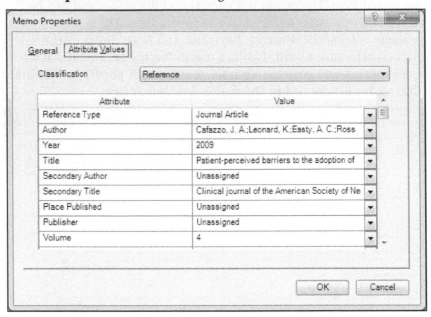

The Classification and Attribute values are identical with those of the linked item.

The External Source Item

Bibliographic records without file attachments (like PDFs) are imported as External source items. These items have a link leading to the external source from where the records were captured. External items have also a linked Memo with similar properties as explained above. Exploring the External Properties you will find that the description field has a copy of the abstract like the Internals have. The Externals are also classified along with the Internals.

External Properties dialog box, the General tab:

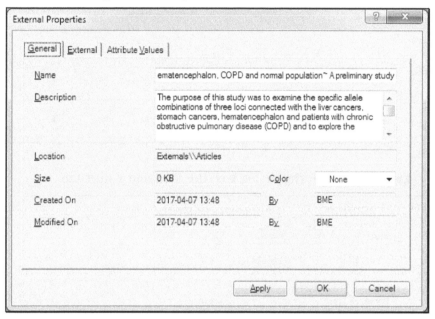

External Properties dialog box, the External tab:

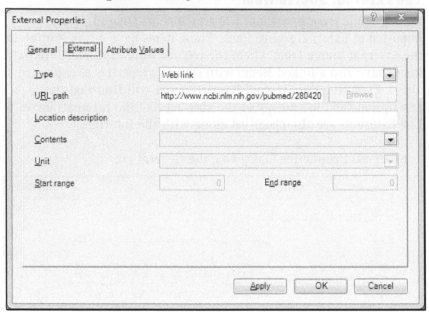

External Properties dialog box, the Attribute Values tab:

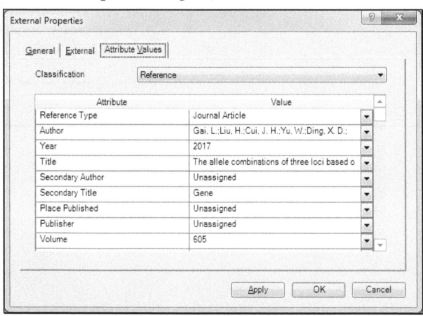

16. ABOUT THE FRAMEWORK METHOD – ONLY FOR PRO & PLUS

Framework is a qualitative data analysis method developed by the UK's largest, independent not-for-profit research institute, the National Centre for Social Research (NatCen) in the 1980's.

The Framework method is used to organize and manage research through the process of summarization, resulting in a robust and flexible matrix output which allows the researcher to analyze data both by case and theme. It's used by hundreds of researchers in areas such as health research, policy development and program evaluation.

NatCen developed specialty software called FrameWork to support this method. This software is no longer developed, but through a partnership between NatCen and QSR, NVivo 11 now provides new functionality to support the Framework method.

Accordingly, the Framework approach will provide you with exciting opportunities to apply this method to textual and non-textual data (audio-visual or images) and adopt other approaches that NVivo also supports such as discourse analysis.

Framework differs from traditional qualitative approaches to analysis as it does not rely on coding and indexing alone.

Introducing the Framework Matrix

Like any matrix, the Framework Matrix consists of rows and columns. Therefore, for those of you who are familiar with Node Matrices (as a result of a Matrix Coding Query) this approach seems familiar. Thus, rows are Nodes, columns are Nodes, and the cell content is the intersection (or cross coding) between two Nodes also understood as the result of an AND operator. The important difference between a Framework Matrix and a Matrix Coding Query is that the cells of a Framework Matrix can display data, or they can display any text you enter along with any links you create.

More than a tool for displaying your data, a Framework Matrix is a Source Item that allows you to quickly and easily view your data and write notes and insights about it. One particularly useful function of a Framework Matrix is viewing your data in the Associated View while recording your insights in cells. A second useful function is the ability to easily view a certain Theme Node in a grid that allows you to quickly compare data to other Theme Nodes or Case Nodes. A third useful function is the ability to create links between cell content and your source material using summary links.

This is the default view of a Framework Matrix:

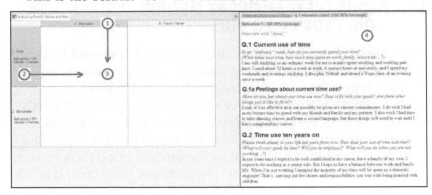

① Rows are defined as Nodes which are often classified Case Nodes. This could be a person or a place or an organization. It could also be literature of any kind for example a set of articles in PDF format. In the latter case PDF Source Items must be created as Cases before they can be used as rows in a Framework Matrix.
Go to **CREATE | Items | Create As Cases**.

② Columns are defined as Nodes, typically topic or theme Nodes. It could also be Nodes representing interview questions from structured interviews.

③ The content of a cell is always blank (default) when the first Framework Matrix in a project is created. Several options are now at hand for the user:
You can type any text.
You can let the cell contain the whole or part of the coded content in the intersection between a row and a column. See Auto Summary, see page 257.
You can create Summary links to any content in the Associated view. See Summary Links, see page 258.

④ The Associated View is a separate window to the right of the Framework Matrix showing the whole or parts of the Case Node of the selected cell or row. There are several options for the Associated View: The whole Node (Row coding), the intersection between a row and a column (Cell coding) or Summary links.

Creating a Framework Matrix

1 Go to **CREATE | Sources | Framework Matrix**.
Default folder is **Framework Matrices**.
Go to 5.

alternatively

1 Click on [**Sources**] in Area 1.
2 Select the **Framework Matrices** folder in Area 2 or its subfolder.
3 Go to **CREATE | Sources | Framework Matrix**.
Go to 5.

alternatively

3Click on any empty space in Area 3.
4Right-click and select **New Framework Matrix...**
or [**Ctrl**] + [**Shift**] + [**N**].

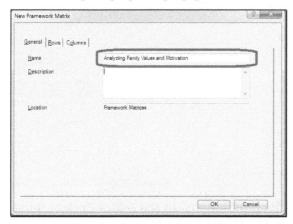

4 In **New Framework Matrix** dialog box type a name (compulsory) and a description (optionally).
5 Click on the **Rows** tab.

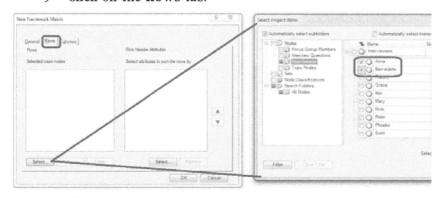

6 Click on the left [**Select**] button and in the **Select Project Items** dialog box select the Cases that you want to become rows in the Framework Matrix, then confirm with [**OK**].

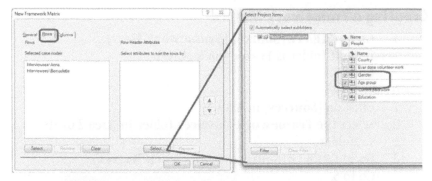

7   Click on the right [**Select**] button and in the **Select Project Items** dialog box select the attributes that you want to become Row Header Attributes in the Framework Matrix, then confirm with [**OK**].

8   Click on the **Columns** tab.

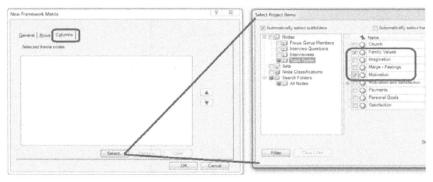

9   Click on the [**Select**] button and in the **Select Project Items** dialog box select the Theme Nodes that you want to become columns in the Framework Matrix, then confirm with [**OK**].

10 When you are finished choosing your Rows and Columns, click [**OK**].

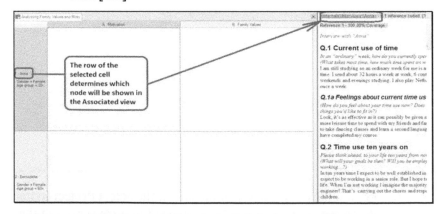

When your Framework Matrix is finished, you will see a screen resembling the above image. The default cell content is blank. A new context dependent Ribbon menu, **FRAMEWORK MATRIX**, has now opened and is opened each time a Framework Matrix is opened.

Remember, a Framework Matrix is a Source Item, so you can create memo-like insights and their attendant links as a way of writing up your insights or generating qualitative data.

Populating Cell Content

With your new Framework Matrix created, you have three options for populating content in the cells:

- auto-populating the cell with all or part of the content at the 'intersection' between a row and a column. (See Auto Summary below)
- creating Summary links to any content in the Associated view. (See Summary Links, page 258)
- typing in any text you wish

Auto Summary

1 Go to **FRAMEWORK MATRIX | Summary | Auto Summarize**.

Using Auto Summarize, all cells (irrespective of which cell is selected) will be automatically filled with the content corresponding to the intersection between a row and a column.

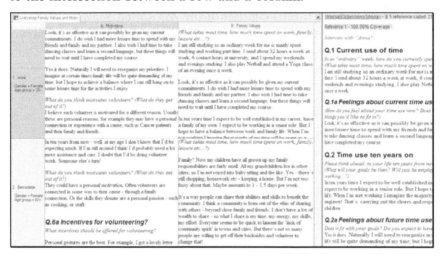

If there is any text in a cell before Auto Summary is applied, then the new content will be pasted after that text. Using Auto Summary will not overwrite extant cell content. Using Auto Summary repeatedly will create repeated content in all cells.

After an Auto Summary, you can modify text in any way you see fit. One best practice we recommend is populating cells with Auto-Summary and then writing your own summary overtop of the content. In this way, you can easily record your insights on aspects of your data.

Summary Links

Summary links are connection points between Framework Matrix content and content from your data sources. Like See Also Links, Summary Links allow for shortcutting across your project and moving seamlessly between summary content and your data.

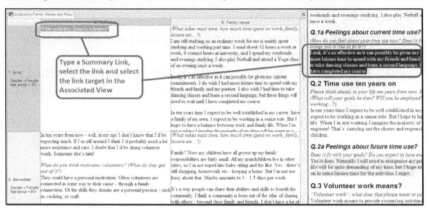

1   If required blank out the current cell content with [**Ctrl**] + [**A**] then the [**Del**] key.
2   Type the text of the new Summary Link.
3   Select this link.
4   Select the linked content in the Associated View.
5   Go to **FRAMEWORK MATRIX** | **Summary** | **New Summary Link**.

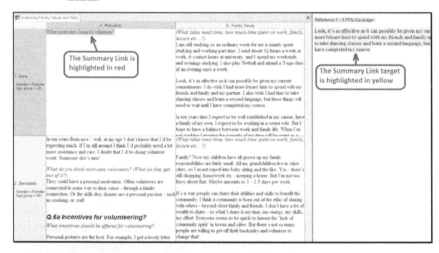

To get the above view you need the following settings:
   Go to **FRAMEWORK MATRIX** | **Associated View** | **Highlight**
→ **Summary Links**
   Go to **FRAMEWORK MATRIX** | **Associated View** | **Content**
→ **Cell Coding**

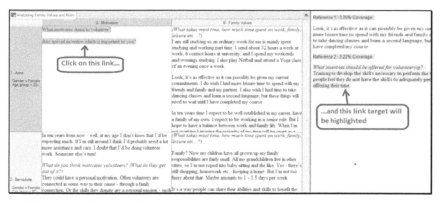

If you need more than one Summary Link in a cell then it is very handy to use the setting:

Go to **FRAMEWORK MATRIX | Associated View | Highlight → Summary Links from Position**

Go to **FRAMEWORK MATRIX | Associated View | Content → Cell Coding**

More on Associated View

The default settings for the ribbon **FRAMEWORK MATRIX | Associated View | Content** and **Highlight** are determined in the **Application Options** dialog box. Go to **FILE → Options → Display** tab, section **Framework Matrix Associated View Defaults**:

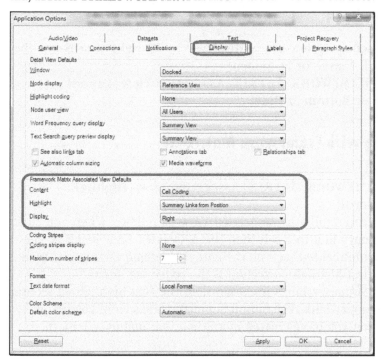

These default settings are restored each time a project is opened and any changes made are kept intact during the current work session.

An alternative setting is:

1   Go to **FRAMEWORK MATRIX | Associated View | Content → Row Coding**

2   Go to **FRAMEWORK MATRIX | Associated View | Highlight → Column Coding**.

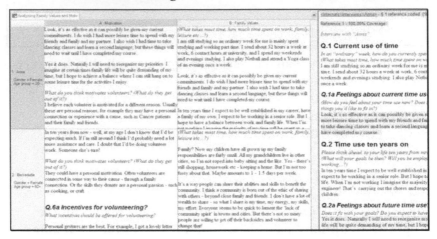

The coded sections are now highlighted depending on which cell has been selected.

- ◆ -

The Associated View can be displayed to the right of or below the Framework Matrix, or be hidden:

Go to **FRAMEWORK MATRIX | Associated View | Layout → Right** or **Bottom** or **Hide**.

Working with Framework Matrices

Auto Scroll

Go to **FRAMEWORK MATRIX | Associated View | Highlight → Auto Scroll**.

Auto Scroll scrolls the Associated View as follows. When you click on a Summary link in a cell then the Associated View displays the currently highlighted section. If Highlight Column Coding is chosen then the first highlighted section is the coded section and if Highlight Summary Links is chosen then the first highlighted section is the Summary Link. The option Summary Links from Position is useful when you have created more than one Summary Link in a cell.

Where is the Cell Summary stored?

The cell Summary is stored in the intersection between two Nodes, one from a row and one from a column in a Framework Matrix. Once created the Summary is stored even if the Framework is deleted. If same combination of two Nodes occurs in another Framework the Summary is identical. Changing the Summary in one Framework is therefore instantly mirrored in the other Framework.

Opening a Framework Matrix

1   Click on [**Sources**] in Area 1.
2   Select the **Framework Matrices** folder in Area 2 or its subfolder.
3   Select the Framework Matrix in Area 3 that you want to open.
4   Go to **HOME | Item | Open**
    or right-click and select **Open Framework Matrix...**
    or double-click on the Framework Matrix in Area 3
    or [**Ctrl**] + [**Shift**] + [**O**].

Please note, you can only open one Framework Matrix at a time, but several matrices can stay open simultaneously.

Editing a Framework Matrix

1   Select a Framework Matrix.
2   Right-click and select **Framework Matrix Properties...**

You can add or delete rows and columns.

Importing Framework Matrices

Framework Matrices can be imported along with another project that you import. All Nodes which constitute the Framework Matrix must either exist in the open project or must be imported with the Framework Matrix. The Framework Matrix will be updated with the updated Nodes.

Exporting Framework Matrices

1   Click [**Sources**] in Area 1.
2   Select the **Framework Matrices** folder in Area 2 or its subfolder.
3   Select the Framework Matrix or Matrices in Area 3 that you want to export.
4   Go to **DATA** | **Export** | **Items**
    or right-click and select **Export** → **Export Framework Matrix...**
    or [**Ctrl**] + [**Shift**] + [**E**].
5   Decide file name, file location, and file type. Possible file types are: .TXT, .XLS, or XLSX. Confirm with [**Save**].

Deleting a Framework Matrix

1   Click on [**Sources**] in Area 1.
2   Select the **Framework Matrices** folder in Area 2 or its subfolder.
3   Select the Framework Matrix or Matrices in Area 3 that you want to delete.
4   Go to **HOME** | **Editing** | **Delete**
    or right-click and select **Delete**
    or [**Del**].
5   Confirm with [**Yes**].

Please note that according to what was said about storing Framework Matrices the content of a matrix is not deleted even when the matrix is. The content is saved as the intersection between two Nodes. When one of those Nodes is deleted the content will be deleted.

Printing Framework Matrices

1   Open a **Framework Matrix**.
2   Go to **FILE** → **Print** → **Print...**
    or right-click and select **Print...**
    or [**Ctrl**] + [**P**].

Undocking the Framework Matrix

Undocking a Framework Matrix is possible with the same command as for other open Project Items. However, the Associated View window is hidden in this view. One way to use more screen space and still keep the Associated view is closing the Navigation View by going to **VIEW** | **Workspace** | **Navigation View**.

Fonts, Font Styles, Size, and Color

The default text style in the Cell Summary is determined by **Project Properties** dialog box, the **Framework Matrices** tab, see page 62:

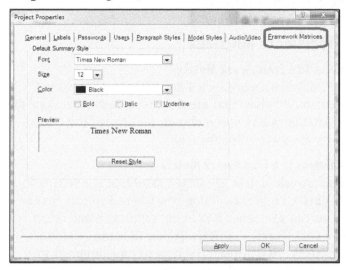

You can add text styles and attributes as an overlay to these default settings:

1 Select the text in a cell.
2 Go to **HOME** | **Format** | and select font, size, color or attribute.

Setting paragraph styles under **HOME** | **Styles** is not available for Framework matrices.

Paragraph alignment, indentation, bulleted or numbered lists under **HOME** | **Paragraph** is not available for Framework Matrices.

Searching and Replacing Words

This feature is the same as when editing Source Items that are documents.

HOME | **Editing** | **Find → Find...**
HOME | **Editing** | **Replace**

However, **HOME** | **Editing** | **Find → Go to...** is not available for Framework Matrices.

Spell Checking

NVivo's native spell checking can be used for Framework Matrices, see page 82.

Inserting Date and Time and Symbols

This feature is the same as when editing Source Items that are documents.

> **HOME | Editing | Insert → Date/Time**
> **HOME | Editing | Insert → Symbol...**

Organizing Framework Matrices

About Sorting Rows in a Framework Matrix

Rows in a Framework Matrix are sorted according to the selected Attributes and attribute values that are displayed under the name of each row. If no Attributes have been chosen for display the Node names of the rows are sorted alphabetically.

About Sorting Columns in a Framework Matrix

Columns in a Framework Matrix are sorted according the setting in the Framework Matrix Properties dialog box where you can change the sort order. You can also select a column, right-click and select **Column → Move Left** (**[Ctrl] + [Shift] + [L]**) or **Column → Move Right** (**[Ctrl] + [Shift] + [R]**). Alternatively, select a column go to **LAYOUT | Rows & Columns | Column → Move Left** or **Move Right**.

Hiding and Filtering Rows and Columns

Hiding and filtering rows and columns in a Framework Matrix (like you could for a matrix Node) is not possible in a Framework Matrix.

Adjusting Row Height and Column Width

1 Select a row or a column.
2 Right-click and select **Row → Row Height (Column Width)**.
3 Enter the row height (column width) in pixels.
4 Confirm with **[OK]**.

The row height and column width can also be adjusted by pointing at the border between rows or between columns and drag with the mouse pointer.

Row heights can also be set to automatically adjust to the amount of text, however maximum value for autofit is 482 pixels:

1 Select a row or rows.
2 Right-click and select **Row → AutoFit Row Height**.

If you need more row height, then use **Row → Row Height** instead.

Row heights and Column widths can be reset to default values (values applied when you create a new Framework Matrix).

1 Select any row, column or cell in the Framework Matrix.
5 Go to **LAYOUT | Tools | Reset Settings**
   or right-click and select **Reset Settings**.

17. ABOUT SURVEYS AND DATASETS - ONLY FOR PRO & PLUS

This section deals with data that originates from both multiple-choice questions and open-ended questions. In NVivo a dataset is a Source Item created when structured data is imported. Structured data is organized in records (rows) and fields (columns). The structured data formats that NVivo can import are Excel spreadsheets, tab-delimited text files and database-tables compatible with Microsoft's Access. A dataset in NVivo is presented in a built-in reader that can display data both as table and as a form. The reader makes it much easier to work on the computer and read and analyze data.

A dataset has two types of fields (columns), namely Classifying and Codable.

Classifying is a field with demographic content of a quantitative nature, often the result of multiple choice questions. The data in these fields is expected to correspond to attributes and values.

Codable is a field with 'open ended content' like qualitative data. The data in these fields should typically be the subject of theme coding.

Datasets can only be created when data is imported. Data is arranged in the form of a matrix where rows are records and columns are fields. Typically, respondents are rows, columns are questions and cells are answers.

Importing Surveys

Structured data of any origin can be imported into NVivo so long as it meets the criteria described above:

1   Go to **DATA | Import | Survey → From Microsoft Excel File...**
    Default folder is **Internals**.
    Go to 5.

alternatively

1   Click [**Sources**] in Area 1.
2   Select the **Internals** folder in Area 2 or its subfolder.
3   Go to **DATA | Import | Survey → From Microsoft Excel File...**
    Go to 5.

alternatively

3   Click on any empty space in Area 3.
4   Right-click and select **Import → Survey → From Microsoft Excel File...**
5   Select the appropriate Excel-file and click [**Open**].

The **Survey Import Wizard – Step 1** appears:

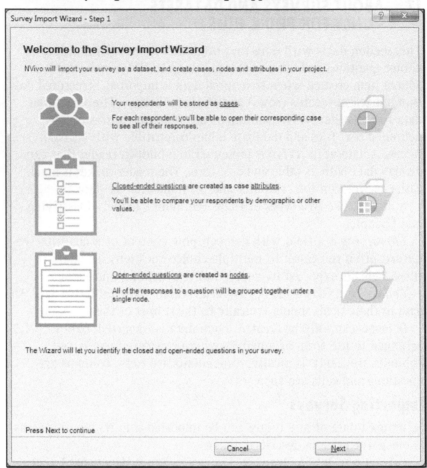

This box informs you how NVivo will handle the data of your imported data.

    6   Click **[Next]**.

The **Survey Import Wizard – Step 2** appears:

The upper section of the dialog box, SheetName, displays the two sheets of the Excel workbook: survey data and variable explanations. Select a sheet and its contents are displayed under Data Preview. The first 25 records of each are displayed. We select the sheet *survey data*.

You can verify the Time and Date formats and the Decimal symbol against the information displayed in the Data Preview.

It is important that the field names of imported data are only in the first row. Certain datasheets have field names in two rows and if so then the two rows must be merged. If you uncheck the option *First row contains field names* the row instead will contain column numbers.

7   Click [**Next**].

The **Survey Import Wizard – Step 3** appears:

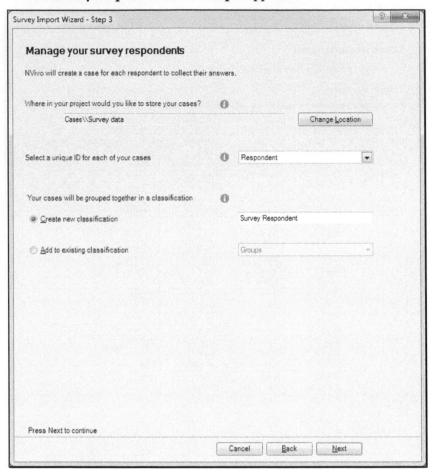

8   Click **[Next]**.

The **Survey Import Wizard** – **Step 4** appears:

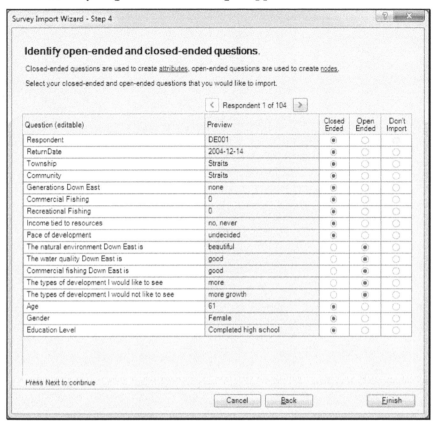

In this dialog box you can change NVivo's interpretation of Closed Ended (Classifying) and Open Ended (Codeable) columns. You can also exclude any column from being imported using the Don't Import marking.

9   Click [**Finish**].

The **Survey Import Wizard** - **Processing survey** appears:

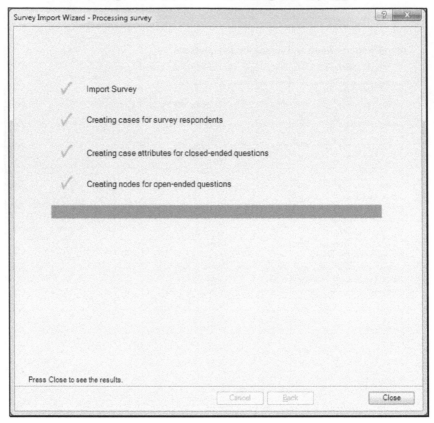

10   When finished then click [**Close**].

A successful import creates a Dataset with the same name as the Excel-file and when it opens in Area 4 and view mode *Table* it appears like this:

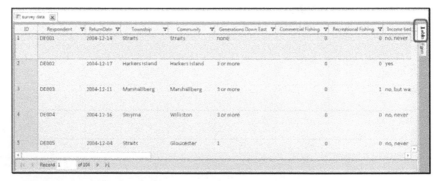

NVivo has created a new leftmost column, ID. A Dataset cannot be edited nor can you create or delete rows or columns. The buttons down left are for browse buttons between records.

View mode *Form* displays one record at a time:

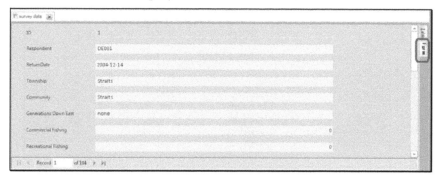

Classifying fields have a grey background and Codable fields a white background, like here in view mode *Table*:

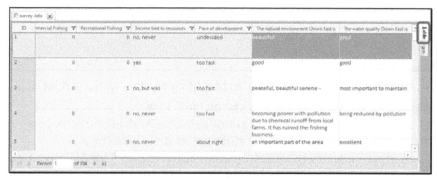

Or here in view mode *Form*:

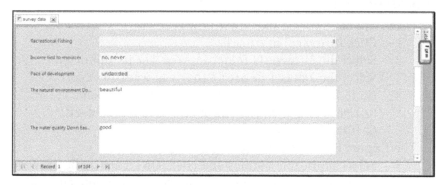

In the **Dataset Properties** dialog box you can do certain modifications to a Dataset's presentation:

Dataset Properties — General | Dataset | Attribute Values

Fields

Name	Analysis Type	Data Type	Visible
(all columns)			✓
Respondent	Classifying	Text	✓
ReturnDate	Classifying	Date	✓
Township	Classifying	Text	✓
Community	Classifying	Text	✓
Generations Down East	Classifying	Text	✓
Commercial Fishing	Classifying	Integer	✓

Move Up   Move Down

Social Media

Origin

Contents   :

OK   Cancel

You can change names of a field, hide a field or move a field, but you cannot change Analysis Type or Data Type.

Alternatively, such modifications can also be made directly in a Dataset, view mode *Table*. All rules are as described for a Classification Sheet (Chapter 11, Classifications), and for Matrices (see page 220 and onwards), including the use of filters apply to Datasets.

Exporting Datasets

Datasets can be exported like other Project Items:

1   Click [**Sources**] in Area 1.
2   Select the **Internals** folder in Area 2 or its subfolder.
3   Select the Dataset in Area 3 that you want to export.
4   Go to **DATA** | **Export** | **Export → Export Dataset...**
     or right-click and select **Export → Export Dataset...**
     or [**Ctrl**] + [**Shift**] + [**E**].

The **Export Options** dialog box now appears.

5   Select applicable options and click [**OK**]. Then a file browser
     opens and you can decide file name, file location, and file
     type. Possible file formats are: Excel, .TXT and HTML.
6   Confirm with [**Save**].

Coding Datasets

Coding Datasets applies all the common rules: select text in codeable fields, right-click and select **Code**.

All coding in a Dataset can be explored like in other Project Items including coding stripes and highlighting.

Autocoding Datasets

Autocoding Datasets is the opportunity to create Cases and Nodes to provide a structure to your Dataset content. Autocoding Datasets is fully described related to Autocoding Social Media Datasets (Chapter 18, see page 288).

The earlier described highly automated import procedure of an Excel worksheet includes autocoding of Cases and Nodes and a classification of Cases why further instructions will be redundant.

Classifying Datasets

From a Dataset you can create and classify Cases based on the Classifying fields. In certain instances there could be reasons to update data and especially when you need to apply the Mapping and Grouping feature described later on. We will consider updating the existing Case Classification created when we imported the survey.

  1   Select the Dataset in Area 3 with the data that you want to use for updating the Case Classification
       or click on the open Dataset in Area 4.

  2   Go to **CREATE | Classifications → Classify Cases from Dataset**
       or right-click and select **Classify Cases from Dataset**.
     The **Classify Cases from Dataset Wizard** – **Step 1** appears:

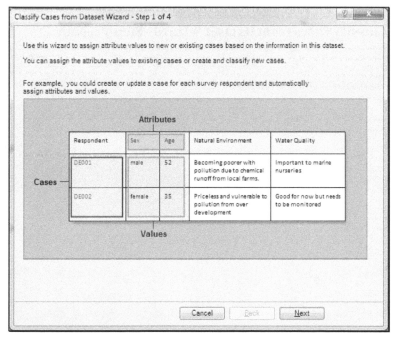

  3   Click [**Next**].

The **Classify Cases from Dataset Wizard – Step 2** appears:

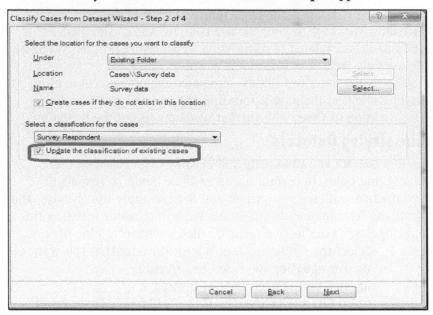

In our example we will update the Classification created during the import. Therefore it is important to check *Update the classification of existing cases.*

    4   Click [**Next**].

The **Classify Cases from Dataset Wizard – Step 3** appears:

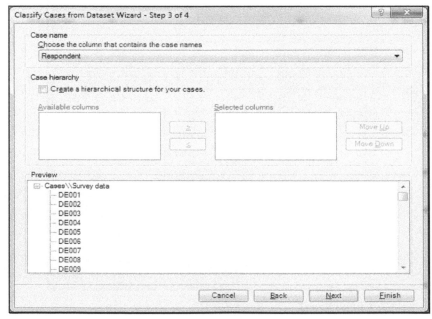

    5   We select the column *Respondent* to correspond to the Cases. Click [**Next**].

The **Classify Cases from Dataset Wizard – Step 4** appears:

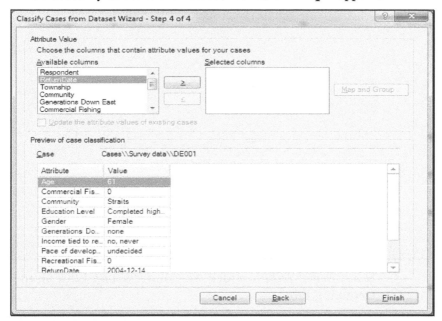

All Classifying fields are listed in the left box, *Available columns*. Use [>] to bring over the fields to the *Selected columns* box. In the section Preview the result from the topmost Node is displayed.

    6   Click [**Finish**].

Mapping and Grouping

We return to the **Classify Nodes from Dataset Wizard – Step 4** above. The [**Map and Group**] button can be used to move (or map) the content from one column to another. There is also an option to group discrete numerical values as intervals, typically discrete ages of people to age groups:

    1   In **Classify Nodes from Dataset Wizard – Step 4** the field *Age* has been moved to the right box, Selected columns.

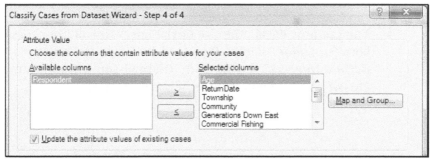

    2   Highlight *Age* and click [**Map and Group...**].

The **Mapping and Grouping Options** dialog box appears:

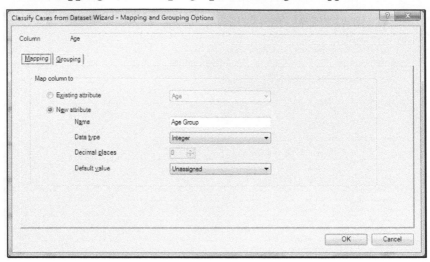

3   Select *New Attribute* which we call *Age Group*. Click on the
     Grouping tab.

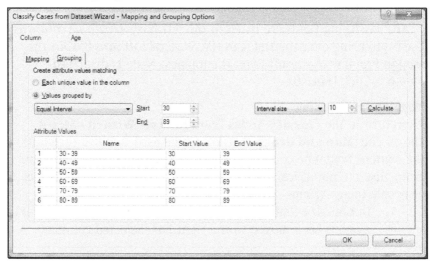

4   You can now decide the size of the interval. You can choose
     between *Equal Interval, Standard Deviation* or *User-
     defined Interval*. Confirm with **[OK]** and you will return to
     Classify Nodes from Dataset Wizard – **Step 4**.

Importing from SurveyMonkey

If you use SurveyMonkey to collect survey responses, you can import the completed responses directly into your NVivo project. The imported data becomes a dataset source that you can sort, filter or auto code. You can exclude particular questions from being imported—for example, if they are not relevant to your analysis or if they contain confidential information. You can also change the field names (column headings).

Importing data from SurveyMonkey:
1   Go to **DATA | Import | Survey → From SurveyMonkey**.
2   In the **SurveyMonkey Authenticator** dialog box enter your SurveyMonkey Username and Password, and then click [**Login**].

Follow the instructions in the **Import from SurveyMonkey Wizard**.

Importing from Qualtrics

If you use Qualtrics to collect survey responses, you can import the completed responses directly into your NVivo project. The imported data becomes a dataset source that you can sort, filter or auto code. You can exclude particular questions from being imported—for example, if they are not relevant to your analysis or if they contain confidential information. You can also change the field names (column headings).

Importing data from Qualtrics:
1   Go to **DATA | Import | Survey → From Qualtrics**.
2   In the **Qualtrics Authenticator** dialog box enter your Qualtrics Username and Password. Type also your API Token if applicable. Finally click [**Allow Access**].

Follow the instructions in the **Import from Qualtrics Wizard**.

18. INTERNET AND SOCIAL MEDIA – ONLY FOR PRO & PLUS

Arguably the most significant upgrade for NVivo 10 and 11 is the ability to import and handle data from internet web pages and social media sites like LinkedIn, Facebook, Twitter, and YouTube. NVivo also features full integration with Evernote and OneNote, the popular cloud-based notetaking/archiving services that will also be discussed in the next chapters.

Introducing NCapture

NCapture is a browser plugin that is delivered and installed with NVivo 11. NCapture exports web content into files called *web data packages* (a .vcx file) that you will import into NVivo. NCapture allows you to export any website including the website's text, images and hyperlinks. Websites import into NVivo as PDF sources. NCapture also allows you to export data from LinkedIn, Facebook and Twitter. Social media data can also import into NVivo as a PDF source, but more importantly social media data can also be imported as an NVivo Dataset. Presently, NCapture is available as addins with Internet Explorer and Google Chrome.

Exporting websites with NCapture

Like most software commands, capturing web data with NCapture in a web-browser can happen in three ways:

1. Select the **NCapture icon** on the toolbar of the web-browser:

2. Select **NCapture for NVivo** from the Tools menu:

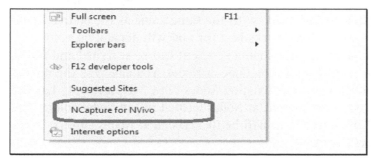

3 Right-click anywhere in your web-browser and select **NCapture for NVivo**.

Importantly, you can export numerous web data packages during your online research. NVivo does not require you to import your web data until you're ready. When you select to import a website to NVivo, the **NCapture** dialog box appears in the web-browser:

For websites, your Source Type will be Web Page as PDF by default as NVivo can currently only create website data packages that will be imported as PDF sources. But a variety of useful options are available for you to customize how your web data package can be imported into NVivo:

Source name will be the name of your new PDF source –the website's name will be the default here.

The *Description/Memo* tab allows you to type custom text that you want to add into *description field* of the PDF Source Item or a newly created *linked memo* with the same name as the Source Item. Which of these options works best for you will depend on your project – remember, linked memo content can be searched and coded; description field text cannot. Code at Nodes: You can type the names of any number of new or existing Nodes here. NCapture only has the ability to code web content at Nodes located in the Nodes folder. The imported PDF Source Item will be 100% coded at Nodes entered in the *Code at Nodes* field.

Importing Websites with NCapture

After NCapture exports your data, you will need to retrieve and import the newly created web data package (.vcx) file(s). When you have returned to NVivo:

1   Go to **DATA | Import | From Other Sources → From NCapture...**
    Default folder is **Internals**.
    Go to 5.

alternatively

1   Click on **[Sources]** in Area 1
2   Select the **Internals** folder in Area 2 or its subfolder
3   Go to **DATA | Import | From Other Sources → From NCapture...**
    Go to 5.

alternatively

3   Click on any empty space in Area 3.
4   Right-click and select **Import → Import from NCapture...**
    The **Import From NCapture** dialog box appears:

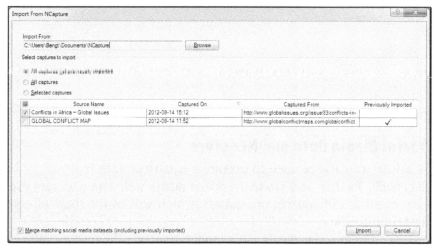

At the bottom of this dialog box, all recently imported items from NCapture are listed. NVivo will detect if there are web data packages that you have already imported, and so the default selection is All captures not previously imported. You can also select to import All captures or Selected captures.

5   Click **[Import]** and the result will be as follows:

The sample PDF Source item below is an export from the website 'Conflicts in Africa – Global Issues'. You'll notice that the webpage title is the same as the name of the PDF source file. Imported NCapture websites are classified with the Source Classification 'Reference'. Values are inserted by default for the following Attributes: Reference Type, Title, keywords, URL and Access Date. As you'll recall from our sample export image above, this entire PDF source will be coded at two Nodes, *Africa* and *Conflicts* and a linked memo will have been created sharing the PDF source's name, *Conflicts in Africa - Global Issues.*

Now you can open the source and hyperlinks are clickable like in any PDF item by using [**Ctrl**] + click

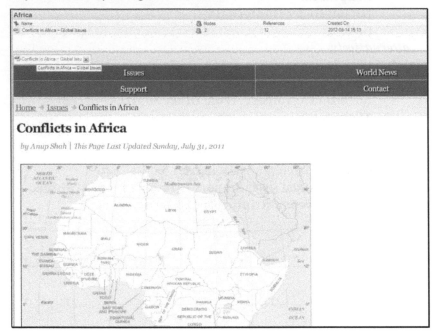

Social Media Data and NCapture

NCapture can also be used to capture a wealth of data from Facebook, Twitter, and LinkedIn. Social media web data packages can be created as PDF sources or Datasets, which will be the focus of our description below.

Due to each social media site's unique structure, NCapture captures different types of data from each site. While a summary of the complete functionality of Facebook, Twitter, and LinkedIn is beyond our purposes here, we will provide an explanation of the types of data you can capture from each site. Importantly, your ability to capture social media data is contingent on the privacy settings of the individual or group whose data you are interested in capturing (e.g., some Twitter users may require you to be their Follower before you can capture their Twitter data).

Importantly, you can use NCapture to gather social media data over a period of time and then easily update the data later. When you import web data packages containing social media data, by default, new data will be merged with old data so long as the original social media properties (e.g., hashtags, usernames, etc.) remains the same.

NCapture for Facebook Data

NCapture allows you to capture Facebook wall posts and data about their authors. Whether from an individual's Facebook wall (e.g., Allan McDougall), a Group wall (e.g., the Stockholm Sailing Club), or a Page wall (e.g., QSR International), NCapture can export wall posts, tags, photos, hyperlinks, link captions, link descriptions, number of 'likes', comments, comment 'likes', dates and times of posts and comments. Further, NCapture can export authors' names, genders, birthdays, locations, relationship statuses, bios, religions, and hometowns.

NCapture for Twitter Data

NCapture allows you to capture Twitter tweets and data about their authors. Unlike Facebook, which is largely based on users being connected as 'friends' or as fans who 'like' a specific page, Twitter profiles and their attendant tweets are (typically) publically available. As a result, along with individual user streams, full Twitter searches can also be exported with NCapture. Whether for user streams or search results, NCapture can export tweets along with their attendant usernames, mentions (usernames within tweets), hashtags (user-driven keywords), timestamps, locations, hyperlinks (if any), retweets (reposts by other users), and usernames of any 'retweeters'. Unlike NCapture's ability to export demographic data from Facebook, NCapture for Twitter captures data associated with a user's influence level (or klout), such as number of tweets, number of followers, and the number of users they are following.

NCapture for LinkedIn Data

Capturing social media data from LinkedIn is more similar to Facebook than Twitter. NCapture allows you to capture discussions and comments from LinkedIn groups, rather than individual user's LinkedIn profile pages. LinkedIn recently limited access to their web service (API), restricting the information available to apps like NCapture. As a result, you can no longer capture a LinkedIn group discussion as a dataset using NCapture. You can still capture a group discussion, and any other page in LinkedIn, as a PDF.

> **Tip:** Although you can't export LinkedIn users' profile data as a dataset with NCapture, you can still export user profiles as a PDF source. While unstructured, these PDF source can still be searched and coded after you import them into NVivo.

NCapture for YouTube

You can capture video clippings from YouTube as a Video item with or without comments or as a PDF.

When importing a video clipping to NVivo it behaves like other video items. However, the video clipping is always external (Not embedded) why Internet must be connected. In all other respects everything is working normally, that is you can create transcript rows and you can code.

When importing comments as a Dataset NCapture will create a number of columns (typical for Video) and will decide that the columns Comment and Reply are the only Codable columns.

The video item and the dataset (but not the PDF) are classified as a Source Classification named YouTube with 13 attributes.

Exporting Social Media Data with NCapture

Once you have found social media data that you need then activate NCapture from Internet Explorer or Google Chrome as described above. For social media web data packages, you can usually select between a Dataset and a PDF-page:

Like exporting websites with NCapture, when you export social media data you can create an item description, linked memo, and Nodes. After completed the **NCapture** dialog box, click [**Capture**].

Importing Social Media Data with NCapture

Now that you've exported your social media data to a web data package, it's time to import:

1   Go to **DATA | Import | From Other Sources → From NCapture...**
    Default folder is **Internals**.
    Go to 5.

alternatively

1   Click on [**Sources**] in Area 1.
2   Select the **Internals** folder in Area 2 or its subfolder
3   Go to **External Data | Import | From Other Sources → From NCapture...**
    Go to 5.

alternatively

3   Click on any empty space in Area 3.
4   Right-click and select **Import → Import from NCapture...**
    The **Import From NCapture** dialog box appears:

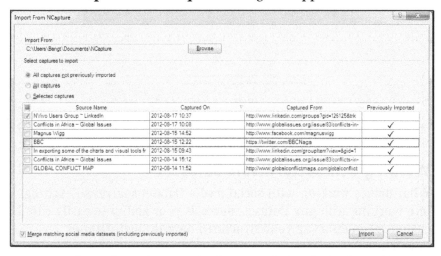

5   Like website data, at the bottom of this dialog box all recently imported items from NCapture are listed. NVivo will detect if there are web data packages that you have already imported, and so the default selection is *All captures not previously imported.*
6   Click [**Import**] and the result will be as follows:

When NCapture exports a photo from Facebook, the photos are stored as separate picture source file in the same folder as the Facebook dataset when imported. The icon shown is a *source shortcut* and a placeholder that allows you to easily navigate between your dataset and the photos.

The sample Dataset Source Item below is an export from the 'NVivo Users Group on LinkedIn'. You'll notice the Dataset Source Item contains the LinkedIn group name. Imported NCapture social media data is classified with the Source Classification 'Reference'. Values are inserted by default for the following Attributes: Reference Type, Title, keywords, URL and Access Date. As you'll recall from our sample export image above, this entire Dataset source will be coded at two Nodes, *Grounded Theory* and *Focus Groups*, and a linked memo has been created sharing the Dataset source's name, *NVivo Users Group on LinkedIn*.

Now you can open the Source and view it in several modes: Table (default), Form, or as a Cluster Analysis. The latter mode is unique for Datasets from Social Media and usually clusters Usernames.

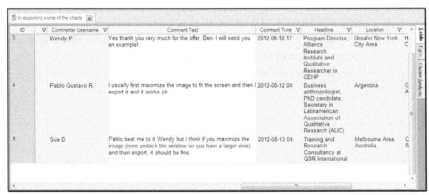

Working with Social Media Datasets

What makes working with social media Dataset sources so exciting, like working with any Dataset source, is your ability to easily edit, customize, and survey your structured data through Dataset Properties:

1   Click on [**Sources**] in Area 1.
2   Select the **Internals** folder in Area 2 or its subfolder.
3   Select the dataset that you want to edit.
4   Go to **HOME | Items | Properties → Dataset Properties**
     or right-click and select **Dataset Properties**
     or [**Ctrl} + [Shift] + [P]**.

alternatively

4   From any open any dataset, go to **HOME | Items | Properties**.

Within the **General** tab you can change the name and description of your social media Dataset.

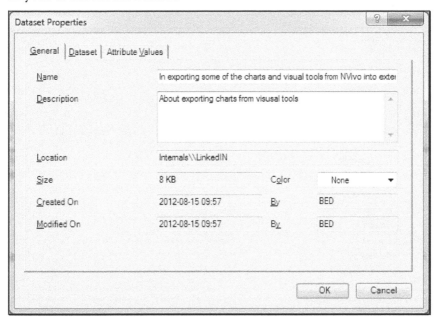

The **Dataset** tab allows you to view your Dataset fields and move some fields up or down. Upon importing your social media web data package, NVivo has already decided which columns are Classifying (a limited set of options) and which columns are Codable (editable text) respectively. Within this tab you can uncheck Visible on any row with data you deem unnecessary, like some demographics (e.g., Hometown for Facebook data).

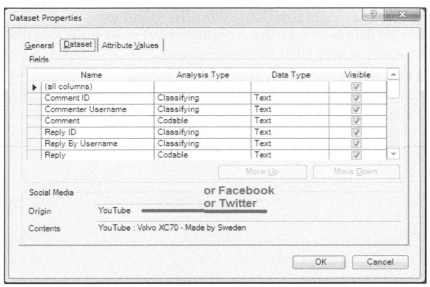

The **Attribute Values** tab allows you to view default Attribute Value information. You can select a custom Classification if that is useful for your project:

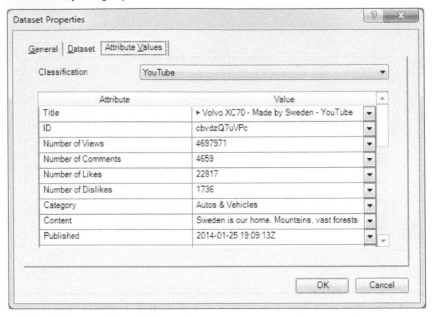

Analyzing Social Media Datasets

A number of exciting methods for analyzing social media Datasets exist in NVivo 11. Like any open Dataset source, you can search for patterns in your data by hiding, sorting, or filtering rows and columns. More advanced analysis functions such as Word Frequency Queries and Text Search Queries can offer insight into some themes in your data as well. Further, visualizations of social media data can be achieved using chart functions (see page 337).

Autocoding a Dataset from Social Media

Perhaps the most useful tool for social media web data is autocoding.

1 Select a Dataset in Area 3 that you want to auto code.
2 Go to **ANALYZE | Coding | Auto Code**
   or right-click and select **Auto Code...**

The **Auto Code Dataset Wizard – Step 1** appears:

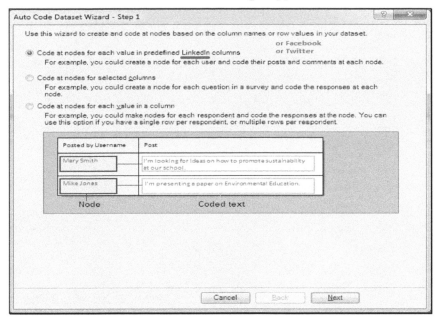

The first option, *Code at Nodes for each value in predefined LinkedIn (or Facebook or Twitter) columns* is unique for importing social media compared to other types of Datasets. For example, using the Auto Code Dataset Wizard we can create Nodes containing all of the content generated by one user, or all of the comments generated during a group discussion.

3   Click [**Next**].

The **Auto Code Dataset Wizard** - **Step 2** appears:

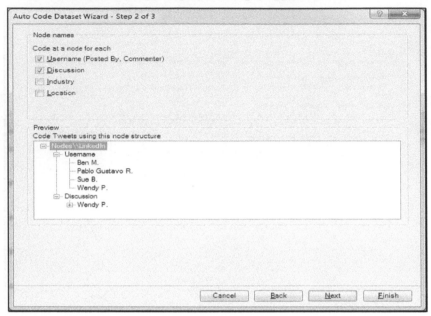

The **Auto Code Dataset Wizard** provides a preview of the resulting Node structure that your autocoding will generate. As you can see in the above image, by selecting to code data at Username and Discussion, Node hierarchies will be created where all of the data generated by each user will be coded into a Node named after that user.

    4   Click **[Next]**.

The **Auto Code Dataset Wizard** - **Step 3** appears:

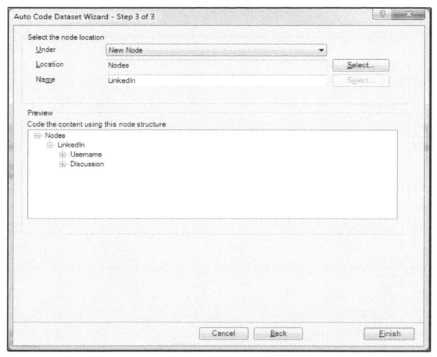

Default settings will create Nodes and apply a Node Classification named LinkedIn User, Facebook User or Twitter User which classifies the users under respective parent Node LinkedIn/Username, Facebook/Username or Twitter/Username. Also other Nodes have been created under the parent Nodes LinkedIn (Discussion), Facebook (Conversation) or Twitter (Hashtags).

Like other NVivo Datasets, the auto code wizard can also allow you to create Nodes based on the columns (e.g., all hashtags would become Nodes within a parent Node called hashtags) and cell values of the Dataset (e.g., all unique hashtags become their own Nodes with each occurrence auto coded).

Privacy levels can vary using social media so contact QSR Support if you have any problems with importing social media data.

   5   Finally click [**Finish**].

The result from these operations is not only a easy-to-handle dataset, a set of case nodes (Usernames) and a set of theme nodes (Comment text, Post, Title) but also a Source Classification and a Case Classification.

The Source Classification **Reference** was created when data from NCapture was imported as a dataset:

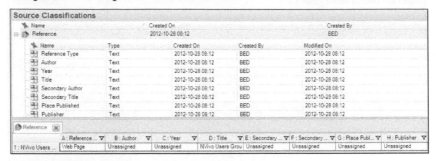

The Case Classification **LinkedIn User** was created when our dataset was autocoded with reference to Username:

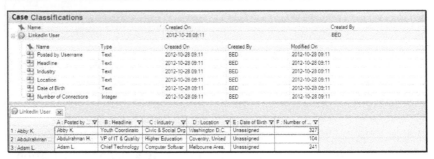

Installing NCapture

For Internet Explorer:
1. Download NCapture.IE.exe from QSR's web page.
2. Close Internet Explorer.
3. Launch NCapture.IE.exe and follow the prompts to complete the installation.

For Google Chrome:
1. Run Google Chrome.
2. Find the link with the installation guide on QSR's web page.
3. Follow the prompts to complete the installation.

Check your Version of NCapture

For Internet Explorer:
Go to **Tools → Manage Add-ons**
View the version number for **NCapture for NVivo** in the list.

For Google Chrome:
Go to **Tools → Extensions**
View the version number for **NCapture for NVivo** in the list.

19. SOCIAL NETWORK ANALYSIS
    – ONLY FOR PLUS

The ability for researchers to build sociograms for social network analysis (SNA) is one of NVivo 11's powerful new features. Social network analysis is an interdisciplinary process for investigating— often by way of visualization—the composition and consistency of social phenomena. Examples of social phenomena studied with social network analysis can include but are not limited to social media communities, networks of friends and families, or more conceptual topics like mapping idea dissemination.

The SNA methodology fits well with NVivo insofar as Nodes form the primary units for analysis. SNA defines a Node as a person or thing, which matches NVivo 11's definition of a Case Node. Sociograms are a mapping tool for visualizing the ways that Case Nodes relate to one another. Sociograms allow researchers to answer questions that involve how elements of a social phenomena interact and connect. They are analytic tool with a variety of applications, such as identifying where ideas have originated, revealing people or indivduals with access to too few resources, or observing how students use a classroom computer. In short, NVivo 11 now allows researchers using SNA to beautifully visualize and dynamically interact with the links between Case Nodes as sociograms.

Making Sociograms

Prior to building sociograms, you will have had to code relationships between your Case Nodes. For more on Relationships see page 144. You can build three types of sociograms in NVivo 11. First, *egocentric sociograms*, which highlight one particular Case Node—the "ego"— and display how other Case Nodes connect to it. Second, *network sociograms*, which display the relationships between a group of your Case Nodes. Third, *Twitter sociograms*, which ostensibly are the same as network sociograms but are accessed as a tab within an open Twitter Dataset detail view.

Creating an Egocentric Sociogram
1   Select any Case Node.
2   Go to **EXPLORE | Social Network Analysis | Egocentric Sociogram** (this button will be grey if a Case Node is not selected)
     or right-click on a Case Node and select **Create Egocentric Sociogram.**
3   The sociogram will appear in the Case Node's detail view (Area 4) with the egocentric Case Node appearing as a star shape.

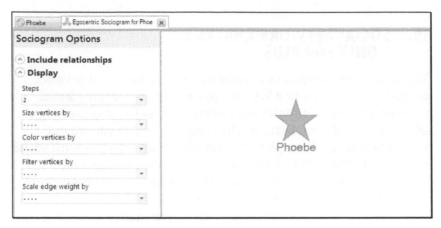

Creating a Network Sociogram

1 Go to **EXPLORE | Social Network Analysis | Network Sociogram**.
2 The **Select Project Items** dialog box will open.
3 Select the Case Nodes you wish to visualize.
4 The Network Sociogram with the Sociogram Options panel will appear in Area 4.

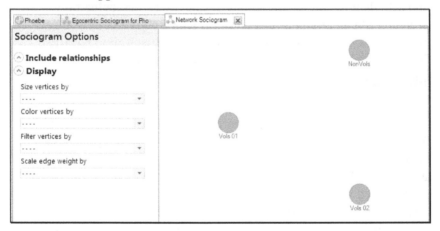

Creating a Twitter Sociogram

1 Open any Twitter Dataset.
2 Select the **Twitter Sociogram** tab in detail view.
3 The Twitter sociogram will appear.

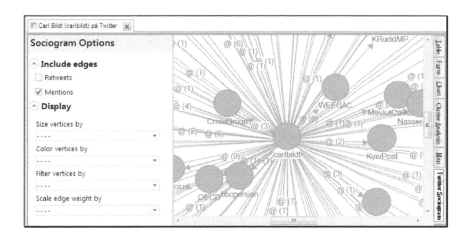

Adjusting Sociograms

When a sociogram opens, you will see Vertices and Edges—the terms used for Case Nodes (Vertices) and the lines that represent the relationships connecting Case Nodes (Edges).

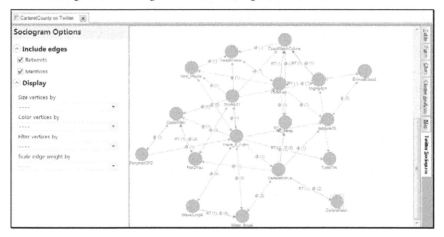

Once you have opened a sociogram, a diverse array of Sociogram Options for filtering this visual data are available. While these filters may adjust which Case Nodes and Edges appear, they do not omit their presence in the overall project—this may seem like a minor point, but the positioning of Case Nodes and Edges directly impacts how NVivo quantifies and calculates sociogram metrics, called *Centrality measures.* More on this below.

Displaying Relationships on your Sociogram

Directly under the heading **Sociogram Options**, a set of filters allow you to adjust the types of relationships between your Case Nodes. For egocentric sociograms and network sociograms, these filters appear under the heading **Include relationships**. Simply check or uncheck a relationship type to include or omit it from your sociogram. Once an adjustment is made, you will need to select **Click to redraw** in order to recreate your sociogram.

For Twitter sociograms, you will have access to only two filters, under the heading **Include edges**: Retweets and Mentions.

Displaying Degrees of Connection on your Sociogram (Egocentric Sociograms only)

As the title indicates, this Sociogram Option filters the number of connective steps between the egocentric Case Node and its connected Case Nodes. For example 1 step will only display Case Nodes that directly connect to the egocentric Case Nodes, whereas selecting 2 steps, etc. show additional degrees of connectivity.

Using Size, Color and Line Weight to distinguish Sociogram Case Nodes and Relationships

The **Display** heading under **Sociogram Options** allows you to adjust how Edges and Case Nodes appear based on three types of *Centrality measures*, the background calculations run by NVivo to quantify how Case Nodes relate with each other. Case Nodes' appearance can be adjusted according to size and color.

When adjusting **Size vertices by** and **Color vertices by**, know that *degree* centrality counts the number of Case Nodes that are connected, *betweenness* counts how often a Case Node lies on the shortest path between two other Case Nodes, and *closeness* is a measure of 'reach' insofar as the speed of information transfer is considered to represent the sum of the shortest distances from a Case Node to all of the other Case Nodes in the sociogram. Case Nodes will be sized and colored depending on *Centrality measures*.

Username	Degree	Degree In	Degree Out	Betweenness	Closeness
Debiffler.	0	0	0	0.000	0.000
EntertaintJs84.	0	0	0	0.000	0.000
FerrymanOf72.	2	1	2	0.000	0.026
Frank_B_Fishn.	10	5	9	102.767	0.042
Shrimp73.	6	2	5	25.083	0.033
CoastWatchCulture.	5	4	2	8.750	0.030
Cookn-Man.	4	4	2	6.333	0.029
WaveJumpd.	2	1	2	0.000	0.026
NC_Nette.	3	3	1	2.500	0.029
Head4Home.	4	4	2	5.483	0.031
Nick_Maybe.	4	3	2	4.067	0.032
LocalRep.	8	2	7	42.090	0.034
Fish2You.	3	3	2	4.917	0.029
CarteretKim.	7	4	5	64.133	0.037
Water_Angel.	3	3	2	3.900	0.029
ladyluck78.	4	4	1	15.483	0.033
Emma8Good.	2	2	1	0.000	0.025
MightyRph.	4	2	3	9.250	0.029
TurtleTim.	2	2	1	3.333	0.028
CarteretKeeth.	1	1	1	0.000	0.023

As you might expect, nodes with higher values will be the largest or colored the darkest. Lower values will be the opposite.

The thickness of Edges (edge weight) can also be adjusted. Select **Scale edge weight by** to make lines more distinct based on the number of relationships associated with a given Case Node.

Filter Case Nodes by Centrality Measure
Case Nodes can also be filtered by *Centrality measure*. Under **Filter vertices by**, you can quantitatively filter Case Nodes based on the extent to which they represent a certain measure. For example, you filter Case Nodes according to a betweeness measure of between 0.05 and 0.1.

Reviewing your Sociogram's Centrality Measures
Selecting Centrality Measures under the contextual Sociogram or Twitter Sociogram tab allows you to view how Edges and Vertices appear based on the three primary types *Centrality measures* described above: degree, betweenness and closenees.

Two more Centrality Measures: Density and Reciprocity
Sociograms use five types of *Centrality measures* as a metric for calculating the influence of Case Nodes in relation to one another, not just the three outlined above. However, density and reciprocity are measurements that reflect an entire sociogram, so they do not feature in the sociogram interface. You can find both shown in the NVivo **Status Bar** when an entire sociogram is selected:

Density is a ratio based on a count of Case Node pairs that are connected in a sociogram divided by the total number of connections possible. The density score is purported to display the level of *connectedness* in a sociogram.

Reciprocity shows the percentage of relationships in a sociogram that are reciprocated. The reciprocity score is purported to represent the level of reciprocal relations within a sociogram.

20. USING EVERNOTE WITH NVIVO

One of the new features in NVivo 10 and 11 that we are most excited about is the software's native capacity for importing data from Evernote. If you aren't already an Evernote user, it is a software suite designed for note taking and archiving. Evernote is cloud-based, which means that your notes are stored on an online server rather than on a local hard drive on a computer. The name Evernote implies that your notes will be archived 'forever' on the Evernote server. Do you have privacy concerns about uploading data to a cloud-based service like Evernote? Check with your institution's IT group or ethics office to find out what kind of data you are allowed to capture on Evernote and other popular cloud-based resources like Dropbox, SkyDrive, and Google Drive.

Evernote for Data Collection

Evernote has gained popularity because of its functionality for smart phone users. As a note taking program that is available on Blackberry, iPhone, iPad, and Android smart phones.

For qualitative researchers, a smart phone with Evernote installed offers a range of new possibilities for data collection. From the same device, researchers can record audio and video, take photos, capture web data, and easily upload all of these multimedia resources into NVivo.

Exporting Notes from Evernote

Evernote notes must be exported as an .ENEX file from the Evernote client, which is basically a XML format, for further import to NVivo. While a tutorial on how to use Evernote is beyond our purposes here, we have included a screen shot below displaying the File menu in Evernote. In order to export this picture note, simply go to **File →
Export → Export as a file in ENEX format**:

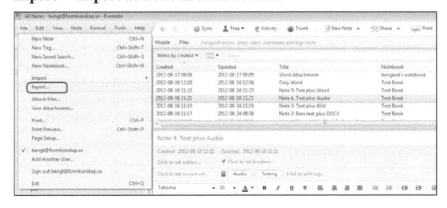

Importing Evernote Notes into NVivo

Remember you can batch import a set of notes or an entire Evernote notebook to an .ENEX file. Once you save your .ENEX file you can easily import its content into NVivo:

1   Go to **DATA | Import | From Other Sources → From Evernote...**
     Default folder is **Internals**.
     Go to 5.

alternatively

1   Click on [**Sources**] in Area 1.
2   Select the **Internals** folder in Area 2 or its subfolder
3   Go to **DATA | Import | From Other Sources → From Evernote...**
     Go to 5.

alternatively

3   Click on any empty space in Area 3.
4   Right-click and select **Import → Import from Evernote...**

The **Import from Evernote** dialog box appears:

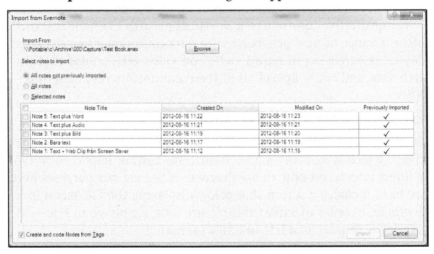

This example shows the import dialog when a notebook has been exported. The bottom of the dialog box contains a list of each individual note included in the .ENEX file. NVivo will detect if there are notes in the .ENEX that you have already imported, and so the default selection is to import *All notes not previously imported*. Alternatively, you can select import *All notes* or import *Selected notes*. Select the notes that you want to import.

5   Click [**Import**].

Evernote Note Formats in NVivo

Not all Evernote data will be imported as internal sources, so it is a good idea to familiarize yourself with the following list of Evernote note types and their attendant locations in NVivo:

- Evernote text notes will become a document Source in the internal Sources folder.
- Evernote notes with file attachments (e.g., PDFs, photos, images, audio files, or video files) will retain their file types. Any text that accompanies these notes will become a linked memo associated with the newly imported Source Item.
- Evernote web clippings (i.e., web page which has been saved to Evernote via an Evernote Web Clipper) will be imported as PDF Source Item.

Autocoding your Evernote Tags

Some Evernote users using note tagging as a way of linking notes together with broad categories for later reference and searching. Evernote tags in this sense are similar to NVivo Nodes. A nice feature for importing your tagged Evernote notes allows you to convert your tags to Nodes when you import the Evernote note. These Nodes are created in the Nodes folder (if they do not already exist). The Node will code the entire imported source. If you do not want to create Nodes when your notes are imported, clear the *Create and code Nodes from Tags* check box in the **Import from Evernote** dialog box.

21. USING ONENOTE WITH NVIVO

NVivo 10 and 11 contain native capacity for importing data from OneNote 2010 or OneNote Online. If you aren't already an OneNote user, it is a software suite designed for note taking and archiving. OneNote is cloud-based, which means that your notes are stored on an online server rather than on a local hard drive on a computer.

Exporting Notes from OneNote

Export to NVivo is made by an Addin component normally installed when NVivo is installed. OneNote pages must be exported as a .NVOZ file from the OneNote client, which is basically a XML format, for further import to NVivo. While a tutorial on how to use OneNote is beyond our purposes here, we have included a screen shot below displaying the **Share** ribbon in OneNote. In order to export these pages, simply go to **Share | NVivo | Export:**

Then the **Export for NVivo** dialog box appears.

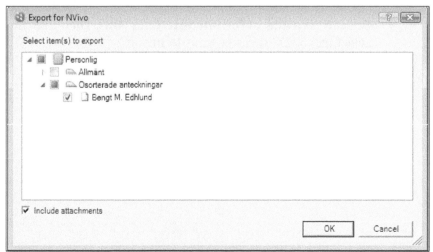

Importing OneNote Notes into NVivo

Once you save your .NVOZ file you can easily import its content into NVivo:

    1   Go to **DATA | Import | From Other Sources → From OneNote...**
        Default folder is **Internals**.
        Go to 5.

alternatively

    1   Click on **[Sources]** in Area 1.
    2   Select the **Internals** folder in Area 2 or its subfolder
    3   Go to **DATA | Import | From Other Sources → From OneNote...**
        Go to 5.

alternatively

    3   Click on any empty space in Area 3.
    4   Right-click and select **Import → Import from OneNote...**

The **Import From OneNote** dialog box appears:

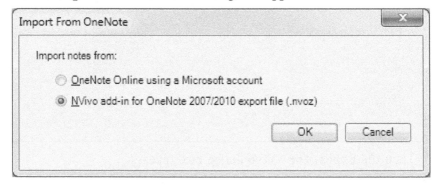

    5   Select **NVivo add-in for OneNote**. Click **[OK]**. Then find and select the .NVOZ file you want to import.

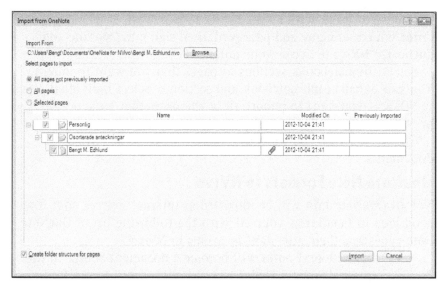

This example shows the import dialog when a notebook has been exported. The bottom of the dialog box contains a list of each individual note included in the .NVOZ file. NVivo will detect if there are notes in the .NVOZ that you have already imported, and so the default selection is to import *All pages not previously imported*. Alternatively, you can select import *All pages* or import *Selected pages*. Select the pages that you want to import.

6　Click [**Import**].

Importing from OneNote Online

Referring to point 5 above. Alternatively select **OneNote Online using a Microsoft account**. Then click [**OK**].

Choose to log in with a Personal account or Work or school account. Enter your user name and password, then sign into OneNote and authorize NVivo to access your notes.

Select the notebooks, sections or pages that you want to import. You can expand each notebook and section to select individual pages.

NOTE: If you want to import all of the pages that have not been previously imported, click All pages not previously imported.

Choose whether you want to import your pages as PDFs or documents.

OneNote Note Formats in NVivo

Not all OneNote data will be imported as internal sources, so it is a good idea to familiarize yourself with the following list of OneNote note types and their attendant locations in NVivo:

- OneNote text notes will become a document Source in the internal Sources folder.
- OneNote notes with file attachments (e.g., PDFs, photos, images, audio files, or video files) will retain their file types.

Installing NVivo Addin for OneNote

1 Download NVivoAddIn.OneNote.exe from QSR's website.
2 Make sure that OneNote is not running.
3 Click **Run**.

Check whether NVivo Addin for OneNote is Installed

For OneNote 2010:
1 Go to **File → Options → Add-Ins**
2 Check if Export for NVivo is on the list.

For OneNote 2007:
1 Go to **Tools → Options → Add-Ins**
2 Check if Export for NVivo is on the list.

22. FINDING AND SORTING PROJECT ITEMS

This chapter is about how to find Project Items. The finding tools in NVivo are *Find* and *Advanced Find*. Another useful function for finding relations between items is *Group Queries,* which is dealt with on page 224. The results of these functions are lists of shortcuts to the found items.

Find

The bar **Find** is always just above the List View heading for Area 3. This bar can be hidden or unhidden with **VIEW** | **Workspace** | **Find** which is a toggling function. The easy function **Find Now** is used for finding names of documents, memos or Nodes, not their contents.

1 At **Look for** you type a whole word or a fragment of a word that is part of the name of an item. Here is free text search applied (not whole words, not case sensitive).
2 The drop-down list **Search In** is used to select to which folder or folders the search shall be restricted.
3 Click [**Find Now**].

The result is a list of shortcuts in Area 3. A shortcut is indicated by a small arrow in the bottom-right corner of the icon. The list cannot be saved but you can create a **Set** from selected items from the list (see page 31).

Advanced Find

Advanced Find gives increased specificity to any given search.

1   In the **Find** bar go to **Advanced Find**
     or key command **[Ctrl]** + **[Shift]** + **[F]**.

The **Advanced Find** dialog box are shown.

The drop-down list **Look For** has the following options:

- Sources
- Documents
- Audios
- Videos
- Pictures
- Datasets
- PDFs
- Externals
- Memos
- Framework Matrices
- Nodes
- Relationships
- Node Matrices
- Source Classifications
- Case Classifications
- Attributes
- Relationship Types
- Sets
- Queries
- Results
- Reports
- Extracts
- Maps
- All

As an example of Advanced Find options, you can limit a text search to just the Description box of a certain type of Project Item.

The Intermediate Tab

The **Intermediate** and **Advanced** tabs are independent of each other. Below is the **Intermediate** tab of the **Advanced Find** dialog box:

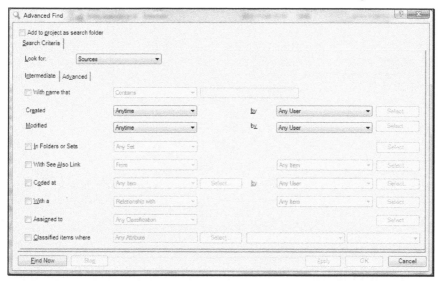

As soon as any option in the Intermediate tab has been chosen the corresponding [**Select...**] button is activated and opens the **Select Project Items** dialog box. The exact shape of this dialog box is determined by the selected option.

This function can be used to create a list with items matching certain criteria, like:

- Nodes created *last week*
- Nodes that are *Male*
- Memos with a 'See Also Link' from the Node *Adventure*
- Documents that are coded at the Node *Passionate*
- Nodes that code the document *Volunteers Group 1*
- Sets containing *Nodes*

The Advanced Tab

The **Advanced** tab offers other types of criteria:

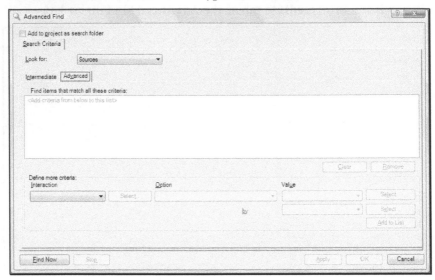

The **Interaction** drop-down list depends on the type of item that you have selected at **Look for**. For example, if *Documents* is selected the drop-down list *Define more criteria, Interaction* has the following options:

- Document
- Name
- Description
- Created
- Modified
- Size (MB)
- Attribute

The contents of a Description can be searched with this tool, but not the contents in an Annotation.

1 Select *Nodes* from the **Look for:** drop-down list. In the section *Define more criteria, Interaction* the drop-down list now has options specifically for Nodes.
In this case, select *Attribute* and then:
Age Group | equals value | 50-59 and the dialog box looks like this:

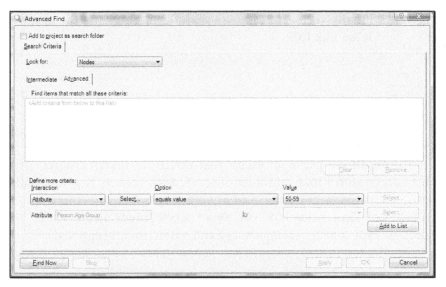

2　　Click [**Add to List**] and the search criteria moves to the box
　　　Find items that match all these criteria.

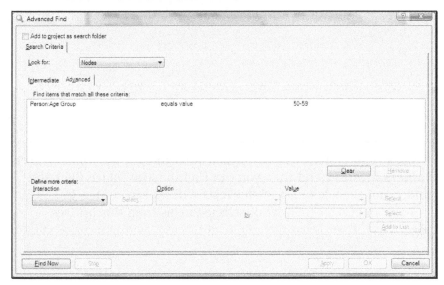

3　　You can now add another criterion for example a
　　　limitation to women. Then again click [**Add to List**].

4 Finally, the search is done with [**Find Now**] and the result looks like this:

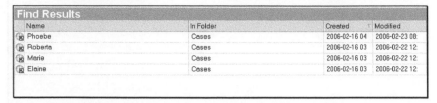

Name	In Folder	Created	Modified
Phoebe	Cases	2006-02-16 04	2006-02-23 08:
Roberta	Cases	2006-02-16 03	2006-02-22 12:
Marie	Cases	2006-02-16 03	2006-02-22 12:
Elaine	Cases	2006-02-16 03	2006-02-22 12:

The result is a list of shortcuts that match the search criteria. This list can be stored in a subfolder of the **Search Folder**. This subfolder can be created by checking *Add to project as search folder* in the **Advanced Find** dialog box. The **New Search Folder** dialog box is shown. Type a name (compulsory) and a description (optional):

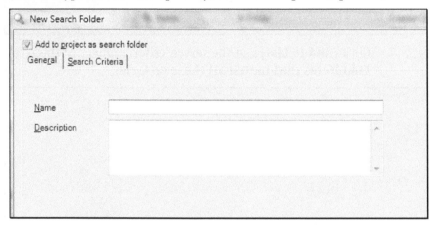

Click [**Folders**] in Area 1 and then you can open the folder **Search Folders** in Area 2 and then you can find the new folder. Click the folder and the whole list of shortcuts will appear in Area 3.

You can also create a set of selected items from this list (see page 31).

Sorting Items

This section applies to all items that can be viewed in a list usually in Area 3, but sometimes also in Area 4. For example, when a Node is opened in view mode Summary, a list is shown in Area 4.

1   Display a list of items in Area 3.
2   Go to **LAYOUT | Sort & Filter | Sort By → <select>**.

The options offered depend on of the type of items in the list. Nodes, for example, can be arranged hierarchically, so for Nodes there is a special sorting option, Custom.

1   Display a list with Nodes in Area 3.
2   Go to **LAYOUT | Sort & Filter | Sort By → Custom**.
3   Select the Node or Nodes that you want to move. If you want to move more than one Node they must be adjacent.
4   Go to **LAYOUT | Rows & Columns | Row → Move Up/ Move Down**
    or **[Ctrl] + [Shift] + [U]/[Ctrl] + [Shift] + [D]**.

This sorting is automatically saved even if you temporarily change the sorting. You can always return to your Custom sorting:

1   Display a list of items in Area 3.
2   Go to **LAYOUT | Sort & Filter | Sort By → Custom**.

This command is a toggling function. When you use the command again it sorts in the opposite order.

You can also use the column heads for sorting. Sorting by commands or sorting with column heads always adds a small triangle to the column head in question. Clicking again on this column head turns the sorting in the opposite order.

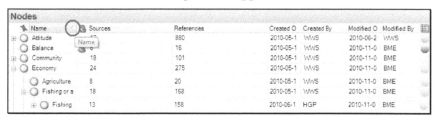

23. COLLABORATING WITH NVIVO
– ONLY FOR PRO & PLUS

As technology and interdisciplinary facilitate more and more complex qualitative studies, teamwork structures and procedures become increasingly important. NVivo allows several users to use the same project file provided that the file is opened by one user at a time. Alternatively, each member can work with his/her own project file that can be merged into a master file at a certain predefined occasion. The focus of this chapter focuses on how a team can operate using a single project file. The first half of this chapter explains some collaboration tools features in NVivo. The second half explains some general insights on collaborating with NVivo.

Collaborating on the same NVivo project can be arranged in a number of ways:

- Team members can use the same data but each individual creates his/her Nodes and codes accordingly – perhaps importing to a master project later.
- Team members use different data but use a common Node structure.
- Team members use both the same data and a common Node structure.

In cases where individual team members plan to merge their analytic progress into a master project file, merging projects is described on page 64. Review the options of the **Import Project** dialog box to find out how it can suite your needs. If Nodes with same names need to merge you can select Merge into existing item. Remember that Nodes and other items must have the same name and must be located on the same level of the folder structure before they can be merged successfully. Further, the contents of the Source Items must be identical.

NVivo includes several useful tools for collaborative data analysis:

- View Coding Stripes by Selected Users.
- View Coding by Users in an open Node (using sub-stripes).
- *Coding Comparison Queries* for comparing two coders working with the same sources and Nodes. This is an important option that improves a project's validity and quantifies inter-rate reliability.

Current User

An important concept for teamwork in NVivo is the **Current User**. In **FILE → Options** and the **Application Options** dialog box, the **General** tab identifies that the current user. When a project is open you can change the current user. However, it is not possible to leave the Name and Initial boxes empty.

If you select the option *Prompt for user on launch* then the **Welcome to NVivo** dialog box is prompted each time NVivo is started:

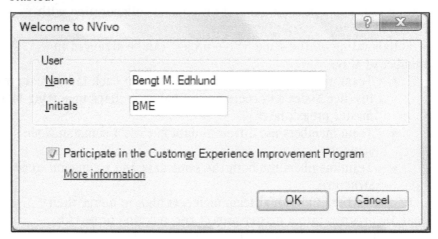

All users who have worked on the project are listed in **FILE →** **Info → Project Properties...** and in the **Project Properties** dialog box, under the **Users** tab:

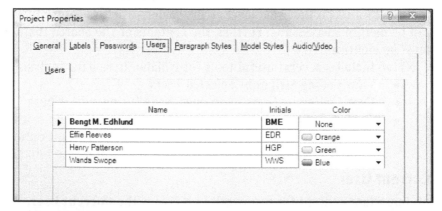

The current user is written in bold. The small triangle in the left column indicates the user who created the current project. In this

box you cannot change the names but the initials. To the left in the status bar the current user is shown:

Initials are used to identify all Project Items created or modified by a certain user.

Viewing Coding by Users

NVivo allows you to view the coding made by a certain member of a team:

1 Open the Node you wish to review.
2 Go to **VIEW | Detail View | Node → Coding by Users → <select>**.
3 Choose any of the options *All Users, Current User, Selected User..., Select Users...*

The default setting is *All Users* and during a work session the selected option will remain. Selecting *Select Users* will show in **bold** the users of this Node. When a certain user has been selected a filter funnel symbol is shown in the status bar.

Viewing Coding Stripes

Coding stripes and sub-stripes can be used to display the coding that individual team-members have made (see page 192):

1 Open the Source Item you wish to review.
2 Go to **VIEW | Coding | Coding Stripes → Selected Items**.

The **Select Project Items** dialog box is shown. Only Nodes used to code the current item have names in **Bold**. When you select **Users** (and select individual users) one coding stripe per user is shown. When you point at one such stripe the names of the Nodes at which each user has coded will show.

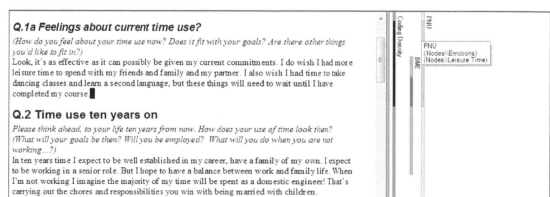

When you instead select **Nodes** (and select some individual nodes) one coding stripe per Node is shown. When you point at one such stripe the names of the users who has coded at those Nodes will show. The sub-stripes are Users.

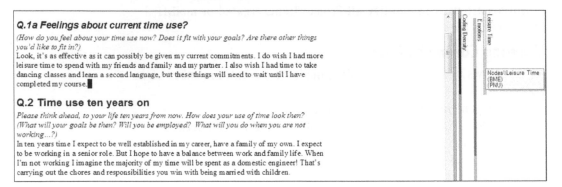

You can also display sub-stripes at the same time as the normal coding stipes by pointing at a coding stripe, right-click and select **Show Sub-Stripes → More Sub-Stripes...** and select one or more sub-stripes that you want to show. Here are some sub-stripes for Users:

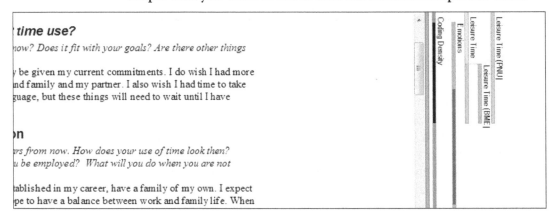

Coding Comparison Query

For projects interested in studying inter-rater reliability it is possible to compare how two people or two groups of people have coded the same material. This is possible provided that the same source material and the same Node structure have been used:

1   Go to **QUERY | Create | New Query → Coding Comparison...**
Default folder is **Queries**.
Go to 5.

alternatively

    1   Click [**Queries**] in Area 1.

    2   Select the **Queries** folder in Area 2 or its subfolder.

    3   Go to **QUERY | Create | New Query → Coding Comparison...**

        Go to 5.

alternatively

    3   Click on any empty space in Area 3.

    4   Right-click and select **New Query → Coding Comparison...**

The **Coding Comparison Query** dialog box appears:

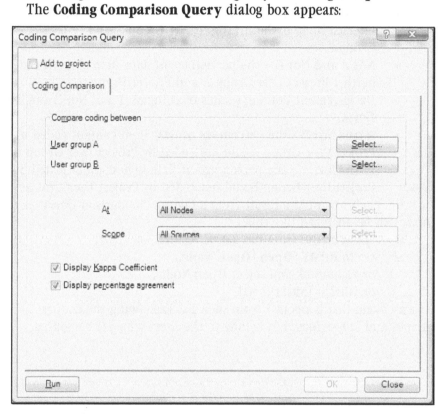

    5   Define User group A and B with the [**Select...**] buttons which give access to all users that have been working in the project.

    6   The **At** drop-down list determines the Node or Nodes that will be compared.

    7   The **Scope** drop-down list determines the Source Item or items that will be compared.

    8   Select at least one of the options *Display Kappa Coefficient* or *Display percentage agreement.*

    9   You can save the query by checking *Add To Project.*

    10   Run the query with [**Run**].

The result can look like this:

Node	Source	Source Fold	Source Size	Kappa	Agreement	A and B (%)	Not A and Not	Disagreeme	A and Not B	B and Not A
Communi	Thomas	Internals\In	4952 chars	0,5929	89,24	9,87	79,36	10,76	0	10,76
Communi	Thomas	Internals\In	4952 chars	0,9456	97,88	25,44	72,44	2,12	0,24	1,88
Economy	Thomas	Internals\In	4952 chars	0,2811	91,3	2,12	89,18	8,7	4,14	4,56
Economy	Thomas	Internals\In	4952 chars	0,9547	98,42	21,61	76,82	1,58	1,53	0,04
Natural e	Thomas	Internals\In	4952 chars	0	91,05	0	91,05	8,95	0	8,95

The percentage agreement columns indicate the following values:

- **Agreement Column** = sum of columns **A and B** and **Not A and Not B.**
- **A and B** = the percentage of data item content coded to the selected Node by both Project User Group A and Project User Group B.
- **Not A and Not B** = the percentage of data item content coded by neither Project User Group A and Project User Group B.
- Disagreement Column = sums of columns A and Not B and B and Not A.
- **A and Not B** = the percentage of data item content coded by Project User Group A and not coded by Project User Group B.
- **B and Not A** = the percentage of data item content coded by Project User Group B and not coded by Project User Group A.

From each row of the result from a Coding Comparison Query any *Node* can be analyzed like this:

1   Select a row from the list of results.
2   Go to **HOME | Open | Open Node...**
     or right-click and select **Open Node...**
     or **[Ctrl]** + **[Shift]** + **[O]**.

Any Node that is opened from such list is showing the coding stripes and sub-stripes that belong to the users who are compared.

From each row of the result from a Coding Comparison Query any *Source Item* can be analyzed like this:

1 Select a row from the list of results.
2 Go to **HOME | Open | Open Source...**
   or right-click and select **Open Source...**
   or double-click on the row.

Any Source Item that is opened from such a list shows the coding stripes and sub-stripes that belong to the users who are compared:

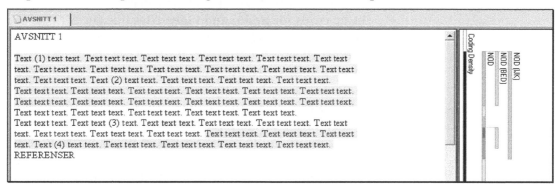

Coding stripes can always display the coding made by an individual user. This is made by pointing at a certain coding stripe, right-clicking and selecting **Show Sub-Stripes** and then selecting one or several users. Hiding sub-stripes is made using **Hide Sub-Stripes**.

Maps and Reports

During team project meetings, mapping can be illustrative and useful. Any Node structure can easily be made understandable using NVivo Maps (see the next chapter).

Reports are created by going to **EXPLORE | Reports | New Report**. These reports can be used to study Nodes and coding made by the different team-members, see Chapter 27, Reports and Extracts.

Tips for Teamwork

Based on our years of experience working with hundreds of qualitative researchers using NVivo, we offer our colleagues the following tips for collaborating with NVivo:

- Appoint **an NVivo coordinator** for the research project.
- Set up **file name protocols**, read-only, storage locations, backup locations, file distribution and archiving.
- Set up **rules for audio and video files** like file formats and file distribution. For example, should you use embedded items or external files?
- Set up a **Node strategy**. Such a strategy can be communicated in a number of ways. It is easy to make a Node template in the form of a project without Source Items. Each Node should have 'instructions' written in the Node's Description field (max 512 characters) or in the form of a linked Memo, which is easier to write, read, print and code. The Node template can be distributed to team-members, saved with a new name and developed into a project in its own right. Importantly, the Node template's structure must not be modified by users. When new ideas are evolved, users should instead create new Nodes in addition to the Node template and create Memo Links.
- Determine how **Node Classifications** and **Source Classifications** will be applied. Such Nodes can be interviewees or other research items like places, professions, products, organizations, phenomena. In some situations it is useful to work with different classifications.
- Set up **rules for the master project** including protocols for merging and updating. Define a new project with a new name that clearly indicates that it is a merged project. Possibly a new set of user names will be defined for this purpose. Import one partial project at a time with **Import Project** and the option 'Merge into existing item'. Items with same name and same location will be merged.
- Hold periodic **team meetings** for the project. Such meetings should compare and analyse data (as described in this chapter), summarize discussions, and make decisions. Distribute minutes from each meeting.
- Assuming that the work has come to a stage where different members have submitted contributions to the project, make sure that the team has the standardized **usernames** when they work with their respective parts.

Continuing to Work on a Merged Project

After exploring a merged project you have two options to proceed:

- Each user continues with the original individual projects and at a certain point of time you make a complete new merger – perhaps archiving the original merger.
- Each user continues to work on the merged project and archives the original individual portions.

We recommend continuing with the first option up to a certain point and then, if the team agrees, deciding to focus on the merged project later.

A Note on Cloud-computing

Some researchers we have worked with use cloud-based file sharing services like Dropbox, SkyDrive and Google Drive as a working solution for collaborating on an NVivo Project. These services allow changes to the NVivo project file to be made across several computers using the 'cloud'. We recommend you turn off the live syncing features of these programs while you are running NVivo. We have been contacted by a number of colleagues and clients who have lost data while simultaneously using NVivo and syncing its attendant (.nvp) file. Again, cloud-based utilities can be useful for team collaboration, but taking the proper precautions can avoid costly loss of analysis time due to software crashes.

When you need to access a project file stored on any cloud service either copy the file to your local drive or create a new project and import the project file. Never open a project file from a USB memory or any cloud service.

A Note on NVivo for Teams

NVivo manufacturer QSR International has developed a collaborative software solution called NVivo for Teams (an earlier ws named NVivo Server). Projects that are stored in NVivo for Teams can be considerably larger, up to 100 GB or more provided storage space is available. NVivo for Teams allows multiple users to work on the same project from different computers simultaneously. While useful, in our experience the logistical challenges associated with working on a server have kept our colleagues and clients from using this tool. While we support NVivo for Teams, it is beyond the purposes of this book to describe it. Feel free to follow contact us directly if you and your team have any interest in NVivo for Teams.

24. MAPS – ONLY FOR PRO & PLUS

Maps are useful tools when a project is developing or when a project is ready to begin reporting findings. Maps present ideas and theories visually. In a research team, maps are also useful for team meetings. NVivo 11 offers three types of maps, Mind Maps, Project Maps, and Concept Maps.

Creating a New Mind Map

A Mind Map reflects what you think about a single topic and is usually created quickly or spontaneously.

At the beginning of your project you might use a mind map to explore your expectations or initial theories. Later on, mind maps can help to confirm the structure of your nodes.

   1   Go to **EXPLORE | Maps | Mind Map**.
       Default folder is **Maps**.
       Go to 5.

alternatively

   1   Click [**Maps**] in Area 1.
   2   Select the **Maps** folder in Area 2 or its subfolder.
   3   Go to **EXPLORE | Maps | Mind Map**.
       Go to 5.

alternatively

   3   Click on an empty space in Area 3.
   4   Right-click and select **New Mind Map...**

The **New Mind Map** dialog box appears:

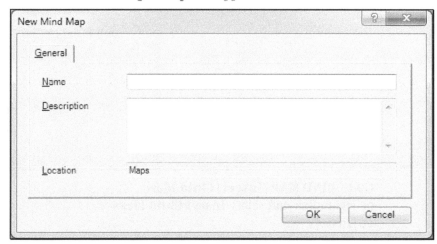

   5   Type a name (compulsory) and a description (optional), then [**OK**].

A new window appears in Area 4 and it is a good idea to undock with **VIEW** | **Window** | **Docked** to give you more space on the screen:

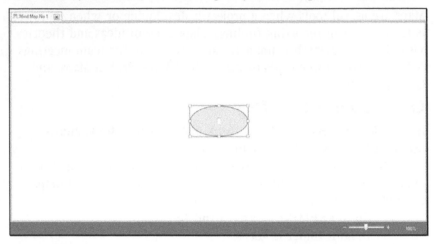

A new context dependent Ribbon menu, **MIND MAP**, has now opened and the new Mind Map and the new Main Idea are shown.

6 Go to **MIND MAP** | **Insert** | **Sibling Ideas**
   or right-click and select **Insert Sibling Ideas**
   or **[Enter]**.

This image shows two added Sibling Ideas:

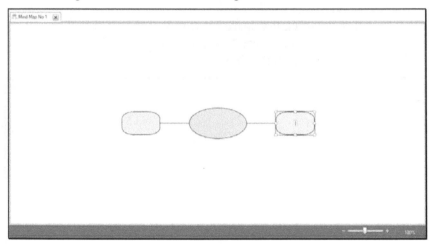

7 Go to **MIND MAP** | **Insert** | **Child Ideas**
   or right-click and select **Insert Child Ideas**
   or **[Ins]**.

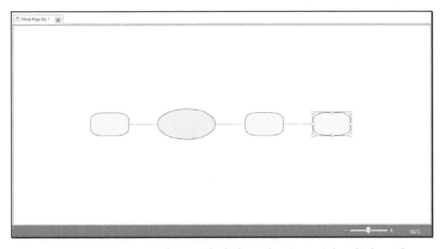

You can insert text in the symbols by selecting, right-click and select **Edit Label** or **[F2]**. Changing fonts, font attribute, color and size you need to select text and to go to **MIND MAP** | **Format Text**:

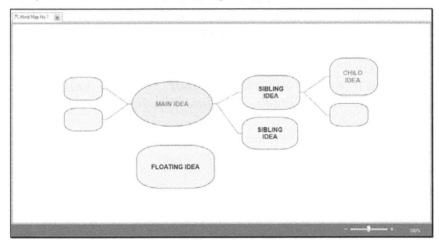

A Floating Idea is inserted by going to **MIND MAP** | **Insert** | **Floating Idea**.

Ideas can also be moved around in e map by using normal **Cut** (or **Copy**) and **Paste** commands.

If you want to create nodes based on your Mind Map you need to go to **MIND MAP** | **Create** | **Creates As Nodes** or right-click and select **Create As Nodes**:

Now you select the folder or the node which will be the location for the new nodes based on your current Mind Map.

Layout

You can modify the layout of a map manually by moving any item with the mouse or drag in a corner of a selection to change the size or the proportions between height and width. The connectors between items will adopt as were they elastic.

There are a few layout templates available in NVivo and they can be applied by going to **MIND MAP | Layout** or by right-clicking and select **Layout** and the options are: *Mind Map, Top Down* or *Left Right*.

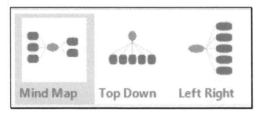

You can also make the items equal in size according to some alternatives from **MIND MAP | Size | Resize**:

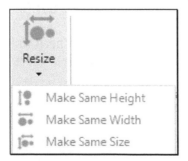

The first selected item becomes the model for the then selected items.

More Formatting Tools

There are also several tools for formatting shapes and text under **MIND MAP | Format Shape** and **Format Text** like Fill, Border Color, Border Width, Fonts, Font Size, and text attributes.

Creating a New Project Map

A Project Map is a way of visually exploring or presenting the data in your project. Project maps are made of shapes that represent the different items in your project and connectors which show links between them.

> 1   Go to **EXPLORE | Maps | Project Map**.
>
> Default folder is **Maps**.
>
> Go to 5.

alternatively

> 1   Click [**Maps**] in Area 1.
> 2   Select the **Maps** folder in Area 2 or its subfolder.
> 3   Go to **EXPLORE | Maps | Project Map**.
>
> Go to 5.

alternatively

> 3   Click on an empty space in Area 3.
> 4   Right-click and select **New Project Map...**

The **New Project Map** dialog box appears:

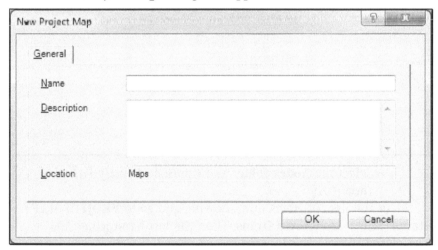

> 5   Type a name (compulsory) and a description (optional), then [**OK**].

A new window appears in Area 4 and it is a good idea to undock with **VIEW | Window | Docked** to give you more space on the screen:

A new context dependent Ribbon menu, **PROJECT MAP**, has now opened.

6   Go to **PROJECT MAP | Items | Add Project Items**
      or right-click and select **Add Project Items...**

The **Select Project Items** dialog box appears:

7   Select the **Nodes** folder and the Node *Family Values*,
      then **[OK]**.

Select the item or items now showing and go to **PROJECT MAP | Items | Show Associated Items**. Then the left hand panel Add Associated Items opens in Area 4.

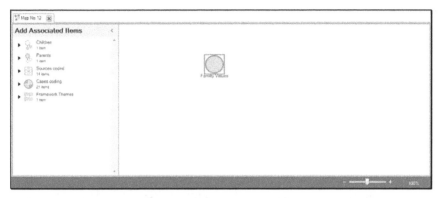

8   Choose some project items in the Add Associated Items panel and drag them to the Project Map:

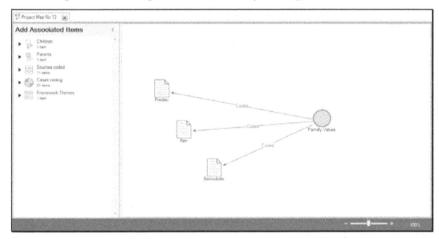

Connections between Items

By default connections are created between all items. You can, however, decide which type of connectors you want to hide or show by going to **PROJECT MAP | Connectors,** presenting the following options:

Layout

You can modify the layout of a map manually by moving any item with the mouse. The connectors between items will adopt as were they elastic.

There are a few layout templates available in NVivo and they can be applied by going to **PROJECT MAP | Layout** or by right-clicking and select **Layout** and the options are: *Layered Directed Graph, Hierarchical, Circular* or *Directed.*

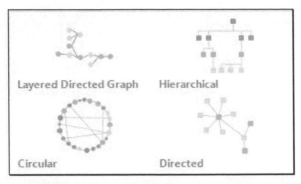

Layered Directed Graph   Hierarchical

Circular   Directed

You can also align the items by going to **PROJECT MAP | Arrange | Align** offering the following options:

The first item you select is the reference for the items then being selected.

Creating a New Concept Map

A Concept Map is a free-form visualization made up of different shapes and connectors. Shapes represent concepts (ideas, people, or data). The connectors between the shapes articulate links such as *this causes..., this requires...* or *this contributes to...*

1   Go to **EXPLORE | Maps | Concept Map**.
    Default folder is **Maps**.
    Go to 5.

alternatively

1   Click [**Maps**] in Area 1.
2   Select the **Maps** folder in Area 2 or its subfolder.
3   Go to **EXPLORE | Maps | Concept Map**.
    Go to 5.

alternatively

3   Click on an empty space in Area 3.
4   Right-click and select **New Concept Map...**

The **New Concept Map** dialog box appears:

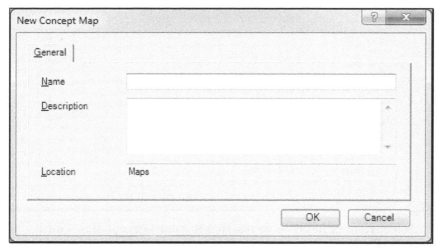

5   Type a name (compulsory) and a description (optional), then [**OK**].

A new window appears in Area 4 and it is a good idea to undock with **VIEW** | **Window** | **Docked** to give you more space on the screen:

A new context dependent Ribbon menu, **CONCEPT MAP**, has now opened.

To insert shapes you drag them from the **Add Shapes** panel to the Concept Map or you right-click and select **Add Shapes**.

You can also insert project items by:

6   Go to **PROJECT MAP** | **Items** | **Add Project Items** or right-click and select **Add Project Items...**

The **Select Project Items** dialog box appears:

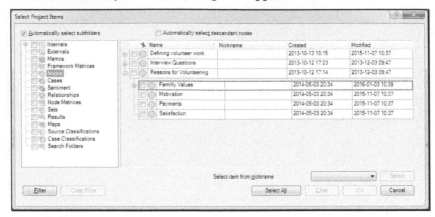

Select item or items to be inserted in your Concept Map. Finish with [**OK**].

Connectors

First you need to select the proper type of pointer by going to **CONCEPT MAPS | Tools | Connector** and the pointer type is changed. Then you select *the from* item and drag the pointer to *the to* item. Then the map can look like this:

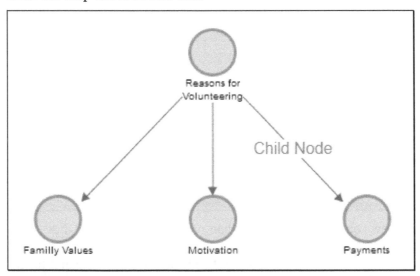

Concept Maps are unique as you may select a region with the pointer and create a rectangular area and all items within this area are thus selected.

The default type of connector is an arrow. This can be modified by selecting a connector and go to **CONCEPT MAP | Connectors | Change Connector** and you will find the following options: *One Way, Symmetrical* and *Associative*.

You can insert text in Shapes and Connectors by selecting, right-click and select **Edit Label** or **[F2]**. Changing fonts, font attribute, color and size you need to select text and to go to **CONCEPT MAP | Format Text**.

Layout

You can modify the layout of a map manually by moving any item with the mouse or drag in a corner of a selection to change the size or the proportions between height and width. The connectors between items will adopt as were they elastic.

You can also align the items by going to **CONCEPT MAP | Arrange | Align** offering the following options:

The first selected item will be reference for the items then selected.

The following layout templates are available from **CONCEPT MAP | Layout** showing these options: *Mind Map, Top Down,* and *Left Right.*

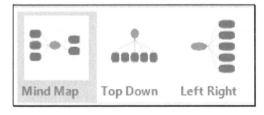

You can also make items equally sized by going to **CONCEPT MAP** | **Size** | **Resize** offering the following options:

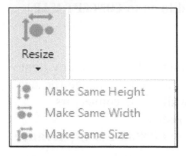

The item first selected is the size reference for the then selected items.

Deleting Graphical Items

1   Select one or more graphical items.
2   Go to **HOME** | **Editing** → **Delete**
     or right-click and select **Delete**
     or the [**Del**] key.

Exporting Maps

Open a Map, go to **DATA** | **Export** | **Items** or right-click and select **Export Map...** or [**Ctrl**] + [**Shift**] + [**E**].

 You can also copy the whole map or selected items and then go to **HOME** | **Clipboard** | **Copy** or [**Ctrl**] + [**C**].

Maps can be exported in the following file formats: .JPG, .BMP, .GIF, TIF, or .PNG.

Final Comment on Graphic Management

Of interest to researchers who also dabble in graphic design software, such as Adobe InDesign or Microsoft Visio, NVivo allows maps and charts to be exported as a Scalable Vector Graphic file format (.SVG). These image files are optimized for web viewing and are suitable for importing into graphic design software. After a small amount of tweaking, your NVivo map could be optimized for your next conference poster presentation. Feel free to follow up with us if you want more information on working with your .SVG files outside of NVivo.

25. CHARTS

Charts

Charts are graphics that easily and clearly can illustrate how sources have been coded. The generic way to create Charts is using the Chart Wizard.

    1   Go to **EXPLORE | Charts | Chart**.

The **Chart Wizard – Step 1** appears:

    2   Click [**Next**].

The **Chart Wizard – Step 2** is shown and the options are:

Coding (Create a chart for coding) and the alternatives are:
    Coding for a source
    Coding by attribute value for a source
    Coding by attribute value for multiple sources
    Coding for a Node
    Coding by attribute value for a Node
    Coding by attribute value for multiple Nodes

Sources (Create a chart for sources) and the alternatives are:
    Sources by attribute value for an attribute
    Sources by attribute value for two attributes

Nodes (Create a chart for Nodes) and the alternatives are:
   Nodes by attribute value for an attribute
   Nodes by attribute value for two attributes

Option	Comments
Coding for a source	Compare the Nodes used to code a particular source. For example, chart any source to show the Nodes which code it by percentage of coverage or number of references.
Coding by Node attribute value for a source	Show coding by Node attribute value for a source. For example chart a source to show coding by one or more Node attribute values.
Coding by Node attribute value for multiple sources	Show coding by Node attribute value for multiple sources. For example chart two or more sources to show coding by one or more Node attribute values.
Coding for a Node	Look at the different sources that are coded at a Node. For example, chart any Node to see which sources are coded at the Node and their corresponding percentage of coverage.
Coding by Node attribute value for a Node	Show coding by attribute value for a Node. For example, chart a Node to show coding by one or more attribute values.
Coding by Node attribute value for multiple Nodes	Show coding by attribute value for multiple Nodes. For example, chart two or more Nodes to show coding by one or more attribute values.
Sources by attribute value for an attribute	Display sources by attribute value for an attribute. For example chart an attribute to see how the sources which have that attribute are distributed across the attribute values.
Sources by attribute value for two attributes	Display sources by attribute value for two attributes. For example chart two attributes to see how the sources which have those attributes are distributed across the attribute values.
Nodes by attribute value for an attribute	Display Nodes by attribute value for an attribute. For example chart an attribute to see how the Nodes which have that attribute are distributed across the attribute values.
Nodes by attribute value for two attributes	Display Nodes by attribute value for two attributes. For example chart two attributes to see how the Nodes which have those attributes are distributed across the attribute values.

3   Click [**Next**].
The **Chart Wizard – Step 3** appears:

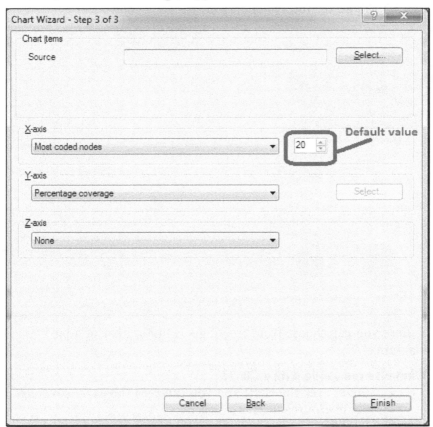

4   Use the [**Select**] button to choose the item that you will
visualize, then [**Finish**].
The result can be like this:

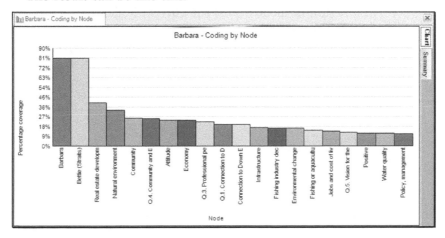

The context dependent ribbon menu **CHART** opens and makes it possible to modify the formatting, zooming and rotating. By going to **CHART | Type** the following drop-down menu shows:

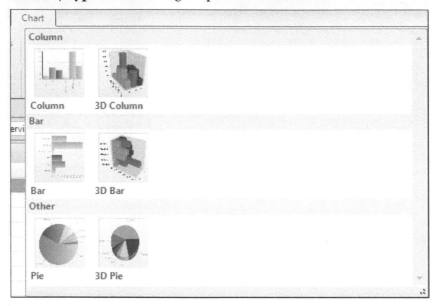

Here you can choose from creating a column, a bar or a pie diagram.

What else can you do with a Chart?
- Hover over the chart and you can read the exact coverage.
- Chart <Source Item> Coding:
  Double-click on a bar and you will open the selected Node in a Highlight mode on for the current Source Item.
- Chart Node Coding:
  Double-click on a bar and you will open the selected source in a Highlight mode on for the current Node.
- Edit and format the Title and Axis.

The *Summary* tab displays a list with Nodes and their coverage:

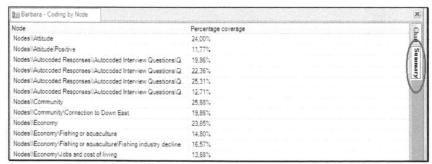

- ◆ -

During a work session you can also start from Area 3:

1   Select the item in Area 3 that you want to visualize.

2   Go to **EXPLORE | Charts | Chart → Chart <Item type>
     Coding**
     or go to **EXPLORE | Charts | Chart → Chart <Item type> by
     Attribute Value**.

alternatively

2   Right-click and select **Charts → Chart <Item type> Coding**
     or **Chart <Item type> by Attribute Value**.

   The graphic is then shown directly when you select **Chart <Item
type> Coding** or the **Chart Options** dialog box appears (same box as
the **Chart Wizard - Step 3**). From there you proceed as above. These
charts cannot be saved as items in the project but can be exported in
the following file formats: .JPG, .BMP, .GIF, .PNG, .PDF, or .SVG.

1   Create a Chart.

2   Go to **DATA | Export | Items → Export Chart**
     or right-click in the graph and select **Export Chart**
     or **[Ctrl] + [Shift] + [E]**.

3   Use the file-browser to decide filename and location, then
     click **[Save]**.

If you want to display more than 20 items in a chart then:

1   Open a chart.

2   Go to **CHART | Options | Select Data**.

The **Chart Options** dialog box appears:

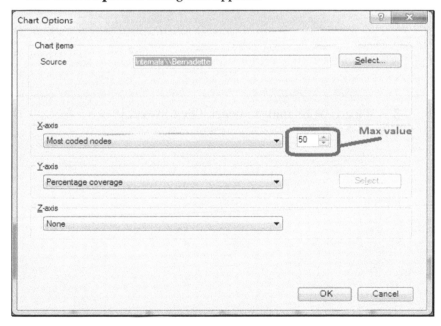

Exporting Charts

Create a Chart and go to **DATA | Export | Items** or right-click and select **Export Chart..** or **[Ctrl] + [Shift] + [E]**.

You can also copy the whole diagram or selected items by going to **HOME | Clipboard | Copy** or **[Ctrl] + [C]**.

Hierarchy Charts – Only for Pro & Plus

Hierarchy Charts makes it possible to visualize how source items and nodes are coded and classified and hierarchically organized with qualitative comparisons. The general method to create Hierarchy Charts is using the Hierarchy Chart Wizard.

1 Go to **EXPLORE | Charts | Hierarchy Chart**.

The **Hierarchy Chart Wizard – Step 1** appears:

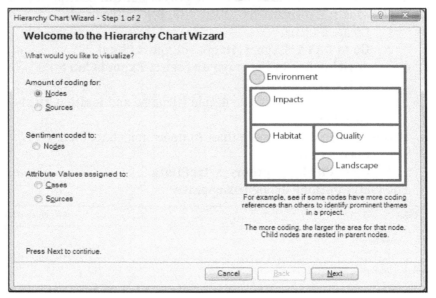

2 We accept to analyze nodes. Click **[Next...]**.

The **Hierarchy Chart Wizard – Step 2** appears:

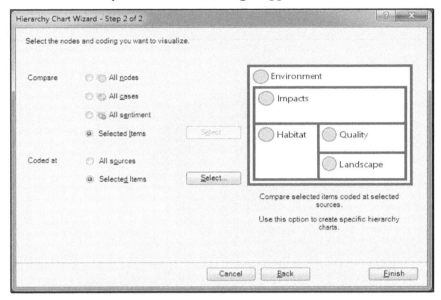

3   With the [**Select...**]-buttons we have selected nodes and cases for analysis. Click [**Finish**].

A new context dependent ribbon, **HIERARCHY CHART,** appears. The result looks like this and the size of the different fields represent the number of references:

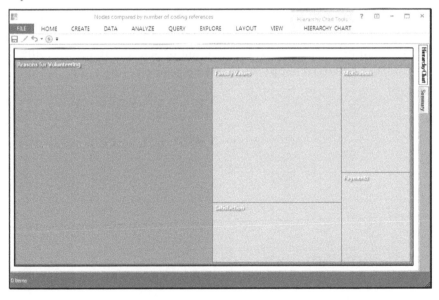

You can change the chart type by going to **HIERARCHY CHART |
Type | Sunburst**:

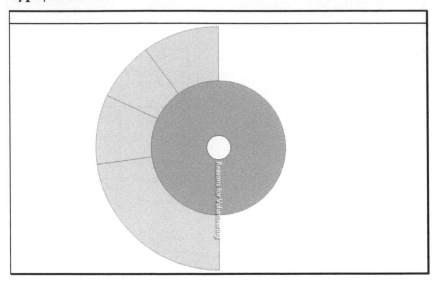

You can open a certain field by right-clicking and selecting **View
References** or **[Ctrl] + [O]**. Then a new Coding Query with a Preview
result will open. If you want to save this result as a new node you
will follow the instructions described earlier.

Exporting Hierarchy Charts

Create a Chart and go to **DATA | Export | Items** or right-click and
select **Export Hierarchy Chart..** or **[Ctrl] + [Shift] + [E]**.

You can also copy the whole diagram or selected items by going
to **HOME | Clipboard | Copy** or **[Ctrl] + [C]**.

26. DIAGRAMS

Explore Diagrams

This type of diagram is a dynamic preview offering a visual analysis of a selected project item and its connections to all other items. Dynamic means that the diagram is updated as soon as any item is modified and preview means that such diagram is created and not saved unless it is exported and saved in any external format.

1   Select an item in Area 3 that you want to analyze.
2   Go to **EXPLORE | Diagrams | Explore Diagram**.

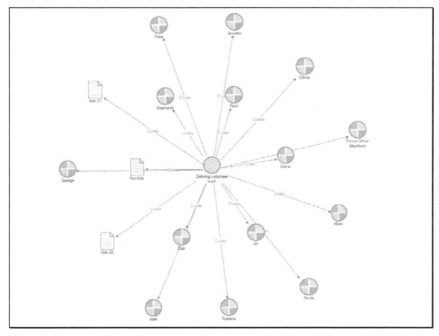

The context dependent **EXPLORE DIAGRAM** ribbon is opened.

You can select which type of connected items you want to display by going to **EXPLORE DIAGRAM | Display** with the following options:

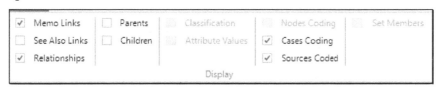

You can also proceed by selecting any item from the diagram and then go to **EXPLORE DIAGRAM | Navigation | Change Focus** or right-click and select **Change Focus**. Then a new diagram is shown with the newly selected item in focus:

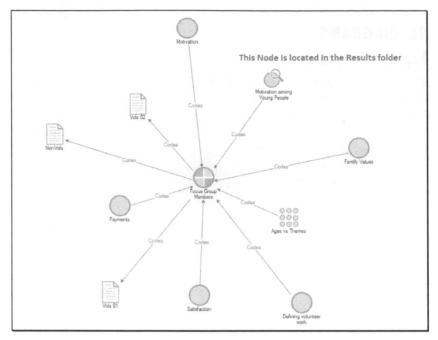

Now you can alternate between these two diagrams using **EXPLORE DIAGRAM** | **Navigation** | **Back** or **EXPLORE DIAGRAM** | **Navigation** | **Forward**. You can also right-click and alternately select **Back** or **Forward**.

From these diagrams you can open any item by going to **HOME** | **Item** | **Open** → **Open Result** or **[Ctrl]** + **[Shift]** + **[O]** or right-click and select **Open Result...**

You can also go on in your analysis and select again a new item and **Change Focus**. With this option you can go backwards or forwards in many steps.

Optional Display Modes

Go to **EXPLORE DIAGRAM** | **Display** and you will access several display options like Classification, Attribute Values, Nodes, Cases, Sources or Set Members.

Exporting Explore Diagram

Create an Explore Diagram and go to **DATA** | **Export** | **Items** or right-click and select **Export Diagram...** or **[Ctrl]** + **[Shift]** + **[E]**.

You can also copy the whole diagram or selected items by going to **HOME** | **Clipboard** | **Copy** or **[Ctrl]** + **[C]**.

Comparison Diagrams

This type of diagram is a dynamic preview offering a visual analysis of two selected project items and how they are related to each other and their connections to all other items. Dynamic means that the diagram is updated as soon as any item is modified and preview means that such diagram is created and not saved unless it is exported and saved in any external format.

1   Select two items in Area 3 for this analysis.
2   Go to **EXPLORE | Diagrams | Comparison Diagram**.

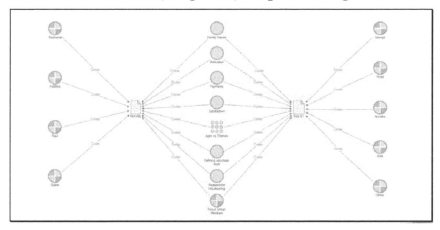

The context dependent **COMPARISON DIAGRAM** ribbon is opened.

The two related items to be compared show the commonly connected items in between and the unique items to the left and to the right respectively.

You can select which related items you want to display by going to **COMPARISON DIAGRAM | Display** with the following options:

From a Comparison Diagram you can open any item by going to **HOME | Item | Open → Open Item** or [Ctrl] + [Shift] + [O] or right-click and select **Open Item...**

Optional Display Modes
Go to **COMPARISON DIAGRAM | Display** and you will access several display options like Classification, Attribute Values, Nodes, Cases, Sources or Set Members.

Exporting Comparison Diagram

Create an Explore Diagram and go to **DATA | Export | Items** or right-click and select **Export Diagram...** or **[Ctrl] + [Shift] + [E]**.

You can also copy the whole diagram or selected items by going to **HOME | Clipboard | Copy** or **[Ctrl] + [C]**.

Cluster Analysis – Only for Pro & Plus

Cluster analysis is an exploratory technique that you can use to visualize patterns in your project by grouping sources or Nodes that share similar words, similar attribute values, or are coded similarly by Nodes. Cluster analysis diagrams provide a graphical representation of sources or Nodes to make it easy to see similarities and differences. Sources or Nodes in the cluster analysis diagram that appear close together are more similar than those that are far apart.

   1   Go to **EXPLORE | Diagrams | Cluster Analysis**.

The **Cluster Analysis Wizard – Step 1** appears:

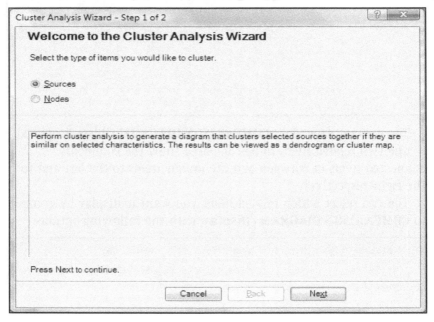

   2   We want to analyze selected Source Items, PDF articles. We select the *Sources* options and click **[Next]**.

The **Cluster Analysis Wizard** – **Step 2** appears:

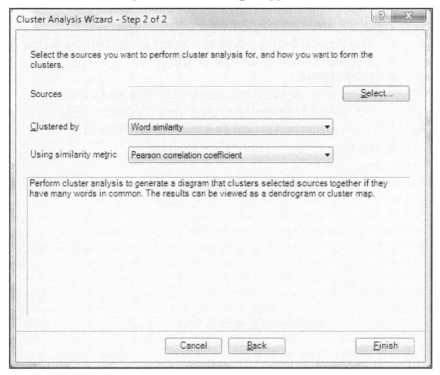

Under the **Clustered by** drop-down list you find the following options: *Word similarity, Coding similarity* and *Attribute value similarity.*

Word similarity: The words contained in the selected sources or nodes are compared.

Sources or nodes that have a higher degree of similarity based on the occurrence and frequency of words are shown clustered together. Sources or nodes that have a lower degree of similarity based on the occurrence and frequency of words are displayed further apart. Stop words are excluded when using this measure of similarity.

Coding similarity: The coding at the selected sources or nodes is compared.

Sources or nodes that have been coded similarly are clustered together on the cluster analysis diagram. Sources or nodes that have been coded differently are displayed further apart on the cluster analysis diagram.

Attribute value similarity: The attribute values of the selected sources or nodes are compared.

Sources or nodes that have similar attribute values are clustered together on the cluster analysis diagram. Sources or nodes that have different attribute values are displayed further apart on the cluster analysis diagram.

Under the **Using similarity metric** drop-down list you find the following options: *Jaccard's coefficient, Pearson correlation coefficient* and *Sørensen coefficient.*

3 The [**Select**] button opens the **Select Project Items** dialog box and we select the PDF articles.

4 Click [**Finish**].

The context dependent Ribbon menu **CLUSTER ANALYSIS** opens and you can choose between 2D Cluster Map, 3D Cluster Map, Horizontal Dendrogram, Vertical Dendrogram or Circle Graph. The default diagram is the Horizontal Dendrogram:

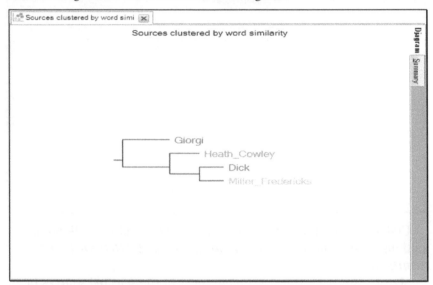

Go to **CLUSTER ANALYSIS | Type | Vertical Dendrogram** and the following diagram is shown:

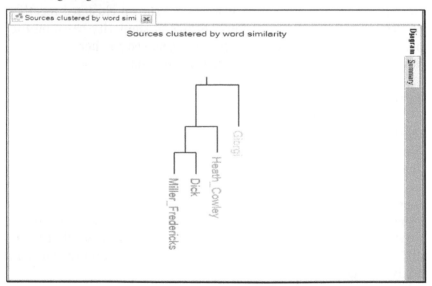

Go to **CLUSTER ANALYSIS | Type | 2D Cluster Map** and the following diagram is shown:

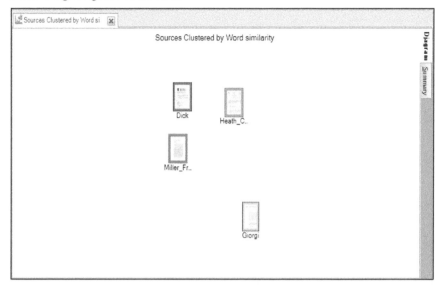

Go to **CLUSTER ANALYSIS | Type | 3D Cluster Map** and the following diagram is shown:

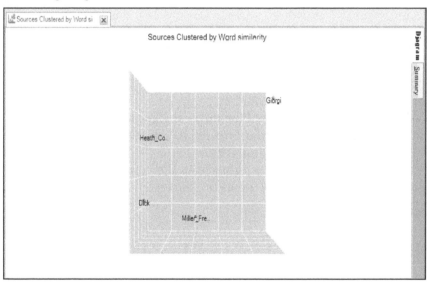

Go to **CLUSTER ANALYSIS | Type | Circle Graph** and the following diagram is shown:

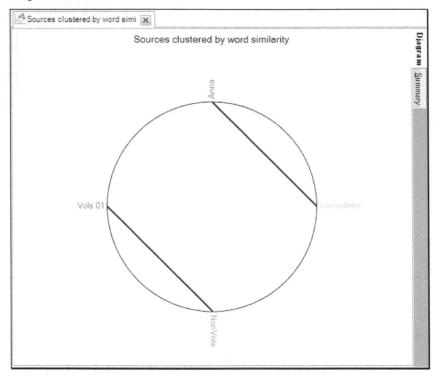

A circle where all the items are represented as points on the perimeter. Realtions between items is indicated by connecting lines of varying thickness and color.

Similarity is indicated by blue lines—thicker lines indicate stronger similarity. Dissimilarity is indicated by red lines—thicker lines indicate stronger dissimilarity.

The **Summary** tab to the right shows the current metric coefficient for each pair of items in the cluster:

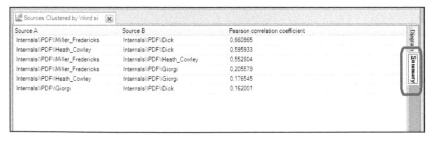

With **CLUSTER ANALYSIS | Options | Select Data** you can choose the metric coefficient.

The Cluster map applies a certain color for each cluster in each type of cluster diagram. In order to study the clustering structure you can vary the number of cluster as any number between 1 and 20

(10 is default) in each type of cluster diagram by going to **Cluster Analysis | Options → Clusters**.

A Cluster map can also be used like this: Select an item in the cluster diagram, right-click and the menu alternatives are: **Open Source** (or double-click or key command **[Ctrl] + [Shift] + [O]**), **Export Diagram, Print, Copy** (the whole graph), **Run Word Frequency Query, Item Properties, Select Data**.

27. REPORTS AND EXTRACTS – ONLY FOR PRO & PLUS

Reports contain summary information about your project that you can view and print. For example, you could check the progress of your coding by running a report that lists your sources and the Nodes that code them.

An extract lets you export a collection of data to a text, Excel or XML file. In some cases you can use this data for complementary analysis in other applications.

Understanding Views and Fields

In reports and extracts, a view is a group of related data fields. There are five different views: Source, Source Classification, Node, Node Classification, and Project Items. When you build a report or an extract, select the view which contains the fields you want to include in your report or extract.

View	Comment
Source	Report on sources including which Nodes code the sources. This view also includes collections, which you could use to limit the scope of your reports.
Source Classification	Report on the classifications that are used to describe your sources. You can create reports that show the classifications in your project or how your sources are classified. This view does not contain any coding information. To report on coding in sources, choose the Source view.
Node	Report on the Nodes in your project including sources they code, coding references, and any classifications assigned to them. This view includes 'intersecting' Nodes which is useful for reporting on how coding at two Nodes coincides—for example see which 'cases' intersect selected themes. This view also includes collections, which you could use to limit the scope of your reports.
Node Classification	Report on the classifications, attributes and attribute values used to describe the people, places and other cases in your project. You can use this view to show the classification structure, or the demographic spread of classified Nodes. This view does not contain any coding information. If you want to report on coding at Nodes, choose the Node view.
Project Items	Use this view to create reports about the structure of your project. Report on your project and the Project Items, including the types of Project Items and who created them.

Report and Extract Templates

NVivo comes with 8 pre-defined Report templates and 8 pre-defined Extract templates ready to be used for any NVivo project. These templates can be deleted or modified by the user. New Reports and Extracts can be created by the user for the current project or be exported to other users working with any other NVivo projects.

The pre-defined Report templates are located in the **Reports** folder under the [**Reports**] navigation button:

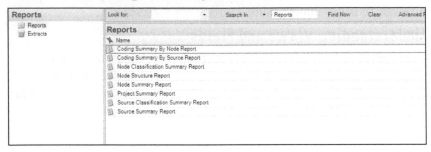

The Report templates that include contents are 'Coding Summary By Node Report' and 'Coding Summary By Source Report'.

The pre-defined Extract templates are located in the **Extracts** folder under the [**Reports**] navigation button:

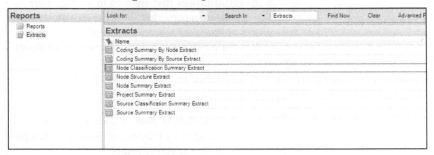

The Extract templates that include contents are 'Coding Summary By Node Extract' and 'Coding Summary By Source Extract'.

Reports

Creating a New Report via the Report Designer

1   Go to **EXPLORE | Reports | New Report → New Report via Designer...**

The **New Report** dialog box appears:

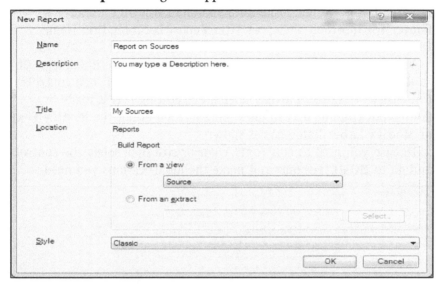

A new context dependent Ribbon menu, **REPORT**, is now opened and is opened each time a Report is opened. If you prefer the option *From an extract* you will need to select an extract from the existing extract templates and you will inherit the view and fields from the chosen extract. We have typed a name and title of the Report and we have selected the View *Source*.

2   Click **[OK]**.

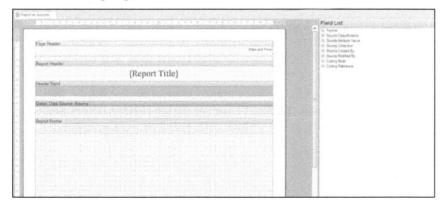

The key to understanding the **Report Designer** is the idea of controls. Controls are static fields with label data or dynamic fields with data. The following graph will explain. First you select a field from the list of field headings in the Field List panel to the right. Then go to **REPORT** | **Add/Modify** or right-click and select **Add Field**. The result is two controls, Label Control and Field Control.

The text or Image controls are created when you click on an empty space immediately below one of the band headers, for example the Report Header. Then an empty control, which is rectangular, is created. From here you go to **REPORT** | **Header & Footer** for insertion of Report Title, Report Location, User Name, Date and Time, Project Name or Page N of M.

You can also create your own text box or an image like a logo. Go to **REPORT** | **Controls** and choose **Text** or **Image**. All such controls can easily be resized, moved, deleted etc. Editing text is made by double-clicking the text in question and then either the **Modify Text** or **Modify Label** dialog box is shown.

In case you need to edit fonts, color or size then select the control and go to **HOME** | **Format** and make the modifications you need.

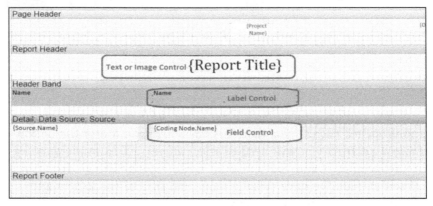

REPORT | **Page** | **Layout** can be used to go between Tabular or Columnar layout for a non-grouped report and Stepped, Blocked or Outlined layout for a grouped report.

A Grouped report is created by going to **REPORT** | **Grouping** | **Group** and then you select the field or fields that will create structural headings in the report.

REPORT | **Sort & Filter** | **Sort** makes it possible to change the sorting principles and **REPORT** | **Sort & Filter** | **Filter** offers an option to introduce a filter either with fixed or user-prompted settings.

Example of a Report based on Source View

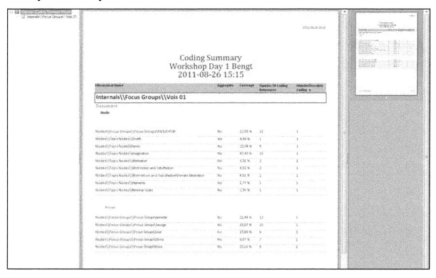

Creating a New Report via the Report Wizard

The Report Wizard provides a systematic method for creating a new, custom report for your project:

1   Go to **EXPLORE | Reports | New Report → New Report via Wizard...**

The **Report Wizard – Step 1** appears:

2   Select *Node Classification* from the **From a view** drop down list. If you prefer the option **From an extract** you will need to select an extract from the existing extract

templates and you will inherit the view and fields from the chosen extract.

3   Click [**Next**].

The **Report Wizard** – **Step 2** appears:

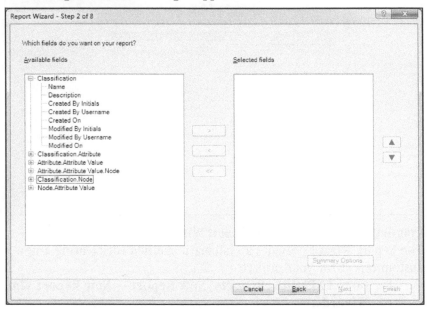

4   Expand the field headings and select the fields from the left box that will form the Report and click the [>] button which brings over the fields to the right box.

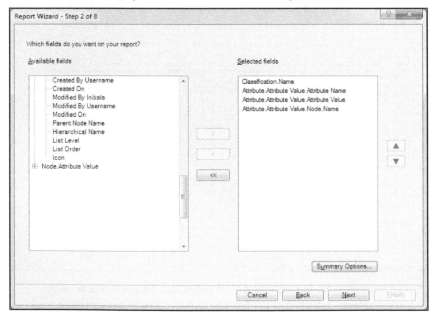

5   Click [**Next**].

The **Report Wizard** – **Step 3** appears:

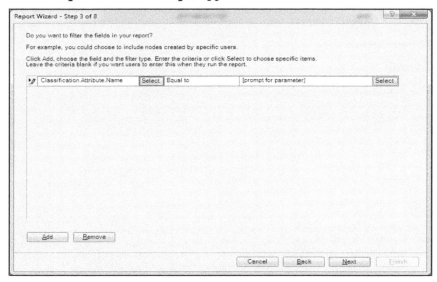

6   Use the **[Add]** button to create the first filter row and then the **[Select]** button to select the field that shall limit the report. If you leave the right textbox as *[prompt for parameter]* then the user will be prompted to select a parameter each time the report is run.

7   Click **[Next]**.

The **Report Wizard** – **Step 4** appears:

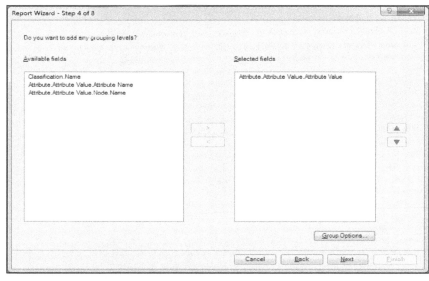

8   Grouping is a way to introduce headings in the Report thus making the report easier to read. We select *Attribute.Attribute Value.Attribute Value* and use the [>] button to bring it over to the right box.

9   Click **[Next]**.

The **Report Wizard** – **Step 5** appears:

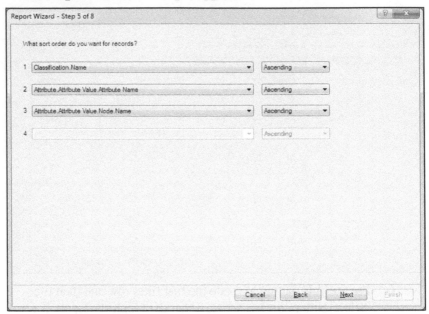

10 We decide the sort order by using the drop-down lists.
11 Click [**Next**].

The **Report Wizard** – **Step 6** appears:

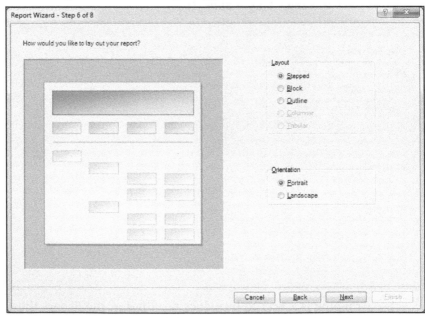

12 We accept the default settings which are *Stepped* layout
    and *Portrait* orientation.
13 Click [**Next**].

The **Report Wizard – Step 7** appears:

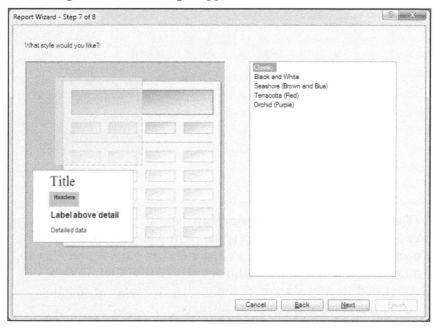

14 We accept the default setting which is the *Classic* style.

15 Click [**Next**].

The **Report Wizard – Step 8** appears:

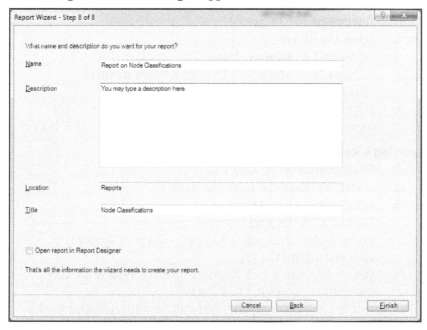

16 Finally, we type the Name and Title of the Report and optionally a Description.

17 Click [**Finish**].

The new **Report** opens:

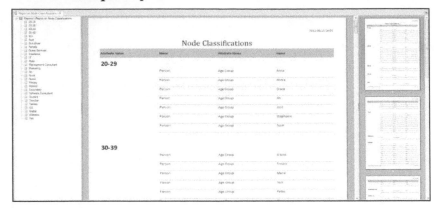

The left panel is called **Report Map** and can be used to easily find a certain headings in the Report. The right panel is called **Thumbnails** and can be used to find a certain page. Report Map and Thumbnails can be hidden/unhidden with **VIEW | Detail View | Report** and **Report Map** or **Thumbnails**, two toggling functions.

From this view you can print the Report or export the Report as a Word document.

Exporting the Result of a Report

1   Click [**Reports**] in Area 1.
2   Select the **Reports** folder in Area 2.
3   Select a report in Area 3.
4   Open the Report.
5   Go to **DATA | Export | Items**
      or right-click and select **Export Report Results**
      or [**Ctrl**] + [**Shift**] + [**E**].
6   Decide file name, file type (Word, text formats, Excel
      formats, PDF, RTF, Web formats) and location. Click [**Save**].

Exporting a Report Template

1   Click [**Reports**] in Area 1.
2   Select the **Reports** folder in Area 2.
3   Select a report in Area 3.
4   Go to **DATA | Export | Items**
      or right-click and select **Export → Export Report**
      or [**Ctrl**] + [**Shift**] + [**E**].
5   Decide file name and location. The file type is already
      determined as .NVR. Click [**Save**].

The result is a Report template that can be imported and used by other projects.

Importing a Report Template

    1   Go to **DATA | Import | Report**.
        Default folder is **Reports**.
        Go to 5.

alternatively

    1   Click on **[Reports]** in Area 1.
    2   Select the **Reports** folder in Area 2 or its subfolder.
    3   Go to **DATA | Import | Report**.
        Go to 5.

alternatively

    3   Click on any empty space in Area 3.
    4   Right-click and select **Import Report...**
    5   The **Import Report** dialog box appears.
    6   Select the Report template .NVR that you want to import.
        Click on **[Open]**.

The **Report Properties** dialog box appears:

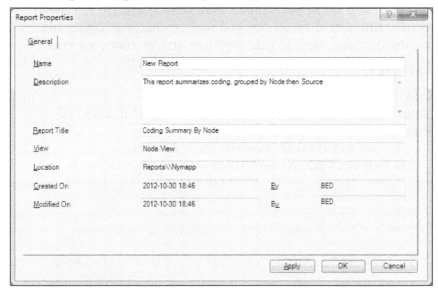

    7   If you need you can change or modify the text in the dialog
        box. Click on **[OK]**.

Editing a Report

By opening a Report in Report Designer you can modify any
parameter except the selected View and Style:

    1   Click **[Reports]** in Area 1.
    2   Select the **Reports** folder in Area 2.
    3   Select a report in Area 3.
    4   Go to **HOME | Item | Open → Open Report in Designer...**
        or right-click and select **Open Report in Designer...**
        or **[Ctrl] + [Shift] + [O]**.

The result may look like this:

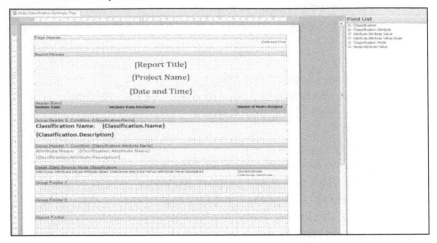

Here you can make any modification that Report Designer allows.

The ribbon tab **Reports** opens. Here you can change the layout, modify filters, modify headers and footers, change grouping and sorting. You can also add your own text and/or your own logo.

Extracts

Creating a New Extract

An extract lets you export a portion of your data to a text file, an Excel spreadsheet, or an XML file.

  1   Go to **EXPLORE | Reports | New Extract...**

The **Extract Wizard – Step 1** appears:

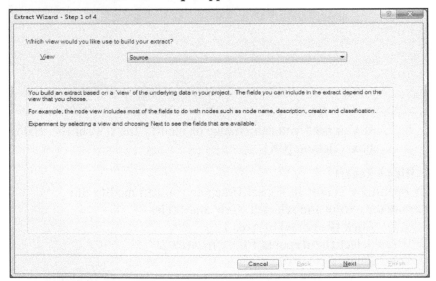

  2   Select *Source* from the View drop down list.
  3   Click [**Next**].

The **Extract Wizard – Step 2** appears:

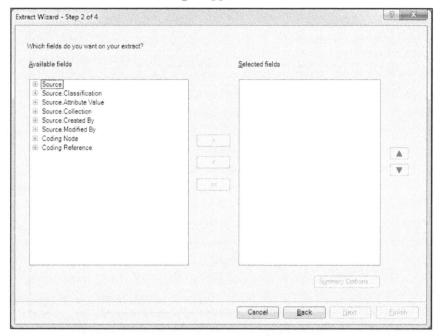

4 Expand the field headings and select the fields from the left box that will form the Extract and click the [>] button which brings over the fields to the right box.

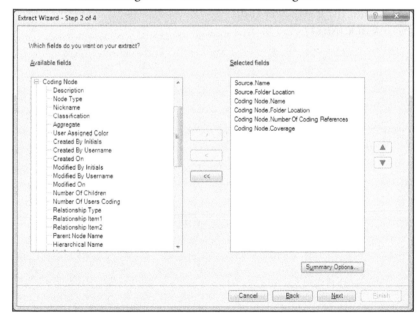

5 Click [**Next**].

The **Extract Wizard** – **Step 3** appears:

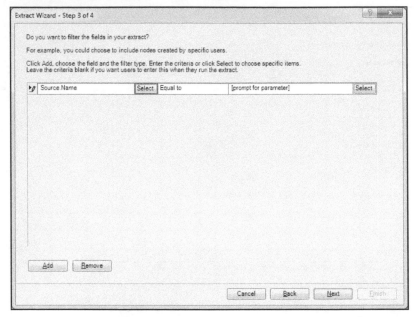

6 Use the [**Add**] button to create the first filter row and then the [**Select**] button to select the field that shall limit the report. Leave the right textbox as *[prompt for parameter]* and the user will be prompted to select a parameter each time the extract is run.

7 Click [**Next**].

The **Extract Wizard** – **Step 4** appears:

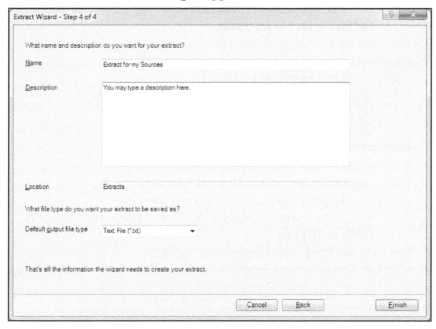

8   Type a name of the Extract (compulsory) and optionally a description. Default file format can also be set but can be changed before you run the Extract. The file formats that you can choose from are: Text, Excel, and XML.

9   Confirm with [**Finish**].

Exporting (Running) an Extract

1   Click [**Reports**] in Area 1.
2   Select the **Extracts** folder in Area 2.
3   Select an Extract in Area 3.
4   Go to **Reports | Run Extract**
    or double-click
    or right-click and select **Run Extract**.
5   Decide file name, file type and location. Click [**Save**].

Exporting an Extract Template

1   Click [**Reports**] in Area 1.
2   Select the **Extracts** folder in Area 2.
3   Select an Extract in Area 3.
4   Go to **DATA | Export | Items**
    or right-click and select **Export → Export Extract**
    or [**Ctrl**] + [**Shift**] + [**E**].

Decide file name and location. The file type is already determined as .NVX. The result is an Extract template that can be imported and used by other projects.

Importing an Extract Template

    1   Go to **DATA | Import | Extract**.
        Default folder is **Extracts**.
        Go to 5.

alternatively

    1   Click on [**Reports**] in Area 1.
    2   Select **Extracts** folder in Area 2 or its subfolder.
    3   Go to **DATA | Import | Extract**.
        Go to 5.

alternatively

    3   Click on any empty space in Area 3.
    4   right-click and select **Import Extract...**
    5   The **Import Extract** dialog box appears.
    6   Select the Extract template .NVX that you want to import.
        Click on [**Open**].

The **Extract Properties** dialog box appears:

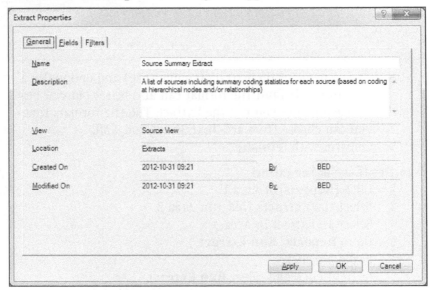

    7   If you need you can change or modify the text in the dialog box. Click on [**OK**].

Editing an Extract

An Extract can be modified by opening its Extract Properties:

    1   Click [**Reports**] in Area 1.
    2   Select **Extracts** folder in Area 2 or a subfolder.
    3   Select an extract in Area 3.
    4   Go to **HOME | Item | Properties → Extract Properties...**
        or right-click and select **Extract Properties**
        or [**Ctrl**] + [**Shift**] + [**P**].

28. HELP FUNCTIONS IN NVIVO

An integral part of NVivo is the variety of help and support functionality for users.

Help Documents Online

1   Go to **FILE → Help → NVivo Help**
    or use the [?] symbol in the upper right corner of the screen
    or [**F1**].

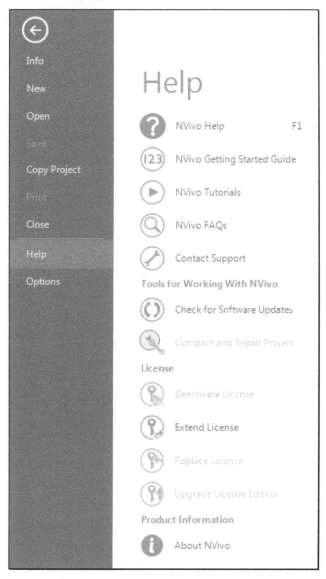

The initial view for **Online Help** is this:

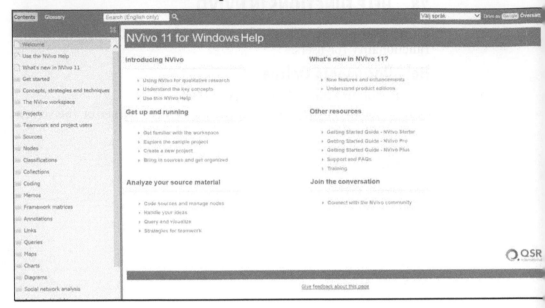

Tutorials

NVivo has some tutorials in the form of video clips:

    1   Go to **FILE → Help → NVivo Tutorials**.

Users can also access QSR's online tutorials. Adobe Flash Player is required to play these tutorials.

Support and Technical Issues

As a holder of this book you are welcome to contact **support@formkunskap.com** or Skype **bengt.edhlund** in any matter that has to do with installation problems or user procedures as described in this book.

In case of performance disturbances like NVivo unintentionally stops, an error log is created automatically. The log files are by default stored in My Documents folder of the current user. Such error log file has the following name structure **'err<date>T<time>.log'**. It is a text file and in case you need technical assistance you may be asked to forward such error log file to QSR Support or the local representative for analysis.

Software Versions and Service Packs

You should always be aware of the software version and Service Pack that you use. A Service Pack is an additional software patch that could carry bug fixes, improvements and new features. Service Packs are free for licensees of a certain software version. Provided that you are connected to the Internet and have enabled *Check for Update every 7 Days* (see page 41) you will automatically get a message on the screen when a new Service Pack has been launched. Always use the latest available Service Pack:

   1   Go to **FILE → Help → About NVivo**.

The image shows the software version and installed Service Pack:

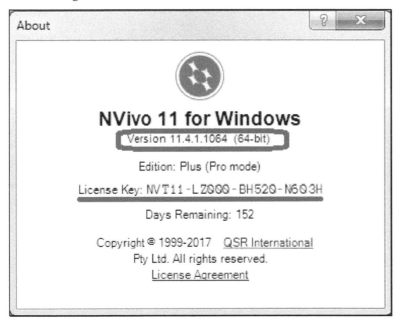

29. GLOSSARY

This is a list of the most common words, terms, and descriptions that are used in this book.

Advanced Find	Search names of Project items like Source items, Memos or Nodes. Use **Find Bar – Advanced Find.**
Aggregate	Aggregate means that a certain Node in any hierarchical level accumulates the logical sum of all its nearest Child Nodes.
Annotation	A note linked to an element of a Source item. Similar to a conventional footnote.
Attribute	A variable that is used to describe individual Source items and Nodes. Example: age group, gender, education.
Autocoding	An automatic method to code documents using names of the paragraph styles.
Boolean Operator	The conventional operators AND, OR or NOT used to create logical search expressions applying Boolean algebra.
Case Node	A Case Node is a member of a group of Nodes which are classified with Attributes and Values reflecting demographic or descriptive data. Case Nodes can be people (Interviewees), places or any group of items with similar properties.
Casebook	Definition used in NVivo 8 corresponding to Classification Sheet in later versions of NVivo.
Classification	A collection of Attributes for Source items or Nodes.
Classification Sheet	A matrix overview of the attributes and values of Source items or Nodes.
Cluster Analysis	Cluster analysis or clustering is the assignment of a set of observations into subsets (called *clusters*) so that observations in the same cluster are similar in some sense. Clustering is a method of unsupervised learning, and a common technique for statistical data analysis used in many fields, including machine learning, data mining, pattern recognition, image analysis, information retrieval, and bioinformatics.

Coding	The work that associates a certain element of a Source item at a certain Node.
Coding Stripe	Graphical representation of coding in a Source item.
Coding Queries	A method to construct a query by using combinations of Nodes or Attribute values.
Compound Queries	A method to construct a query by using combinations of various query types.
Concept Map	A Concept Map is a free-form visualization made up of different shapes and connectors. Shapes represent concepts (ideas, people, or data). The connectors between the shapes articulate links such as *this causes...*, *this requires...* or *this contributes to...*
Coverage	The fraction of a Source item that has been coded at a certain Node.
Dataset	A structured matrix of data arranged in rows and columns. Datasets can be created from imported Excel spreadsheets or captures social media data.
Dendrogram	A tree-like plot where each step of hierarchical clustering is represented as a fusion of two branches of the tree into a single one. The branches represent clusters obtained at each step of hierarchical clustering.
Discourse Analysis	In semantics, discourses are linguistic units composed of several sentences — in other words, conversations, arguments or speeches. Discourse Analysis studies how texts can be structured and how its elements are interrelated.
Document	An item in NVivo that is usually imported from a Source document.
Dropbox	A cloud-based software solution that allows file syncing across several computers.
EndNote	A powerful and convenient reference handling software tool.
Ethnography	The science that examines characteristics of different cultural groups.
Evernote	A popular cloud-based notetaking platform that creates text and voice memos.

Facebook	A social networking platform where users can become 'friends' and post content on one another's personal page ('walls'). Social groups are also available in Facebook (pages).
Filter	A function that limits a selection of values or items in order to facilitate the analysis of large amounts of data.
Find Bar	A toolbar immediately above the List View.
Focus Group	A selected, limited group of people that represents a larger population.
Folder	A folder that is created by NVivo is a virtual folder but has properties and functions largely like a normal Windows folder.
Framework	A data matrix that allows you to easily view and summarize areas of your data you wish to more closely explore.
Grounded Theory	Widely recognized method for qualitative studies where theories emerge from data rather than a pre-determined hypothesis.
Grouped Find	A function for finding items that have certain relations to each other.
Hushtag	A 'keywording' convention that places a number sign ($^{\#}$) before a term in order to allow text-based searches to distinguish searchable keywords from standard discourse (see also, Twitter).
Hyperlink	A link to an item outside the NVivo-project. The linked item can be a file or a web site.
In Vivo Coding	In Vivo coding is creating a new Node when selecting text and then using the *In Vivo* command. The Node name will become the selected text (max 256 characters) but the name (and location) can be changed later.
Items	All items that constitutes a project. Items are Sources, Nodes, Classifications, Queries, Results, and Maps.
Jaccard's Coefficient	The **Jaccard index**, also known as the **Jaccard similarity coefficient** (originally coined *coefficient de communauté* by Paul Jaccard), is a statistic used for comparing the similarity and diversity of sample sets

Kappa Coefficient	**Cohen's kappa coefficient, (K),** is a statistical measure of inter-rater agreement. It is generally thought to be a more robust measure than simple percent agreement calculation since **K** takes into account the agreement occurring by chance. Cohen's kappa coefficient measures the agreement between two raters who each classify *N* items into *C* mutually exclusive categories. If the raters are in complete agreement then **K** = 1. If there is no agreement among the raters (other than what would be expected by chance) then **K** ≤ 0.
LinkedIn	A professional social networking site where users become 'connections' and participate in group discussions in 'groups'.
Matrix Coding Query	The method to construct queries in a matrix form where contents in each cell are the result of a row and a column combined with a certain operator.
Medline	The world's most popular health research database.
Memo Link	Only *one* Memo Link can exist from an item to a memo.
Memo	A text document that could be linked from *one* Source item or from *one* Node.
MeSH	MeSH (Medical Subject Headings), the terminology or controlled vocabulary used in PubMed and associated information sources.
Mind Map	A Mind Map reflects what you think about a single topic and is usually created quickly or spontaneously. At the beginning of your project you might use a mind map to explore your expectations or initial theories.

Mixed Methods	My thoughts on mixed methods include two aspects. First is the integration of survey, test, rating, demographic data with qualitative media (and all interaction with those media in terms of excerpting and tagging). When done well, database queries can draw upon all data points in filtering, creating data visualizations to explore pattern, and basic retrieval. The second is the various ways of quantifying qualitative data in terms of creating new descriptor variables and the scaling or indexing of coded content across meaningful dimensions.
NFS	**Network File System (NFS)** is a distributed file system protocol originally developed by Sun Microsystems in 1984, allowing a user on a client computer to access files over a computer network much like local storage is accessed.
Node	Often used in the context of a 'container' of selected topics or themes. A Node contains pointers to whole documents or selected elements of documents relevant to the specific Node. Nodes can be organized hierarchically.
OCR	Optical Character Recognition, a method together with scanning making it possible to identify characters not only as an image.
OneNote	Microsoft's cloud-based notetaking platform that creates text and voice memos.
Pearson Correlation Coefficient	A type of correlation coefficient that represents the relationship between two variables that are measured on the same interval or ratio scale.
Phenomenology	A method which is descriptive, thoughtful, and innovative and from which you might verify your hypothesis.
Project	The collective denomination of all data and related work.
Project Map	Graphical representation of Project items and their relations.
PubMed	A popular health research database (cf. Medline).

Qualitative Research	Research with data originating from observations, interviews, and dialogs that focuses on the views, experiences, values, and interpretations of participants.
Qualtrics	**Qualtrics** is a private research software company, based in Provo, Utah, in the United States. The company was founded in 2002 by Scott M. Smith, Ryan Smith, Jared Smith and Stuart Orgill. Qualtrics software enables users to do many kinds of online data collection[j] and analysis including market research, customer satisfaction and loyalty, product and concept testing, employee evaluations and website feedback. In 2012, the company received a $70 million investment from Sequoia Capital and Accel Partners, generally considered two of the top venture capital firms in the country. It was the largest joint investment to date by these two firms. In September 2014, Sequoia Capital and Accel Partners returned in Series B funding, led by Insight Venture Partners worth $150 million, a record for a Utah-based company. In May 2016 Qualtrics acquired statistical analysis startup Statwing for an undisclosed sum. Statwing is a San Francisco based company that created point-and-click software for advanced statistical analysis. Quantitative statistical analysis performed with Qualtrics is cited in a number of professional and academic journals.
Quantitative Research	Research that collects data through measurements and conclusions through calculations and statistics.
Ranking	The organization of results according to ascending or descending relevance.
RefWorks	A popular reference handling software tool.
Relationship	A Node that defines a relation between two Project items. A relationship is always characterized by a certain relationship type.

Relationship Type	A concept (often a descriptive verb) that defines a relationship or dependence between two Project items.
Relevance	Relevance in a result of a query is a measure of success or grade of matching. Relevance may be calculated as the number of hits in selected sections of the searched item.
Research Design	A plan for the collection and study of data so that the desired information is reached with sufficient reliability and a given theory can be verified or rejected in a recognized manner.
Result	A result is the answer to a query. A result may be shown as *Preview* or saved as a *Node*.
Saving Queries	The possibility to save queries in order to re-run or to modify them.
See Also Link	A link established between two items. A See Also Link is created from a certain area or text element of an item to a selected area or the whole of another item.
Service Pack	Software updates that normally carry bug fixes, performance enhancements, and new features.
Set	A subset or 'collection' of selected Project Items. A saved set can be displayed as a list of shortcuts to these Project Items.
Sociogram	A **sociogram** is a graphic representation of social links that a person has. It is a graph drawing that plots the structure of interpersonal relations in a group situation. Sociograms were developed by Jacob L. Moreno to analyze choices or preferences within a group. They can diagram the structure and patterns of group interactions. A sociogram can be drawn on the basis of many different criteria: Social relations, channels of influence, lines of communication etc.
Sørensen Coefficient	The **Sørensen index**, also known as **Sørensen's similarity coefficient**, is a statistic used for comparing the similarity of two samples. It was developed by the botanist Thorvald Sørensen and published in 1948.

Stop Words	Stop words are less significant words like conjunctions or prepositions that may not be meaningful to your analysis. Stop words are exempted from Text Search Queries or Word Frequency Queries.
SurveyMonkey	**SurveyMonkey** is an online survey development cloud-based company, founded in 1999 by Ryan Finley. SurveyMonkey provides free, customizable surveys, as well as a suite of paid back-end programs that include data analysis, sample selection, bias elimination, and data representation tools. In addition to providing free and paid plans for individual users, SurveyMonkey offers more large-scale enterprise options for companies interested in data analysis, brand management, and consumer-focused marketing. Since releasing its enterprise in 2013, business-focused services, SurveyMonkey has grown dramatically, opening a new headquarters in downtown Palo Alto.
Twitter	A social networking website where users post 'tweets' that contain a maximum of 140 characters.
Uncoding	The work that deletes a given coding of a document at a certain Node.
Validity	The validity of causal inferences within scientific studies, usually based on experiments.
Value	Value that a certain Attribute can have. Similar to 'Controlled Vocabulary'. Example: male, female.
Zotero	A reference handling software tool.

APPENDIX A – THE NVIVO SCREEN

The NVivo Screen

1. The Navigation Buttons
2. The Virtual Explorer
3. The List View
4. The Details – Opened Items

The NVivo Screen is similar to that of Microsoft Outlook. Normally you start with the Navigation Buttons (1) and select a certain group of folders (2). Clicking a folder lists its contents of documents or items (3). An item is opened with a double-click and is shown in area (4). This window can also be undocked.

For continued work you can either right-click with the mouse (depending on its position), use Ribbon menus, or key board commands.

APPENDIX B – KEYBOARD COMMANDS

Listed below are some of the most useful keyboard commands. Many adhere to general Windows rules. Others are specific for each program.

Windows	Word	NVivo 11	Keyboard Command	Desription
✓	✓	✓	[Ctrl] + [C]	Copy
✓	✓	✓	[Ctrl] + [X]	Cut
✓	✓	✓	[Ctrl] + [V]	Paste
✓	✓	✓	[Ctrl] + [A]	Select All
✓	✓	✓	[Ctrl] + [O]	Open Project
	✓[13]	✓	[Ctrl] + [B]	Bold
	✓[13]	✓	[Ctrl] + [I]	Italic
	✓[13]	✓	[Ctrl] + [U]	Underline
	✓[13]		[Ctrl] + [K]	Insert Hyperlink
		✓	[Ctrl] + [E]	Switch between Edit mode and Read Only
	✓	✓	[Ctrl] + [Z]	Undo
	✓		[Ctrl] + [Y]	Undo - Undo
	✓	✓	[Ctrl] + wheel	Zoom in and out
		✓	[Ctrl]+[Shift]+[K]	Link to New Memo
		✓	[Ctrl]+[Shift]+[M]	Open Linked Memo
		✓	[Ctrl]+[Shift]+[N]	New Folder/Item
		✓	[Ctrl]+[Shift]+[P]	Folder/Item Properties
		✓	[Ctrl]+[Shift]+[O]	Open Item
		✓	[Ctrl]+[Shift]+[I]	Import Item
		✓	[Ctrl]+[Shift]+[E]	Export Item
		✓	[Ctrl]+[Shift]+[F]	Advanced Find
		✓	[Ctrl]+[Shift]+[G]	Grouped Find
		✓	[Ctrl]+[Shift]+[U]	Move Up
		✓	[Ctrl]+[Shift]+[D]	Move Down
		✓	[Ctrl]+[Shift]+[L]	Move Left

[13] Only for English version of Word.

Windows	Word	NVivo 11	Keyboard Command	Description
		✔	[Ctrl]+[Shift]+[R]	Move Right
		✔	[Ctrl]+[Shift]+[T]	Insert Time/Date
	✔	✔	[Ctrl] + Click	Open an hyperlink
	✔	✔	[Enter]	New paragraph
	✔	✔	[Shift] + [Enter]	Line Break
	✔	✔	[Ctrl] + [Enter]	New Page
	✔	✔	[Ctrl] + [Home]	Go to beginning of document
	✔	✔	[Ctrl] + [End]	Go to end of document
	✔	✔	[Ctrl] + [G]	Go to
✔	✔	✔	[Ctrl] + [N]	New Project
✔	✔	✔	[Ctrl] + [P]	Print
✔	✔	✔	[Ctrl] + [S]	Save
		✔	[Ctrl] + [M]	Merge Into Selected Node
		✔	[Ctrl] + [1]	Go Sources
		✔	[Ctrl] + [2]	Go Nodes
		✔	[Ctrl] + [3]	Go Classifications
		✔	[Ctrl] + [4]	Go Collections
		✔	[Ctrl] + [5]	Go Queries
	✔		[Ctrl] + [6]	Unlink
		✔	[Ctrl] + [6]	Go Reports
		✔	[Ctrl] + [7]	Go Maps
		✔	[Ctrl] + [8]	Go Folders
✔	✔		[Ctrl] + [W]	Close Window
✔	✔		[Ctrl]+[Shift]+[W]	Close all Windows of same Type
	✔	✔	[F1]	Open Online Help
		✔	[F4]	Play/Pause
		✔	[F5]	Refresh
	✔	✔	[F7]	Spell Check
		✔	[F8]	Stop
		✔	[F9]	Skip Back
		✔	[F10]	Skip Forward

Windows	Word	NVivo 11	Keyboard Command	Description
		✓	[F11]	Start Selection
		✓	[F12]	Finish Selection
✓	✓		[Ctrl] + [Z]	Undo
✓			[Ctrl] + [Y]	Redo
✓		✓	[Ctrl] + [F]	Find
✓		✓	[Ctrl] + [H]	Replace (Detail View)
		✓	[Ctrl] + [H]	Handtool (Print Preview)
		✓	[Ctrl] + [Q]	Go to Quick Coding Bar
		✓	[Ctrl]+[Shift]+[F2]	Uncode
		✓	[Ctrl]+[Shift]+[F3]	Uncode from This Node
		✓	[Ctrl]+[Shift]+[F9]	Uncode at current Nodes
		✓	[Ctrl] + [F2]	Code
	✓	✓	[Ctrl] + [F4]	Close Current Window
		✓	[Ctrl] + [F8]	Code In Vivo
		✓	[Ctrl] + [F9]	Code at current Nodes
		✓	[Alt] + [F1]	Hide/Show Navigation View
		✓	[Ctrl] + [Ins]	Insert Row
		✓	[Ctrl] + [Del]	Delete Selected Items in a Map
		✓	[Ctrl]+[Shift]+[T]	Insert Date/Time
		✓	[Ctrl]+[Shift]+[Y]	Insert Symbol
	✓		[Ctrl]+[Alt]+[F]	Insert Footnote
		✓	[Ctrl] + [Enter]	Carriage Return in certain text boxes

INDEX